Sandra F. Rief

DATE DUE

DEC 2 0 2010		
MAY 1 1 2011		
JUL 27 2012		
AUG 1 3 2019		

Demco, Inc. 38-293

JOSSEY-BASS
A Wiley Imprint
www.josseybass.com

Published by Jossey-Bass
A Wiley Imprint
989 Market Street, San Francisco, CA 94103–1741—www.josseybass.com

Jossey-Bass books and products are available through most bookstores. To contact Jossey-Bass directly call our Customer Care Department within the U.S. at 800-956-7739, outside the U.S. at 317-572-3986, or fax 317-572-4002.

Jossey-Bass also publishes its books in a variety of electronic formats. Some content that appears in print may not be available in electronic books.

Library of Congress Cataloging-in-Publication Data

Rief, Sandra F.
    The ADD/ADHD checklist / by Sandra F. Rief.—2nd ed.
        p.   cm.
    Includes bibliographical references and index.
        ISBN 978-0-4701-8970-2 (pbk.)
            1. Attention-deficit-disordered children—Popular works.   2. Attention-deficit-disordered children—Education.   3. Attention-deficit-disordered children—Behavior modification.   I. Title.
    RJ506.H9R54   2008
    618.92'8589—dc22

                                                                                2008006603

Printed in the United States of America
SECOND EDITION
PB Printing   10 9 8 7 6 5 4 3

──⁓── Contents

—ᵃᵃᵃ— Preface

Approximately 5 to 9 percent of school-age children in the United States have attention deficit disorders. Every classroom teacher most likely has at least one or two students with ADHD in his or her classroom each year, and these educators need to understand the nature of the disorder, as well as the most effective strategies for reaching and teaching these students.

To make well-informed decisions on how to best help their son or daughter, parents of children with ADHD must learn as much as they can about the disorder and research-validated treatments. They must also be equipped with the skills and strategies that help in managing their child's ADHD symptoms and often challenging behaviors.

It is often not easy to live with or teach a child who has ADHD. The better we understand this disorder, the more tolerant, empathetic, and empowered we all will be to help.

The purpose of this book is to help parents and teachers gain insights into and better understanding of children and teenagers with ADHD, as well as the support and intervention that will help them succeed. Although the book is primarily written for parents and teachers, many others interested in children and teens with ADHD (physicians, mental health professionals, other school personnel, and relatives, for example) should find the information useful as well. Most of the book focuses on specific strategies, supports, and interventions that have been found to be effective in minimizing the typical problems associated with ADHD and helping these children and teens achieve their potential.

This new edition of my original *ADD/ADHD Checklist,* first published in 1998, has been completely updated with the most current information on the disorder. It is designed in a simple, concise, user-friendly format of checklists that address a number of topics. The checklists are divided into five sections.

Section One provides general information about the disorder, its likely causes, common coexisting conditions, and the diagnosis and treatment of ADHD—what most experts in the field believe about it, based on the scientific evidence available at this time. It also includes information about educational rights for students with ADHD.

Section Two is specifically for parents. It looks at topics that are relevant to managing ADHD behavior at home and in other settings, how to pursue an evaluation for ADHD, and strategies for homework, organization skills, and other areas for helping their children to be successful at school as well.

Section Three is geared toward teachers, with checklists on classroom strategies, supports, and accommodations (behavioral, instructional, and environmental). Teachers should note that the strategies suggested in this section are beneficial for all students, not just those with ADHD.

Section Four offers information about common academic difficulties in students with ADHD. It also provides a host of strategies, supports, and accommodations in the areas of reading, math, and written language that both teachers and parents can use to help strengthen their children's skills and boost academic achievement.

Section Five contains other important information on ADHD, such as boosting memory, relaxation, exercise, and other self-regulation strategies, and social skill interventions. It also contains specific information and strategies related to ADHD in early childhood and in adolescence, as well as several recommended resources.

I learned a number of the strategies and recommendations in this book from my many wonderful students with ADHD, their families, and my colleagues in my twenty-three years of teaching. In addition, during my consulting in schools, speaking engagements, and training, I have had the extraordinary privilege of observing hundreds of classrooms and working with scores of educators and other practitioners across the United States and internationally. I am grateful to them all and awed by their dedication and commitment.

It is always preferable to be able to identify children with ADHD or any other special needs early, initiating interventions and supports at a young age in order to avoid some of the frustration, failure, and subsequent loss of self-esteem. However, it is never too late to help. Fortunately, we know a lot from the enormous amount of research about the interventions that are effective in managing ADHD. Also, in many cases, the kind of help that makes a difference does not take a huge effort. For example, awareness of and simple changes in structuring the environment or responding to the child's behaviors can lead to significant improvements. If I am able to convey any message throughout this book, I wish for it to be one of hope and optimism. When we (parents, teachers and other school professionals, and clinicians) work together—providing intervention, appropriate strategies, encouragement, and support—every child can succeed.

Although I am maintaining the use of ADD/ADHD in the book's title (as in the first edition), I have chosen throughout the rest of this book to refer to this disorder as just ADHD, which is the way it is currently best known. Checklist 1.1 explains the differences in terminology. Please be aware that all references to ADHD encompass all types of the disorder.

June 2008   Sandra F. Rief
San Diego, California

In memory of my beloved son, Benjamin, and to all of the children who face obstacles in their young lives each day with loving, trusting hearts, determination, and extraordinary courage

My deepest thanks and appreciation to

- My precious, loving family: Itzik, Ariel, Jackie, Jason, Daniella, Sharon, and Gil
- All of the wonderful educators, doctors, and families of children with ADHD who have shared their insights and ideas with me over the years and have been an inspiration
- The extraordinary parents (especially the wonderful volunteers in CHADD and other organizations worldwide) whose tireless efforts have raised awareness about ADHD and as a result have improved the care and education of our children
- My editor, Margie McAneny, and the great team at Jossey-Bass.

⎯⎯ The Author

Sandra Rief, M.A., is an internationally known speaker, teacher trainer, educational consultant, and author. Her areas of focus include effective strategies and interventions for helping students with learning, attention, and behavioral challenges. Sandra is a popular presenter at seminars and workshops for educators, and keynotes nationally and internationally on the topics of ADHD and learning disabilities.

Previously an award-winning teacher with over twenty-three years' experience in the classroom, Sandra is the author of several popular books including *How to Reach and Teach Children with ADD/ADHD, Second Edition; The ADHD Book of Lists; How to Reach and Teach All Children in the Inclusive Classroom, Second Edition* (coauthored with Julie A. Heimburge); and *How to Reach and Teach All Children Through Balanced Literacy* (coauthored with Julie A. Heimburge)

Sandra also developed and presented these acclaimed educational videos: *ADHD & LD: Powerful Teaching Strategies and Accommodations; How to Help Your Child Succeed in School: Strategies and Guidance for Parents of Children with ADHD and/or Learning Disabilities; ADHD: Inclusive Instruction and Collaborative Practices,* and together with Linda Fisher and Nancy Fetzer, the videos *Successful Classrooms: Effective Teaching Strategies for Raising Achievement in Reading and Writing* and *Successful Schools: How to Raise Achievement & Support "At-Risk" Students.*

Sandra is an instructor for continuing education courses offered through California State University, East Bay, and Seattle Pacific University. For more information, visit her Web site at www.sandrarief.com.

Basic Information on ADHD

1.1 ADD, ADHD, AD/HD: WHAT'S THE DIFFERENCE?

• *AD/HD* stands for *Attention Deficit/Hyperactivity Disorder*. Sometimes it is written with the slash mark (*AD/HD*) and sometimes without (*ADHD*). This is the current and official term that is used when referring to this disorder, and it is the umbrella term for the three types of AD/HD: the Predominantly Inattentive type (AD/HD-I), the Predominantly Hyperactive and Impulsive type (AD/HD-HI), and the Combined type (AD/HD-C). Most people diagnosed with ADHD have the combined type of the disorder with significant symptoms in inattention, impulsivity, and hyperactivity.

• *ADD* stands for *Attention Deficit Disorder* and has been a term associated with this disorder for many years. Many people use *ADD* interchangeably with *ADHD* when referring to all types of the disorder, and it is also the term of choice by many when referring to the Predominantly Inattentive type of ADHD, that is, individuals without hyperactivity.

• The federal special education law (Individuals with Disabilities Education Act, IDEA) regulations that govern educational rights of children with disabilities refer to both ADD and ADHD among the "other health impairments" that may qualify a student for special education and related services (if they meet all of the other eligibility criteria).

• It is likely that there will be changes in the name and abbreviation of this disorder (or among some types of the disorder) in the future.

• Throughout the remainder of this book, I just use *ADHD* (without the slash mark), which is inclusive of all three types.

1.2 DEFINITIONS AND DESCRIPTIONS OF ADHD

There are several descriptions or definitions of ADHD based on the research evidence and most widely held belief of the scientific community at this time, including the following from leading experts and researchers in the field:

• ADHD is a neurobiological behavioral disorder characterized by chronic and developmentally inappropriate degrees of inattention, impulsivity, and in some cases hyperactivity.

• ADHD is a chronic biochemical, neurodevelopmental disorder that interferes with a person's capacity to regulate and inhibit behavior and sustain attention to tasks in developmentally appropriate ways.

• ADHD is a neurological inefficiency in the area of the brain that controls impulses and is the center of executive functions—the self-regulation and self-management functions of the brain.

• ADHD is a developmental delay or lag in inhibition, self-control, and self-management.

• ADHD is a brain-based disorder that arises out of differences in the central nervous system in both structural and neurochemical areas.

• ADHD is a pattern or constellation of behaviors that are so pervasive and persistent that they interfere with daily life.

• ADHD is a dimensional disorder of human behaviors that all people exhibit at times to certain degrees. Those with ADHD display the symptoms to a significant degree that is maladaptive and developmentally inappropriate compared to others that age.

• ADHD is a developmental disorder of self-control. It consists of problems with regulating attention, impulse control, and activity level.

• ADHD represents a condition that leads individuals to fall to the bottom of a normal distribution in their capacity to demonstrate and develop self-control and self-regulatory skills.

• ADHD is a disorder of inhibition (being able to wait, stop responding, and not respond to an event). Inhibition involves motor inhibition, delaying gratification, and turning off or resisting distractions in the environment while engaged in thinking.

• ADHD is a neurobiological behavioral disorder causing a high degree of variability and inconsistency in performance, output, and production.

• ADHD is a common although highly varied condition. One element of this heterogeneity is the frequent co-occurrence of other conditions.

1.3 RISK FACTORS ASSOCIATED WITH ADHD

ADHD places those who have this disorder at risk for a host of serious consequences. Numerous studies have shown the negative impact of this disorder without early identification, diagnosis, and proper treatment. Compared to their peers of the same age, youth with ADHD (those untreated for their disorder) experience:

• More serious accidents, hospitalizations, and significantly higher medical costs

• More school failure and dropout

• More delinquency and altercations with the law

• More engagement in antisocial activities

• More teen pregnancy and sexually transmitted diseases

• Earlier experimentation with and higher use of alcohol, tobacco, and illicit drugs

• More trouble socially and emotionally

• More rejection, ridicule, and punishment

• More underachievement and underperformance at school or work

Prevalence of ADHD

• Estimates of the prevalence in school-age children range from 3 percent to 12 percent. Most sources agree that somewhere between 5 and 9 percent of children are affected.

• Approximately 2 to 4 percent of adults are believed to have ADHD.

• The worldwide prevalence of ADHD in children is estimated at approximately 5 percent. The U.S. prevalence rate falls somewhere in the middle range of other reporting countries.

• Although this disorder can have serious negative outcomes affecting millions of people when untreated, it is estimated that at least half of the children with ADHD are not receiving treatment, and far more adults remain unidentified and untreated.

More Statistics Associated with ADHD

• Between 50 and 75 percent of individuals with ADHD have at least one other disorder or coexisting condition such as anxiety, depression, oppositional defiant disorder, learning disabilities, or speech and language impairments. *See checklist 1.7.*

• Barkley (2000), a leading researcher in the field, cites these statistics:

> • Almost 35 percent of children with ADHD quit school before completion.
>
> • Up to 58 percent have failed at least one grade in school.
>
> • At least three times as many teens with ADHD as those without ADHD have failed a grade, been suspended, or been expelled from school.
>
> • For at least half of the children with ADHD, social relationships are seriously impaired.
>
> • Within their first two years of independent driving, adolescents with a diagnosis of ADHD have nearly four times as many auto accidents and three times as many citations for speeding as young drivers without ADHD (Barkley & Murphy, 1996).

• For more information, go to the Web sites of CHADD (Children and Adults with Attention Deficit/Hyperactivity; www.chadd.org), the National Resource Center on ADHD (www.help4adhd.org), and the National Institute of Mental Health (www.nimh.nih.gov/health/).

References

Barkley, R. A. (2000). *Taking charge of ADHD* (Rev. ed.). New York: Guilford Press.

Barkley, R. A., Murphy, K. R., & Kwasni, D. (1996). Motor vehicle driving competencies and risks in teens and young adults with ADHD. *Pediatrics, 98*(6 Pt. 1), 1089–1095.

1.4 BEHAVIORAL CHARACTERISTICS OF ADHD

The fourth edition of the *Diagnostic and Statistical Manual of Mental Disorders* (DSM-IV) and the text revised edition (DSM-IV-TR), published by the American Psychiatric Association, is the source of the official criteria for diagnosing ADHD. The DSM lists nine specific symptoms under the category of inattention and nine specific symptoms under the hyperactive/impulsive category. Part of the diagnostic criteria for ADHD is that the child or teen often displays at least six of the nine symptoms of *either* the inattentive *or* the hyperactive-impulsive categories *or* six of the nine symptoms in *both* categories.

The checklists that follow contain symptoms and characteristics common in children and teens with ADHD. The specific behaviors listed in the DSM-IV (1994) and DSM-IV-TR (2000) are italicized. Additional symptoms and characteristics associated with ADHD are also included; they are not italicized.

Predominantly Inattentive Type of ADHD

• This type of ADHD is what many prefer to call ADD because those diagnosed with it do not have the hyperactive symptoms. They may show some, but not a significant amount of symptoms in the hyperactive-impulsivity category.

• These children and teens often slip through the cracks and are not as easily identified or understood. Since they do not exhibit the disruptive behaviors that command attention, it is easy to overlook these students and misinterpret their behaviors and symptoms as "not trying" or "being lazy."

• Most people display any of the following behaviors at times and in different situations to a certain degree. Those who truly have an attention deficit disorder have a history of frequently exhibiting many of these behaviors—far above the normal range developmentally. They are pervasive symptoms, exhibited in different settings and environments, and they cause impairment in functioning at school, at home, and in other settings.

• Many children with ADHD and significant difficulties with inattention are often able to be focused and sustain attention for long periods of time when they play video games or are engaged in other high-interest, stimulating, and rapidly changing activities.

CHARACTERISTICS AND SYMPTOMS OF INATTENTION

- *Easily distracted by extraneous stimuli* (for example, sights, sounds, movement in the environment)
- *Does not seem to listen when spoken to directly*
- Difficulty remembering and following directions
- *Difficulty sustaining attention in tasks and play activities*
- Difficulty sustaining level of alertness to tasks that are tedious, perceived as boring, or not of one's choosing
- *Forgetful in daily activities*
- *Does not follow through on instructions and fails to finish schoolwork, chores, or duties in the workplace (not due to oppositional behavior or failure to understand instructions)*
- Tunes out; may appear "spacey"
- Daydreams (thoughts are elsewhere)
- Appears confused
- Easily overwhelmed
- Difficulty initiating or getting started on tasks
- Does not complete work, resulting in many incomplete assignments
- *Avoids, dislikes, or is reluctant to engage in tasks requiring sustained mental effort such as schoolwork or homework*
- Difficulty working independently; needs a high degree of refocusing attention to task
- Gets bored easily
- Sluggish or lethargic (may fall asleep easily in class)

- *Fails to pay attention to details and makes many careless mistakes* (for example, with math computation, spelling, and written mechanics such as capitalization and punctuation)

- Poor study skills

- Inconsistent performance; one day is able to perform a task and the next day cannot; the student is "consistently inconsistent"

- *Loses things necessary for tasks or activities (for example, toys, school assignments, pencils, books, or tools)*

- *Difficulty organizing tasks and activities* (for example, planning, scheduling, preparing)

ACADEMIC DIFFICULTIES RELATED TO INATTENTION
Reading

- Loses his or her place when reading

- Cannot stay focused on what he or she is reading (especially if the text is difficult, lengthy, boring, or not of his or her choice reading material), resulting in missing words, details, and spotty comprehension

Writing

- Off topic as a result of losing train of thought

- Poor spelling, use of capitalization and punctuation, and other mechanics and a poor ability to edit written work as a result of inattention to these details

Math

- Numerous computational errors because of inattention to operational signs (plus, minus, multiplication, division), decimal points, and so forth

- Poor problem solving due to inability to sustain the focus to complete all steps of the problem with accuracy

Predominantly Hyperactive-Impulsive Type of ADHD

- Individuals with this type of ADHD have a significant number of hyperactive-impulsive symptoms; they may have some but not a significant number of inattentive symptoms considered developmentally inappropriate. This type of ADHD is most commonly diagnosed in early childhood, and many of those receiving this diagnosis will be reclassified as having the combined type of ADHD when they get older and the inattentive symptoms become developmentally significant.

• Children and teens with ADHD may exhibit many of the characteristics in the lists that follow. Although each of these behaviors is normal in children at different ages to a certain degree, for those with ADHD, the behaviors far exceed that which is normal developmentally (in frequency, level, and intensity). Again, the behaviors written in italics are those listed in the DSM-IV and DSM-IV-TR.

• Most children, teens, and adults with ADHD have the combined type of the disorder. That means they have a significant number of inattention, impulsive, and hyperactive symptoms that are chronic and developmentally inappropriate, evident from an early age, and are impairing evident from an early age and are impairing their functioning in at least two environments (such as home and school).

CHARACTERISTICS AND SYMPTOMS OF HYPERACTIVITY

- *"On the go" or acts as if "driven by a motor"*
- *Leaves seat in classroom or in other situations in which remaining seated is expected*
- Cannot sit still (instead, jumps up and out of chair, falls out of chair, sits on knees, or stands by desk)
- *Talks excessively*
- Highly energetic; almost nonstop motion
- *Runs about or climbs excessively in situations in which it is inappropriate (in adolescents or adults, may be limited to subjective feelings of restlessness)*
- A high degree of unnecessary movement (pacing, tapping feet, drumming fingers)
- Restlessness
- Seems to need something in hands; finds or reaches for nearby objects to play with or put in mouth
- *Fidgets with hands or feet or squirms in seat*

- Is not where he or she is supposed to be (for example, roams around)
- *Difficulty playing or engaging in leisure activities quietly*
- Intrudes in other people's space; difficulty staying within own boundaries
- Difficulty settling down or calming self
- Overall difficulty regulating motor activity

CHARACTERISTICS AND SYMPTOMS OF IMPULSIVITY

- Much difficulty in situations requiring waiting patiently
- Difficulty with raising hand and waiting to be called on
- *Interrupts or intrudes on others* (for example, butts into conversations or games)
- *Blurts out answers before questions have been completed*
- *Has difficulty waiting for his or her turn in games and activities*
- Cannot keep hands and feet to self
- Cannot wait or delay gratification; wants things immediately
- Knows the rules and consequences but repeatedly makes the same errors or infractions of rules
- Gets in trouble because he or she cannot stop and think before acting (responds first, thinks later)
- Difficulty standing in lines
- Makes inappropriate noises
- Does not think or worry about consequences, so tends to be fearless or gravitate to high-risk behavior
- Engages in physically dangerous activities without considering the consequences (for example, jumping from heights, riding bike into the street without looking); hence, a high frequency of injuries
- Accident prone and breaks things
- Difficulty inhibiting what he or she says, making tactless comments; says whatever pops into his or her head and talks back to authority figures
- Begins tasks without waiting for directions (before listening to the full direction or taking the time to read written directions)

- Hurries through tasks, particularly boring ones, to get finished, and consequently makes numerous careless errors
- Gets easily bored and impatient
- Does not take time to correct or edit work
- Disrupts, bothers others
- Constantly drawn to something more interesting or stimulating in the environment
- Hits when upset or grabs things away from others (not inhibiting responses or thinking of consequences)

OTHER COMMON CHARACTERISTICS IN CHILDREN AND TEENS WITH ADHD

- Disorganized, frequently misplaces or loses belongings; desks, backpacks, lockers, and rooms extremely messy and chaotic
- Little or no awareness of time; often underestimates length of time a task will require to complete
- Procrastinates
- A high degree of emotionality (for example, temper outbursts, quick to anger, gets upset, irritable, moody)
- Easily frustrated
- Overly reactive
- Difficulty with transitions and changes in routine or activity
- Displays aggressive behavior
- Difficult to discipline
- Cannot work for long-term goals or payoffs
- Low self-esteem
- Poor handwriting, fine motor skills, written expression, and output—getting their ideas down on paper and amount of work produced
- Overly sensitive to sounds and other stimuli in the environment
- Motivational difficulties
- Receives a lot of negative attention and interaction from peers and adults

• Learning and school performance difficulties; not achieving or performing to level that is expected given his or her apparent ability

References

American Psychiatric Association. (1994). *Diagnostic and statistical manual of mental disorders* (4th ed.). Washington, DC: Author.

American Psychiatric Association. (2000). *Diagnostic and statistical manual of mental disorders—IV-TR* (4th ed., text rev.). Washington, DC: Author.

1.5 ADHD AND THE EXECUTIVE FUNCTIONS

• Many of the difficulties associated with ADHD center on the ability to employ the *executive functions* of the brain. It is now understood that ADHD is more than a disorder of the three core symptoms of inattention, impulsivity, and hyperactivity; it affects the executive functions of the brain as well. Much of what we have learned since the 1990s about the developmental delay in executive functioning and the significant impact it has on the academic performance of students with ADHD comes from the work of leading ADHD researchers and authorities (particularly Dr. Russell Barkley, Dr. Martha Denckla, and Dr. Thomas E. Brown).

• Executive functions are:

  • The management functions ("overseers") of the brain

  • The self-directed actions individuals use to help maintain control of themselves and accomplish goal-directed behavior

  • The range of central control processes in the brain that activate, organize, focus, integrate, and manage other brain functions

  • Brain functions that have to do with self-regulation of behavior

  • The higher-order cognitive processes involved in the regulation of behavior, inhibition of impulses, planning, and organizing

• For all people, the executive functions are the last part of the brain to develop fully. Research shows that children and teens with ADHD lag in their development of executive functioning skills. This developmental delay is estimated to be approximately 30 percent compared to other children their age. In other words, a fifteen-year-old with ADHD is developmentally more like a ten-year-old and a ten-year-old is more like a seven-year-old in their behaviors related to executive functioning and self-management. It is important that teachers and parents understand that children with ADHD are immature in their self-regulation and self-management abilities in spite of how intelligent they may be. They will need more adult supports, monitoring, and supervision than other children or teens their age will require.

• It has not yet been determined exactly what constitutes all of the executive functions of the brain. However, some of these functions are believed to involve:

- Working memory (holding information in your head long enough to act on it)
- Organization of thoughts, time, and space
- Planning and prioritizing
- Arousal and activation
- Sustaining alertness and effort
- Self-regulation
- Emotional self-control
- Internalization of speech and language (using inner speech to guide behavior)
- Inhibiting verbal and nonverbal responding
- Quick retrieval and analysis of information
- Developing and following through on a plan of action
- Strategy monitoring and revising

• Children whose executive functions are immature and not working efficiently face a number of challenges, particularly with regard to schoolwork and homework. For example, weaknesses in executive functioning often cause difficulties to varying degrees with:

- Time awareness and time management
- Organization and study skills

- Perseverance on tasks and work production
- Delaying immediate gratification for long-term gain
- Decision making based on thoughtful weighing of consequences
- Planning for and completing long-term projects
- Forgetfulness and holding information in mind
- Moderating their emotions
- Using their metacognitive skills
- Ability to resist distractions
- Complex problem solving

• Executive functioning weaknesses commonly cause academic challenges to some degree (mild to severe), regardless of how intelligent, gifted, and capable the person may be. Consequently most children and teens with ADHD need some supportive strategies or accommodations, or both, to compensate for their deficit in executive functioning whether they are part of a written plan or not.

1.6 WHAT WE DO AND DO NOT YET KNOW ABOUT ADHD

What We Know

• ADHD has been the focus of a tremendous amount of research. Literally thousands of studies and scientific articles have been published (nationally and internationally) on ADHD.

• There is no quick fix or cure for ADHD, but it is treatable.

• Proper diagnosis and treatment can substantially decrease ADHD symptoms and impairment in functioning.

• The evidence from an overwhelming amount of worldwide research indicates that ADHD is a neurobiological, brain-based disorder.

• ADHD exists across all populations, regardless of race, ethnicity, gender, nationality, or socioeconomic level.

• ADHD symptoms range from mild to severe.

• There are different types of ADHD with a variety of characteristics. No one has all of the symptoms or displays the disorder in the exact same way.

• A very high percentage (approximately 50 to 75 percent) of children, teens, and adults with ADHD have additional coexisting disorders or conditions. *See checklist 1.7.*

• Many children and teens with ADHD slip through the cracks without being identified or receiving the intervention and treatment they need. This is particularly true of racial and ethnic minorities and girls.

• Although ADHD is diagnosed more frequently in boys than girls, research is showing that many more girls actually have ADHD but are not being diagnosed because they often do not have the disruptive behaviors associated with hyperactivity and impulsivity. *See checklist 1.4.*

• The challenging behaviors that children with ADHD exhibit stem from their physiological, neurobiological disorder. Rarely are these behaviors willful or deliberate. Children with ADHD are often not even aware of their behaviors and their impact on others.

• Children with ADHD are more likely than their peers to be suspended or expelled from school; retained a grade or drop out of school; have trouble socially and emotionally; and experience rejection, ridicule, and punishment. *See checklist 1.3.*

• ADHD is typically a lifelong disorder. The majority of children with ADHD (about 70 to 80 percent) continue to have substantial symptoms into adolescence, and many continue to exhibit symptoms into adulthood. In the past, ADHD was believed to be a childhood disorder. We now know that this is not the case.

• Although ADHD is most commonly diagnosed in school-age children, it can be and is diagnosed in younger children and adults as well.

• The prognosis for ADHD can be alarming if it is not treated. Without interventions, those with this disorder are at risk for serious problems in many domains: social, emotional, behavioral, academic, health, safety, employment, and others. *See checklist 1.3.*

• The prognosis for ADHD when treated is positive and hopeful. Most children who are diagnosed and provided with the help they need are able to manage the disorder. Parents should be optimistic because ADHD does not limit their child's potential. Countless highly successful adults in every profession and walk of life have ADHD.

• ADHD has been recognized by clinical science and documented in the literature since 1902 (having been renamed several times). Some of the previous names for the disorder were Minimal Brain Dysfunction, Hyperactive Child Syndrome, and ADD with or without Hyperactivity.

• Children with ADHD can usually be taught effectively in general education classrooms with proper management strategies, supports, and accommodations, and engaging, motivating instruction.

• ADHD is not the result of poor parenting or lack of caring, effort, and discipline.

• ADHD is not laziness, willful misbehavior, or a character flaw.

• Medication therapy and behavioral therapy are effective treatments for ADHD. *See checklists 1.12, 1.13, and 1.14.*

• Stimulant medications are proven to work effectively for reducing the symptoms and impairment in 70 to 95 percent of children diagnosed with ADHD. They are effective in adults as well. *See checklists 1.12, 1.13, and 1.15.*

• The use of behavioral programs, such as a token economy or a daily report card system between home and school, are beneficial for students with ADHD. *See checklist 1.14.*

• A number of other conditions, disorders, or factors (for example, learning, medical and health, social, emotional) may cause symptoms that look like but are not ADHD. *See checklist 1.9.*

• ADHD causes problems with performance and work production.

• A number of factors can intensify the problems of someone with ADHD or lead to significant improvement, such as the structure in the environment, support systems, or level of stress.

• ADHD can be managed best by a multimodal treatment and a team approach. We know that it takes a team effort of parents, school personnel, and health and mental health professionals to be most effective in helping children and teens with ADHD. *See checklists 1.12 and 5.1.*

• No single intervention will be effective for treating and managing ADHD. It takes vigilance, ongoing treatment and intervention plans, as well as revision of plans.

• The teaching techniques and strategies that are necessary for the success of children with ADHD are good teaching practices and helpful to all students.

• There are many resources available for children, teens, and adults with ADHD, as well as those living with and working with individuals with ADHD. *See checklists 5.7 and 5.8.*

• There is need for better diagnosis, education, and treatment of this disorder that affects so many lives.

• We are learning more and more each day due to the efforts of the many researchers, practitioners (educators, mental health professionals, physicians), and others committed to improving the lives of individuals with ADHD.

• Fortunately, we know a great deal about:

- Which behavior management techniques and discipline strategies are effective in the home and school for children with ADHD. *See checklists 1.14, 2.2–2.5, and 3.1–3.4.*
- The classroom interventions, accommodations, and teaching strategies most helpful for students with ADHD. *See checklists 3.6–3.10, and 3.13–3.17.*
- Specific parenting strategies that are most effective with children who have ADHD. *See checklists 2.1–2.12.*
- Research-validated treatments that have been proven effective in reducing the symptoms and improving functioning of individuals with ADHD. *See checklists 1.12, 1.13, 1.14, and 5.4.*
- Many additional strategies that help those with ADHD build skills and compensate for their weaknesses (for example, with self-regulation, academics, study skills, and interpersonal relationships). *See checklists 4.2, 4.4, 4.6, 4.7, 4.8, 4.9, 4.10, 4.11, 5.2, 5.3, and 5.4.*

What We Do Not Yet Know

• A lot about ADHD is still unknown, and there is much that we do not know enough about at this time. Among other things, research is needed to learn more about the following:

- The causes
- How to prevent ADHD or minimize the risk factors and negative effects
- The inattentive type of ADHD
- The disorder in certain populations (early childhood; adults; females; racial and ethnic minorities)
- More conclusive tests for diagnosing ADHD
- Long-term treatment effects
- What may prove to be the best, most effective treatments and strategies for helping individuals with ADHD

1.7 ADHD AND COEXISTING CONDITIONS AND DISORDERS

ADHD is often accompanied by one or more other conditions or disorders: psychiatric, psychological, developmental, or medical. Because symptoms of these various disorders commonly overlap, diagnosis and treatment can be complex in many individuals. The word *comorbidity* is the medical term for having coexisting disorders.

• At least half, and as high as two-thirds, of children and teens with ADHD have at least one other coexisting disorder, such as learning disabilities, oppositional defiant disorder, Tourette syndrome, anxiety disorder, or depression.

• Coexisting disorders can cause significant impairment above and beyond the problems caused by ADHD.

• Coexisting conditions make diagnosis, intervention, and management more complicated.

• In order to effectively treat the child or teen, an accurate diagnosis must first be made. That is why it is so important for the clinician making the diagnosis to be skilled and very knowledgeable about ADHD and coexisting conditions. It will be important to tease out what is ADHD and what may be something else—such as a different condition with similar symptoms or additional disorders or conditions that accompany or coexist with the ADHD. *See checklist 1.9.*

• Determining the proper diagnosis requires that the evaluator takes the time and is thorough in obtaining information and data about the child from multiple sources and perspectives and carefully reviewing the history and behaviors. It also can take time for all of the pieces of the puzzle to come together, and parents, teachers, and clinicians need to monitor the child's development and any emerging concerns.

Common Coexisting Conditions and Disorders

• The prevalence of specific coexisting conditions and disorders accompanying ADHD varies depending on the source. Most sources indicate the following ranges:

• Oppositional defiant disorder—approximately 40 to 65 percent

• Anxiety disorder—approximately 25 to 30 percent of children and 25 to 40 percent of adults

- Conduct disorder—approximately 10 to 25 percent of children, 25 to 50 percent of adolescents, and 20 to 25 percent of adults

- Bipolar—approximately 1 to 20 percent

- Depression—approximately 10 to 30 percent in children and 10 to 47 percent in adolescents and adults

- Tics, Tourette syndrome—about 7 percent of those with ADHD have tics or Tourette syndrome, but 60 percent of Tourette syndrome patients also have ADHD

- Learning disabilities—a range from 20 to 60 percent, with most sources estimating that between one-quarter and one-half of children with ADHD have a coexisting learning disability

- Sleep problems—approximately 40 to 50 percent

- Secondary behavioral complications—up to 65 percent of children with ADHD may display secondary behavioral complications such as noncompliance, argumentativeness, temper outbursts, lying, blaming others, and being easily angered

• Go to the Web site of the National Resource Center on AD/HD (www.help4adhd.org) for the most up-to-date and reliable information about coexisting disorders with ADHD and recommended treatment.

Consequences of Comorbidities

• Most children with ADHD have school-related achievement, performance, or social problems.

• Because such a high percentage of children with ADHD also have learning disabilities, a psychoeducational evaluation by the school team is very important when a possible learning disability is suspected. *See checklists 1.20, 2.17, and 3.1.*

• Parents, educators, and medical and mental health care providers should be alert to signs of other disorders and issues that may exist or emerge, often in the adolescent years, especially when current strategies and treatments being used with the ADHD child or teen are no longer working effectively. For example, children with the combined type of ADHD are at a much higher risk than the average child of developing a more serious disruptive behavior disorder (oppositional defiant disorder or conduct disorder). There is also a high rate of coexisting depression and anxiety disorder in teenage girls with ADHD that can easily be overlooked.

• It is important to recognize the risks, identify coexisting conditions, and provide the necessary treatment and support to address the problems that stem from ADHD and any other disorders or conditions that exist.

• Early identification of ADHD and implementing appropriate interventions can help significantly in all respects, reducing the risk for future problems developing and increasing overall successful outcomes.

1.8 POSSIBLE CAUSES OF ADHD

ADHD has been researched extensively in the United States and a number of other countries throughout the world. Hundreds of well-designed and controlled scientific studies have tried to determine the causes and most effective treatments for those with ADHD. Sophisticated brain-imaging technologies and recent genetic research have provided a lot of information and hold promise of much more to come. To date, however, the causes of ADHD are not fully known or understood and there are a number of theories. Nevertheless, based on the enormous amount of research so far, there is a lot of consensus in the scientific community about most probable causes.

Heredity

• Based on the evidence, heredity is the most common cause of ADHD: believed to account for about 80 percent of children with ADHD.

• ADHD is known to run in families, as found by numerous studies (for example, twin studies with identical and fraternal twins, adopted children, family studies, and molecular genetic studies).

• It is believed that a genetic predisposition to the disorder is inherited. Children with ADHD frequently have a parent, sibling, grandparent, or other close relative with ADHD or whose history indicates they had similar problems and symptoms during childhood.

• Molecular genetic studies and candidate-gene studies have identified certain genes linked to ADHD. Since ADHD is a complex disorder with multiple traits, future research will likely identify multiple genes involved in ADHD.

• It is hypothesized that the child may inherit a biochemical condition in the brain that influences the expression of ADHD symptoms. An abnormality in one or more genes associated with ADHD may be inherited, such as one of the genes that regulates dopamine activity in the brain. Others suggest that what is inherited is a tendency toward problems in the development of the brain region associated with executive functioning and self-regulation.

Diminished Activity and Lower Metabolism in Certain Brain Regions

• Numerous studies measuring electrical activity, blood flow, and brain activity have found differences between those with ADHD and control groups (those without ADHD), including:

- • Decreased activity level in certain regions of the brain (mainly the frontal region and basal ganglia). These regions that are underactivated are known to be responsible for controlling activity level, impulsivity, attention, and executive functions.

- • Lower metabolism of glucose (the brain's energy source) in the frontal region.

- • Decreased blood flow to certain brain regions associated with ADHD.

- • Less electrical activity in these key areas of the brain.

• These differences have been identified using brain activity and imaging tests and scans—for example, functional magnetic resonance imaging (MRI), single photon emission computed tomography (SPECT), positron emission tomography (PET), and electroencephalograms (EEGs).

• Although imaging and other brain tests are used in researching ADHD, they are not used in diagnosing it.

Chemical Imbalance or Deficiency in Neurotransmitters

• There is strong scientific evidence that those with ADHD have a deficiency, imbalance, or inefficiency in brain chemicals (neurotransmitters) that affect certain brain regions associated with ADHD—particularly the prefrontal cortex. The two main neurotransmitters involved in ADHD are dopamine and norepinephrine, and their levels in those affected brain regions are believed to influence attention, inhibition, motivation, and motor activity.

• The neurotransmitters are the chemical messengers of the brain. The neurons in the brain are not connected. They have a "synapse" or gap between them. The neurotransmitters help carry messages between two neurons by releasing into the synapse and then being recycled or taken back to the first neuron once the message gets across. It is believed that with ADHD, those brain chemicals (dopamine and norepinephrine) may not be efficiently releasing and staying long enough in the synapse in order to do their job in that region and circuits of the brain effectively.

• Stimulant medications for ADHD are believed to work by normalizing the brain chemistry of the neurotransmitters and increasing the availability of the dopamine and norepinephrine in underactivated regions of the brain. *See checklist 1.13.*

Prenatal Exposure to Certain Toxins

There has been found to be an association between prenatal exposure to some environmental toxins and ADHD. Certain substances the pregnant mother consumes or exposes the developing fetus to are believed to increase risk factors and may be a contributing cause for ADHD in some children. This includes fetal exposure to alcohol, nicotine from cigarettes, and high levels of lead.

Birth Complications, Illnesses, and Brain Injury

• For a very small percentage of children with ADHD, some causes may be related to:

- Birth complications, such as toxemia or significantly premature birth and low birthweight
- Trauma or head injury to the frontal part of the brain
- Certain illnesses that affect the brain, such as encephalitis

Structural Brain Differences and Delays in Brain Development

• There is evidence of some slight structural differences in certain brain regions believed responsible for ADHD:

  • As a group, children with ADHD show slightly smaller volume in brain regions (approximately 3 to 4 percent) compared to those without ADHD but follow a normal growth curve.

  • Recent evidence supports that ADHD may involve a delay in the brain development of some areas, particularly maturation in areas of the cortex.

Environmental Factors

• Lead poisoning, which can occur prenatally or later, is one environmental factor that increases a child's chances of developing ADHD. Many people wonder about exposure to other unknown toxins that may have harmful effects on the brain's development.

• The scientific community generally believes that environmental factors influence the severity of ADHD symptoms and their expression and can play a role in increasing symptoms but that they typically are not the cause of ADHD.

• Research has not supported many of the suggested causes that continue to be popular beliefs (for example, consuming too much sugar or poor parenting). These are not causes of ADHD.

• There is evidence that for a very small subgroup of children who have super sensitivities, certain food additives and preservatives may cause allergic reactions and hyperactive symptoms.

1.9 ADHD LOOK-ALIKES

• Not everyone who displays symptoms of ADHD has an attention deficit disorder. A number of other conditions and factors can cause inattentive, hyperactive, and impulsive behaviors. The following list contains some disorders or conditions that might coexist with ADHD (*see checklist 1.7*) or that may produce some symptoms that look like or mimic ADHD:

Learning disabilities

Sensory impairments (hearing, vision, motor problems)

Substance use and abuse (of alcohol and drugs)

Oppositional defiant disorder

Conduct disorder

Allergies

Posttraumatic stress disorder

Anxiety disorder

Depression

Obsessive-compulsive disorder

Sleep disorders

Bipolar disorder

Thyroid problems

Rare genetic disorders (for example, fragile X syndrome)

Seizure disorders

Lead poisoning

Hypoglycemia

Anemia

Fetal alcohol syndrome, fetal alcohol effects

Chronic illness

Language disorders

Tourette syndrome

Pervasive developmental disorder

Asperger's syndrome

Autism

Developmental delays

Sensory integration dysfunction

Low intellectual ability

High intellectual ability, giftedness

Severe emotional disturbance

Side effects of medications being taken (for example, antiseizure medication, asthma medication)

• Emotional and environmental factors that have nothing to do with ADHD can also cause a child or teen to be distracted, unable to concentrate, and have acting-out or aggressive behaviors—for example:

- Experiencing or witnessing physical or sexual abuse or violence
- Family stresses (for example, divorce and custody battles)
- Bullying or peer pressure and other peer and social issues
- A chaotic, unpredictable, unstable, or neglectful home life with inappropriate expectations placed on the child

• Inattention and disruptive classroom behaviors can be school related and have nothing to do with ADHD. Students may display those behaviors if they are in a school environment that has:

- A pervasive negative climate
- Poor instruction and low academic expectations

• Nonstimulating and unmotivating curriculum
• Ineffective classroom management

1.10 GIRLS WITH ADHD

• Many girls with ADHD are undiagnosed or misdiagnosed. They are often overlooked or labeled and written off as being "space cadets," "ditzy," or "scattered."

• Most have the inattentive type of ADHD. They do not have the hyperactive, disruptive behaviors that are problematic in the classroom. In fact, they may be shy and timid.

• Girls who *do* have the combined type of ADHD with hyperactivity are very recognizable because their behavior is significantly out of norm compared to other girls their age.

• Girls with ADHD often struggle with learning difficulties, social problems, and low self-esteem.

• Girls have the propensity to be overwhelmed, disorganized, forgetful, and self-critical.

• It is common for girls to exhibit anxiety-related behaviors (pulling hair, biting nails, picking at cuticles).

• Girls with ADHD often put a lot of effort into trying to hide their academic difficulties and please their teachers, which contributes to why their struggles often go undetected and may not have raised the concern of their teachers when they should.

• Girls with the combined type of ADHD often demonstrate much giggling and silly behavior and their hyperactivity is commonly manifested as being hyperverbal, hypersocial (cannot stop talking, chatting, commenting on everything), and hyperemotional or reactive.

• Girls have the tendency to unleash frustrations at home that were kept hidden at school. Parents may see behaviors in their daughter such as temper tantrums and meltdowns that would never be exhibited at school.

• Research has begun to reveal the significance of gender differences and issues and will undoubtedly result in changes and improvements in the diagnosis and treatment for girls and women with this disorder.

• It is now known that:

- Females with ADHD have a greater likelihood of anxiety and depression.

- Girls with ADHD often have impaired social skills and tend to experience more peer rejection than boys with ADHD.

- Symptoms often increase rather than decrease at puberty, and although DSM-IV criteria for diagnosis require an onset of symptoms by age seven, girls may not show their symptoms until later.

- Hormones from puberty onward have a great impact on girls with ADHD. Premenstrual syndrome, for example, presents additional problems, worsening ADHD symptoms by adding to irritability, low frustration, mood swings, and emotionality.

- Impulsivity in girls can lead to binge eating and engaging in other high-risk activities, such as smoking, drinking, drugs, sexual promiscuity, and engaging in unprotected sex.

• Much of the awareness about gender differences in ADHD comes from the work of Kathleen Nadeau and others (2000), Patricia Quinn (2002), and others who have strongly advocated on behalf of females with ADHD. There is excellent information specific to issues and treatment of girls and women with ADHD found in books, publications, and web resources. For example, see the Web sites of the National Center for Girls and Women with AD/HD (www.ncgiadd. org) and http://www.ADDvance.com and others in *checklist 5.7*.

References

Nadeau, K., Littman, E., & Quinn, P. (2000). *Understanding girls with AD/HD*. Silver Spring, MD: Advantage Books.

Quinn, P., & Nadeau, K. (eds.). (2002). *Gender issues and AD/HD: Research, diagnosis, and treatment*. Silver Spring, MD: Advantage Books.

1.11 MAKING THE DIAGNOSIS: A COMPREHENSIVE EVALUATION FOR ADHD

The diagnosis of ADHD is not a simple process. There is no single laboratory test or measure to determine if a person has ADHD, and no particular piece of information alone can confirm or deny the existence of ADHD. Nevertheless, ADHD can be diagnosed reliably following the guidelines of medical and psychiatric associations. In future years, we may see the use of genetic testing, brain imaging, or other more conclusive tools and methods used for diagnostic purposes, but currently this is not the case.

The Diagnosis

• The cornerstone of an ADHD diagnosis is meeting the criteria described in the most current edition of the *Diagnostic and Statistical Manual of Mental Health Disorders,* published by the American Psychiatric Association: the DSM fourth edition (DSM-IV) and text-revised fourth edition (DSM-IV-TR). *See checklist 1.4.*

• The diagnosis is made by gathering and synthesizing information obtained from a variety of sources in order to determine if there is enough evidence to conclude that the child meets all of the criteria for having ADHD.

• The evaluator must collect and interpret data from multiple sources, settings, and methods and use his or her clinical judgment to determine if DSM-IV criteria have been met:

- The child has a sufficient number of ADHD symptoms (at least six out of the nine characteristics listed) in the categories of inattention or hyperactivity-impulsivity, or both.

- The symptoms are to a degree that is "maladaptive and inconsistent with the child's developmental level."

- Symptoms are serious enough to be causing significant impairment in the child's life and affecting the child's successful functioning in more than one setting (for example, at home, in school, or in social situations in other environments).

- These symptoms are chronic and have been evident from an early age (at least some of the characteristics are evident before age seven).

- Other factors, disorders, or conditions do not better account for these symptoms.

• An appropriate evaluation for ADHD takes substantial time. It is *not sufficient* for a child to be seen by a community physician for only a brief office visit without gathering and analyzing the necessary diagnostic data from the parents, school, and other sources.

• The guidelines of the American Academy of Pediatrics and American Psychiatric Association for diagnosing ADHD require obtaining sufficient evidence about symptoms and resulting impairment. These data or the evidence are to be obtained from parents or caregivers and from the school. If the school has not been communicated with and has not provided the evaluator information about the student's current functioning and school history, that is an inappropriate assessment for ADHD.

• Evaluation of the child with ADHD should include screening or assessment for coexisting conditions when indicated.

Qualifications for Evaluating a Child for ADHD

• A number of professionals have the qualifications to assess children for ADHD: child psychiatrists, pediatricians, child neurologists, clinical psychologists, clinical social workers, family practitioners, and other licensed medical and mental health professionals.

• Specialists in childhood medical and mental health, such as child psychiatrists, child neurologists, and developmental or behavioral pediatricians, are recommended for complex cases.

• The school psychologist and multidisciplinary team conduct a school-based assessment when indicated eligibility for special education, related services, or accommodations based on a disability causing educational impairment. *See checklist 1.20.*

Components of a Comprehensive Evaluation for ADHD

HISTORY

• An evaluation for ADHD requires taking a thorough history. This is the single most important feature of the evaluation process. The history is obtained through:

- Interviewing the parents or guardians
- Use of questionnaires, generally filled out by parents prior to office visits
- A review of previous medical and school records

• By using these techniques and instruments, the evaluator obtains important data regarding:

- The child's medical history (for example, fetal development, birth, illnesses, injuries)
- The child's developmental and school history
- The child's behavioral history
- Family medical and social history
- Any significant family circumstances such as death, serious illness in the family, or divorce
- Sense of the parents' style of discipline and interactions with the child
- Parents' perceptions of the child's strengths as well as difficulties

BEHAVIOR RATING SCALES

• These are useful in determining the degree to which various ADHD-related behaviors or symptoms are observed in different key environments (for example, home and school). In addition to information from teachers and parents, rating scales may be filled out by others who spend time with the child, such as the school counselor, special education teacher, child care provider, or other relative.

• A variety of scales and questionnaires can be used in the diagnosis of ADHD for obtaining information from parents and teachers. Some include: Vanderbilt Assessment Scales, Conners Parent and Teacher Rating Scales, ADD-H Comprehensive Teacher's Rating Scale (ACTeRS), Barkley Home and School Situations Questionnaires, SNAP-IV, Behavior Assessment System for Children (BASC-2), SWAN Rating Scale, and Brown ADD Scales.

CURRENT SCHOOL INFORMATION

• A key part of the diagnostic process is reviewing information supplied by the school that indicates current student performance (academic, behavioral, social). No one is in a better position than the teacher to report on the child's school performance compared to other children of that age and grade. This includes the teacher's observations, perceptions, and objective information indicating the child's academic productivity and social, emotional, and behavioral functioning. The teacher should share information regarding the student's ability to exhibit self-control, stay focused and on task, interact with peers and adults, initiate and follow through on assignments, and other behaviors.

• In an appropriate evaluation for ADHD, teachers will be asked to report their observations about the student through rating scales, questionnaires, narrative statements, phone interviews, or other measures.

• Other indicators of a student's current school performance (academic and behavioral) might be useful as well—for example, disciplinary referrals (among the records of guidance counselors or administrators) and work samples, particularly written samples.

INFORMATION ABOUT THE SCHOOL HISTORY

• Information indicating the existence of symptoms and difficulty the student experienced in his or her school history can be obtained from the school records. A great deal of useful data is located in the student's school records, which might include past report cards, district and state achievement testing, other school evaluations (psychoeducational, speech/language), referrals to the school team, and intervention plans such as individualized education plans.

OBSERVATIONS

• Directly observing the child's functioning in a variety of settings can provide helpful diagnostic information. Most useful are observations in natural settings where the child spends much of his or her time, such as school. How a child behaves and performs in an office visit is not indicative of how that same child performs and behaves in a classroom, on the playground, or in the cafeteria or other natural setting. Because most clinicians do not have the time to make visits to observe the child in the school setting, school personnel can make some observations and provide those observational reports to the evaluating doctor.

• Be aware:

> • The evaluator may or may not read through much supplementary data such as a lot of observational notes that the school sends due to time constraints. Schools should be sure to highlight the main points and supporting evidence. Schools should summarize the key information to communicate to the doctor or other clinician that best reports the student's behaviors and symptoms and how those behaviors are impairing the child's functioning (for example, academically, socially, and behaviorally).

- The school may not communicate or provide any information regarding a student without first obtaining from the parents or guardians their permission in writing. Parents need to fill out a release of information form granting the school permission to do so.

PHYSICAL EXAM
- A clinical evaluation for ADHD generally includes a routine examination to rule out other possible medical conditions that could produce ADHD symptoms. Based on the child's physical exam, as well as medical history (through interview and questionnaire), a physician may look for evidence of other possible causes for the symptoms or additional issues that may need to be addressed, such as sleep disturbances, bedwetting, or anxiety. Other medical tests (bloodwork, electroencephalogram, CT scans) are not done in an evaluation for ADHD. It is the doctor's responsibility to determine the need for additional medical testing or referral to other specialists if indicated.

ACADEMIC AND INTELLIGENCE TESTING
- An evaluator should have at least a general indication of a child's academic achievement levels and performance, as well as a rough estimate of his or her cognitive (thinking and reasoning) ability. This can partly be determined through a review of the student's report cards, standardized test scores, classroom work samples, informal screening measures, and reports from the teacher, parents, or student.
- If the child is exhibiting learning difficulties and struggles academically, a full psychoeducational evaluation needs to be done to determine ability, academic achievement levels, and information about how the child learns. Parents should request this evaluation from the school, which is the beginning of the individualized education program (IEP) process. *See checklist 1.20.*

PERFORMANCE TESTS
- Additional tests are sometimes used in a comprehensive evaluation to obtain more information about how a child functions on various performance measures. Some clinicians use computerized tests that measure the child's ability to inhibit making impulsive responses and to sustain attention to tasks. These tests, however, are not routinely done in ADHD assessments.

Finding a Professional to Evaluate Your Child

Parents are advised to investigate before selecting the professional to evaluate their child. It is important to find someone well qualified, preferably recommended by others.

Parents seeking professionals to evaluate and treat their child may wish to first speak with other parents of children who have ADHD (for example, through the local chapter of CHADD—Children and Adults with Attention Deficit/Hyperactivity Disorder) regarding recommended professionals in the community. School nurses and school psychologists are excellent resources and knowledgeable in most cases about health care providers in the community who have expertise in ADHD.

Parents should discuss with the individual the methods he or she will be using in the diagnostic process. It is important that this professional:

- Adheres to recommended diagnostic guidelines for ADHD
- Conducts a comprehensive and multidimensional evaluation
- Is knowledgeable about ADHD and coexisting conditions
- Takes the time to answer questions about assessment, treatment, and management to the parents' satisfaction

- Parents who are concerned about symptoms that are affecting their child's functioning and suspect that it may be the result of ADHD or another disorder or disability should pursue an evaluation. *See checklist 2.17.* At any point, they should communicate their concerns with their child's primary care physician and teachers.

- Parents should set up an appointment to meet with the classroom teacher and discuss his or her observations regarding the child's academic achievement, performance, and behavior.

- A school-based assessment can be done concurrent with, before, or after the clinical evaluation for ADHD. It is best to coordinate efforts. In pursuing a school evaluation, parents should let the teacher know why they want their child evaluated. They should also speak with the principal or other school team member (school psychologist, school nurse, special education teacher, or school counselor) regarding this request for testing.

- It is likely that the parent will be asked to meet with the school's multidisciplinary team. This team goes by various names in districts around the country, for example, the student support team (SST). During the SST meeting, information and concerns are reviewed as a team (classroom teacher, support staff, administrator, and parents). *See checklist 3.18.*

• The SST meeting is recommended protocol, particularly if the child has never been referred before and there has not yet been an intervention plan developed to address the student's difficulties in the classroom. It is especially helpful to have an SST meeting when considering an evaluation for ADHD for the following reasons:

> • The school can share with parents its role in the assessment of ADHD and obtain parental permission in writing to begin gathering data on such matters as the child's school history and current functioning.
>
> • Better coordination and communication usually follow if parents and school staff meet prior to initiating the diagnostic process.

• As long as the school arranges to meet with the parents in a reasonable time frame, it is often best if parents channel their concerns and request for testing through the SST (if such a team exists at the school). However, parents may choose not to go through this process and can request school testing at any time.

• The school has the responsibility of initiating and following through with a comprehensive evaluation if the child is suspected of having ADHD or any other disability impairing educational performance. If the student is found to be eligible under either of the two federal laws: Individuals with Disabilities Education Act (IDEA) or Section 504 of the Rehabilitation Act of 1973, the school must provide the appropriate supports, services, and accommodations the student needs. *See checklist 1.20.*

• In an ADHD evaluation and potential treatments and interventions, teachers can provide valuable insights and observations regarding:

> • The child's school performance difficulties (academic, social, behavioral)
>
> • How and to what degree the symptoms and behaviors are causing the student impairment in school functioning

- The most problematic times and environments (for example, transition times, the playground)
- The child's strengths, interests, and motivators
- Environmental, instructional, and behavioral strategies and interventions that have been tried and their degree of success

• In an ADHD evaluation and potential treatments and interventions, parents can provide valuable insights and observations regarding:

- The child's difficulties in learning, behavior, health, and social interactions (past and present)
- The child's strengths, interests, and motivators
- Responses to discipline and disciplinary techniques used in the home
- How the child responds when upset, angry, or frustrated
- How the child gets along with siblings, neighborhood children, and others
- The child's feelings: worries, fears, and other feelings

1.12 MULTIMODAL TREATMENT FOR ADHD

Once a child is diagnosed with ADHD, there are many ways to help. A multifaceted or multimodal treatment approach is the most effective. It is important to keep the following points in mind.

• Parents are the primary case managers for their children. When they receive the child's diagnosis, they need to start the journey of becoming an ADHD expert, learning all they can about the disorder and treatment options in order to make the best-informed decision for their child's care and management.

• Most positive outcomes for youngsters with ADHD are achieved when parents, teachers and other involved school personnel, and treating medical and mental health providers have good communication and collaborate well. *See checklist 5.1.*

• All parties involved in the care and education of the child with ADHD should be working together in establishing target outcomes (goals), formulating plans to reach the goals, and monitoring the effectiveness of the interventions being used.

• Since ADHD often lasts throughout one's lifetime, a person may need some of the supports and interventions at different times in life (for example, treatment from medical and mental health professionals, various school interventions, out-of-school tutoring or coaching services).

• The two research-validated interventions known at this time are *medication* and *psychosocial (or behavioral) therapy.* One, the other, or combination of both are the main treatments for ADHD, as the scientific evidence clearly shows these treatments to make the biggest difference with regard to improvement of symptoms and degree of impairment. These interventions have been extensively tested with controlled studies and proven effective in managing ADHD.

• Educational supports and interventions are a critical component in the success of students with ADHD as well.

• There are additional supports and interventions to enhance the plan and benefit the individual with ADHD.

Multimodal Intervention

• A multimodal treatment program may include a number of components.

• *Medical/pharmacological intervention.* Pharmacological treatment is the use of medication to manage ADHD symptoms. Stimulant medications (there are various types) have been proven effective in 70 to 95 percent of children with ADHD and in adults as well. They are called *stimulants* because they stimulate the underactivated parts of the brain, increasing the neurotransmitters or brain chemicals in those brain regions and circuits. Appropriate medical treatment requires well-managed and carefully monitored use of medication(s) for ADHD. When there are coexisting disorders, various medications may be prescribed in the treatment of those other conditions, as well. *See checklists 1.13, 1.15, and 1.7.*

• *Behavior modification and specific behavior management strategies implemented at home and school.* Both parents and teachers learn how to provide clear, consistent structure, follow-through, and effective use of rewards and consequences. These strategies also include specific techniques (for example, token economies, good communication between home and school, incentive systems, and positive reinforcement) to help increase the child's positive, appropriate behaviors and reduce the undesirable, unwanted behaviors. Among the research-validated behavioral interventions for children with ADHD are the use of daily report cards. See descriptions of daily report cards and a token economy system in *checklist 1.20*. Also see the many behavioral supports and strategies in *checklists 2.2–2.8 and 3.1–3.6*.

• *Parent training.* This is a key and crucial component of ADHD treatment, as parents must learn and be provided with:

- Accurate and reliable information about ADHD in order to understand the impact and developmental course of the disorder, the treatment options, and available resources
- A new set of skills for managing their child's challenging behaviors
- Training in effective behavioral techniques and how to structure the home environment and other aspects of their child's life

• The Parent-to Parent training program offered through CHADD (Children and Adults with Attention Deficit/Hyperactivity Disorder) is highly recommended. See www.chadd.org.

Other Psychosocial Interventions

• *Social skills training.* This training is usually provided in small groups with curriculum addressing specific skills that children with ADHD tend to have difficulties with in their interpersonal relationships. The children then practice the skills they have learned in natural settings where they have difficulty in their day-to-day life with feedback and reinforcement. *See checklist 5.4.*

• *Family counseling.* The whole family is often affected in the homes of children with ADHD (*see checklist 1.16*). Family therapy can address issues that affect parents and siblings and improve family relationships.

• *Individual counseling.* Counseling can teach the child coping techniques, self-monitoring and self-regulation strategies, problem-solving strategies, and how to deal with stress or anger.

• *Psychotherapy for teens and adults.* This counseling helps the person with ADHD and a history of school, work, personal, or relationship problems talk about his or her feelings and deal with self-defeating patterns of behavior.

• *Vocational counseling.* This can be a helpful intervention for teens and adults.

Educational Interventions

• *Differentiated instruction.* Teachers who recognize that one size does not fit all embrace the challenge of providing instruction and designing lessons that reach and teach diverse learners.

• *Providing accommodations* (environmental, academic, instructional, behavioral) as needed enables students to achieve success. *See checklists 3.6–3.17, 4.2, 4.4, 4.6–4.11, 5.2,* and others throughout this book.

• *Special education and related service.* Some students with ADHD who meet the eligibility criteria for special education benefit from these programs and services provided through the school district. *See checklist 1.20.*

• *Other school services and supports.* Various interventions and safety nets may be available at the school that any student may access (not just those in special education), such as homework or organizational assistance, mentoring, and academic tutorials.

• *Tutoring or academic supports.* This may be available both in and outside school.

Other Helpful Interventions

• *ADHD coaching.* This is a service that many teens and adults find beneficial in learning strategies to be more focused and productive and to help them with organization and time management. Coaching generally assists with scheduling, breaking work tasks down into reasonable short-term goals, checking in regularly (often over the phone or by e-mail), and keeping the ADHD client on target with his or her individual short- and long-term goals.

• *Support groups and opportunities to share with others and network.* Support organizations such as CHADD and the Attention Deficit Disorder Association (ADDA) are highly recommended resources (*see checklist 5.7*). CHADD has local chapters throughout the United States, and such groups are an excellent source of information and support. Online discussion groups and other vehicles to interact with others with similar concerns and experiences can be helpful.

• *Exercise.* It is important for children and teens with ADHD to build their physical skills and competencies (for example, in swimming, martial arts, gymnastics, track and field, dance, hiking, and other sports) and have an outlet for their need to move. Among the many benefits to medical and mental health is regulating mood. *See checklist 5.3.*

• *Building on their interests and developing their areas of strengths.* Arts and crafts, sports, scouts, dance, music, and the performing arts contribute to self-esteem and motivation and provide a creative outlet and fun.

• *Healthy diet and lifestyle.* Environmental factors can worsen ADHD symptoms and their expression. All children and teens (including those with ADHD) need to be health conscious and have a well-balanced diet, high in nutrition (plenty of protein, fruits, vegetables). Nutritionists point out that a balanced diet can help control behavioral swings related to surges in blood sugar or hunger. Getting a good night's sleep is also very important and can be very important but often problematic for some children and teens with ADHD. More outdoor activities as opposed to indoor ones (glued to a screen of some type) are good choices for everyone and may be even more important for those with ADHD.

Complementary and Alternative Treatments

• A number of alternative treatments have been claimed to be effective in treating ADHD: megavitamins, antimotion sickness medication, antioxidants, chiropractic adjustment and bone realignment, and others. These are unproven treatments without scientific evidence, however, and some have been discredited. In addition, a variety of "natural" products claim in their advertisements that they are effective in treating ADHD.

• Parents are cautioned that some so-called natural products can be harmful because they have not been through rigorous scientific testing for effectiveness or safety.

• Some treatments, for example, elimination diets, may be beneficial for certain children with sensitivities. Parents should always discuss this and other dietary concerns they may have with their physician.

• Neurofeedback (also called *biofeedback*) and used as a complementery or alternative treatment has been available for a number of years. These are brain exercises that take place during a series of sessions during which the child wears headgear lined with electrodes and performs video games and computerized tasks while brain wave activity in the frontal lobe (the part of the brain that is underaroused in those with ADHD) is measured. The treatment is supposed to increase the activation of brain waves in that part of the brain and train patients to eventually produce the brain-wave patterns associated with focus on their own. This is not yet a research-validated intervention for ADHD with sufficient scientific proof, but a number of experts in the field believe it does hold promise (particularly when used along with medication).

• A computer-based intervention called Cogmed Working Memory Training Program is generating interest internationally. This software program is designed to increase working memory— one of the key executive functions that is weak in children with ADHD (*see checklist 1.5*). It involves several exercises in a video game format. Although lacking sufficient research at this time, preliminary studies indicate that it is promising as a complementary intervention.

• For reliable information regarding alternative and complementary interventions, go to these Web sites: National Resource Center on AD/HD (www.help4adhd.org) and National Institutes of Health, National Center for Complementary and Alternative Medicine (http://nccam.nih.gov/).

Additional Points to Keep in Mind

• When pursuing any treatment, seek professionals who are knowledgeable and experienced in treating individuals with ADHD and coexisting conditions.

• The intervention plan should be designed not just to focus on areas of weakness, but also to help the child or teen recognize and build on his or her strengths.

• Parents need to be educated about ADHD and treatments, as well as their legal rights in the educational system (*see checklists 1.13, 1.14, 1.20, and 2.15*). This is necessary in order to advocate effectively for their child in both the educational and health care systems.

• Children, especially teens, should be included as active partners in their treatment program so that they will be willing to cooperate and participate in the program. They need to understand the disorder, the reason for various interventions, and how those treatments are intended to have a positive effect on their daily lives.

1.13 MEDICATION TREATMENT FOR ADHD

• Medications have been used safely for decades to treat ADHD. They do not cure the disorder but do help in controlling and reducing the symptoms. The most commonly used medications for treating ADHD are the stimulants.

• There continues to be much attention (media sensationalism and public controversy) regarding the use of stimulant medication in treating children with ADHD. A great deal of misinformation exists, which makes it difficult for parents trying to make an informed decision.

• Parents should consult with their physician or other medical professionals about any medication issues, questions, or concerns. This checklist is meant only as a general reference.

Stimulant Medications in the Treatment of ADHD

• Stimulant medications have been used since the 1930s in the treatment of children with behavioral disorders. Hundreds of controlled scientific studies demonstrating their effectiveness in children have been conducted.

• Stimulants have been proven to work for 70 to 95 percent of children with ADHD. They are also effective in adults. There are very few people who do not respond to stimulant medications, and the results can be dramatic.

• Because the scientific evidence so strongly supports the effectiveness of stimulants in managing the symptoms and reducing impairment, they are recommended as the first choice of medications used in treating children with ADHD.

• There are two main classes of stimulants: the methylphenidate formulas and the amphetamine formulas.

HOW STIMULANTS ARE BELIEVED TO WORK

• Researchers suspect that stimulant medications act to normalize biochemistry in the parts of the brain involved in ADHD (primarily the prefrontal cortex and basal ganglia).

• Stimulants increase (or stimulate) the production of neurotransmitters, which are the brain chemicals, to a more normalized level in these key brain regions.

• The brain chemicals mostly involved are dopamine and norepinephrine (*see checklist 1.6*). Scientists believe that medications that increase the availability of these neurotransmitters help nerve-to-nerve communication, thereby boosting the "signal" between neurons.

• The stimulants are thought to be working within the system involved in the release of dopamine into the synapse (the gap between two neurons), and reuptake or recyling of dopamine out of the synapse. Stimulants are believed to help in keeping the proper level of dopamine in the synapse long enough to do the job of transmitting messages from one neuron to the next efficiently.

• Stimulants (while in the bloodstream) work to activate the areas of the brain that are underactive and not working efficiently in those with ADHD. These are the regions responsible for attention, inhibition of behavior, regulation of activity level, and executive functions.

STIMULANT MEDICATIONS PRESCRIBED FOR TREATING ADHD

• There are several stimulant medications—some are methylphenidates and some are amphetamines. In the following list, the italicized name is the generic name, and the names in parentheses are the brand names. Also, SR stands for "sustained release," LA is "long acting," and ER and XR mean "extended release":

Methylphenidate Stimulants

- *Methylphenidate* (Ritalin, Ritalin LA, Ritalin SR, Concerta, Metadate CD, Metadate ER, Methylin, Methylin ER, Daytrana Patch)
- *Dexmethylphenidate* (Focalin, Focalin XR)

Amphetamine Stimulants

- *Dextroamphetamine* (Dexedrine, Dexedrine Spansule, DextroStat)
- *Mixed amphetamine salts* (Adderall, Adderall XR)
- *Methamphetamine hydrochloride* (Desoxyn)
- *Lisdexamfetamine dimesylate* (Vyvanse)

• Methylphenidates are among the most carefully studied drugs on the market. Thousands of children have been involved in research evaluating their use in the treatment of ADHD.

• Each of the stimulants has a high response rate. A child who does not respond well (in symptom improvement) to one stimulant medication will often respond well to another.

• Physicians have a number of possibilities of stimulants to choose from. The initial choice is generally a matter of doctor and parent preference.

• The different stimulant prescriptions vary in their onset (when they begin working), how they are released into the body (immediately or over an extended or sustained period), and how long the effects last (from a few hours to as high as twelve hours).

• The short-acting formulas of the stimulants:

> • Start to work about twenty to thirty minutes from the time the medication is taken
>
> • Metabolize quickly and are effective for approximately three to four hours
>
> • Generally require an additional dosage to be administered at school
>
> • May require a third dose (often a smaller one) to enable the child to function more successfully in the late afternoon and evening hours

• The longer-acting stimulants have a time-release delivery system. They:

> • Take longer for the effect to begin
>
> • Vary from approximately five to seven hours of coverage for some of the medications to lasting as long as ten to twelve hours for others
>
> • Provide a smoother, sustained level of the drug throughout the day
>
> • Minimize fluctuations (peak and trough) in blood levels
>
> • Minimize rebound phenomena (a worsening of symptoms as the effects of the drug wear off)
>
> • Eliminate the need for a midday dose at school, which is very beneficial for many children and teens, particularly those who are forgetful or embarrassed to take medication at school

BENEFITS OF STIMULANT MEDICATIONS
• They take effect quickly (generally within thirty minutes).

• Children often experience significant improvement once they are on stimulant medications. For the lucky ones, their initial prescription and dosage will work well. But many others require adjustments in dosage or trying others among the stimulant medications and formulas to get the best effect.

• Stimulants are found to improve the core symptoms (hyperactivity, impulsivity, inattention) and many of the secondary or associated problems these children experience (for example, oppositional behavior, interpersonal relationships, work production, and school performance).

SIDE EFFECTS OF STIMULANT MEDICATIONS
• The side effects that are most common are reduction of appetite, headache, stomachache, and mild sleep disturbances. Other possible side effects are irritability, moodiness, agitation, tics, and a rebound effect.

• Rebound, a worsening of ADHD symptoms as the medication wears off, usually lasts for about fifteen to forty-five minutes. The physician generally can adjust the dosage or the times when medication is given or prescribe a different medication.

• Most side effects from stimulant medications are mild, diminish over time, and respond to changes in dosage or the particular stimulant prescribed.

• Research studies have found that stimulant medication can cause some growth suppression (slightly less height and weight gain) compared to children not receiving stimulant treatment for their ADHD, which is a factor parents should discuss with their doctor.

• Medication treatment begins with a titration phase: a trial period when the physician is trying to determine the appropriate medication and dosage. It involves:

> • Close monitoring of symptoms and behavioral changes (at home and school) while progressively changing the dosages and sometimes adjusting the timing of medication administered
>
> • Starting typically with a very low dosage and raising it gradually
>
> • Trying to achieve the most improvement in symptoms and optimal effects from the medication with a minimum of side effects

• Parents and teachers communicate with the physician and provide the feedback necessary for the doctor to determine the child's response to the medication and benefits that are being achieved at each dosage level. *See checklist 1.15.*

Other Medications for Treating ADHD

ATOMOXETINE (STRATTERA)

• *Atomoxetine* (brand name Strattera) works differently from stimulants. It is a selective norepinephrine reuptake inhibitor, believed to work by blocking the reuptake or recycling of norepinephrine and increasing the availability of this brain chemical in the affected areas of the brain. Whereas the stimulants mostly work to improve the level of dopamine, Strattera works on increasing the norepinephrine level and activity.

• This is the first treatment for ADHD approved by the Food and Drug Administration that is not a stimulant.

• Atomoxetine has demonstrated effectiveness for improving ADHD symptoms in children and adults, and has the advantage of providing smooth, continuous coverage, potentially for twenty-four hours. It can help functioning around the clock.

• As Strattera was only released in 2002, it does not have the advantage of many years of study, as do the stimulants.

• Also, unlike stimulants that start working right away and show positive effects on symptoms that are readily apparent, Strattera takes weeks of daily use before it shows its benefits.

• Most common side effects are upset stomach, nausea, sleep problems, fatigue, and nervousness.

Other Medications

• Certain types of antidepressants are used in the treatment of children with ADHD as a second-line choice of medication. These drugs may be prescribed for a child who is not responding to the stimulant medications or Atomoxetine, or if they cannot tolerate the side effects of those drugs.

• In this category are the tricyclic antidepressant medications: *imipramine* (Tofranil), *desipramine* (Norpramin), and *nortriptyline* (Pamelor).

• The tricyclic antidepressants take some time to build up in the bloodstream and reach a therapeutic level.

• They are used primarily for ADHD symptoms of hyperactivity and impulsivity and tic disorders. They also help with insomnia, mood swings, and emotionality. They are not typically used for treating depression in children.

• Some side effects are fatigue, stomachache, dry mouth, rash, dizziness, accelerated heart rate, and possible risk of cardiac arrhythmias.

• Another drug used sometimes in the treatment of ADHD that is also an antidepressant, but a different type—not a tricyclic, but what is called an atypical antidepressant—is Wellbutrin *(bupropion)*.

• In more complicated cases of ADHD, much less commonly used medications may be prescribed, such as *clonidine* (Catapres) and *guanfacine* (Tenex), which are antihypertensives.

Additional Information

• Because of the comorbidities (coexisting conditions) with ADHD, medical treatment may require a combination of medications.

• All medications can have adverse side effects. Parents need to be well informed of the risks versus benefits in any medical treatment.

• There are excellent resources about medication treatment for ADHD. Consult with your physician or other medical professionals. Other reliable resources are found at www.chadd.org, www.help4adhd.org, and other sites listed in *checklist 5.8*. Timothy Wilens's (2006) book is also an excellent resource on this topic.

Reference

Wilens, T. (2006). *Straight talk about psychiatric medications for kids* (Rev. ed.). New York: Guilford Press.

1.14 BEHAVIORAL TREATMENT AND MANAGEMENT OF ADHD

• Behavioral treatments are one of the two research-validated interventions proven effective in the management of ADHD. They require training and commitment to implement, and this is not easy.

• Parents of children with ADHD must become far more knowledgeable and skilled in behavior management principles and techniques than other parents. They need training in how to cope with and handle the daily challenges and behavioral difficulties resulting from their child's disorder.

- Psychosocial or behavioral interventions for ADHD include:

  - Proactive parenting and classroom management and effective discipline practice at home and school, as described in *checklists 2.2 and 3.1*

  - Communicating in ways to increase compliance—that is, helping the child listen to and follow parent and teacher directions (*see checklists 2.7 and 3.3*)

  - Structuring the environment and being aware of antecedents or triggers to misbehavior to prevent problems at home and school (*see checklists 2.3, 2.8, 3.2, and 3.6*)

  - Using strategies to best deal with the challenging behaviors associated with ADHD in school environments and inside and outside the home (*see checklists 2.4, 2.5, 3.4, and 3.10*)

  - Improving the child's social skills (*see checklist 5.4*)

- Behavior modification techniques are a cornerstone of behavioral intervention for ADHD. Children with ADHD require more external motivation, including the chance to earn rewards with higher frequency, than other children typically need because their internal controls are less mature and they have trouble delaying gratification.

- Negative consequences or punishments are also effective in changing behavior, particularly use of time-out procedures and loss of privileges when they are implemented correctly and judiciously. *See checklists 2.2 and 3.1.*

- A key behavioral approach for children with ADHD is to reward their success in meeting specific goals through well-designed behavioral programs such as daily report cards, token economies or token programs, and individual contracts.

Daily Report Cards

- Daily report cards (DRCs) are excellent tools for tracking school performance and motivating a student to improve specific behaviors that are interfering with his or her success. They are highly effective for communicating between home and school and monitoring a child's daily performance.

- DRCs can be powerful motivators for students when parents and teachers are willing and able to consistently follow through with positive reinforcement for the child's successful performance on the DRC goals. Any means to forge a partnership between home and school and work together on improving specific behavioral goals is very beneficial for children with ADHD.

• Daily report cards have been validated by research as an effective intervention for students with ADHD. Basically, DRCs involve selecting and clearly defining one or a few target behaviors or goals to be the focus for improvement. The teacher is responsible for observing and rating daily how the child performed on each target behavior and sending home the DRC at the end of the day.

• Parents are responsible for asking to see the DRC every day and reinforcing school behavior and performance at home. "Good days" in school (as indicated by meeting the criteria of the DRC) earn the child designated rewards at home on a nightly basis. A good week (for example, at least three out of five good days initially and then four out of five days) may also earn the child or teen extra privileges on the weekend.

• Using this system, parents will provide the agreed-on reward at home when their son or daughter has had a successful day according to the DRC. On days the child failed to meet the goal on their DRC, it is *not* recommended that parents punish their child, but be sure that the reward for success is only provided on those days the child earned it.

• Parents may, however, wish to back up the expectation that their son or daughter will bring the DRC home daily by enforcing with some mild punishment (for example, being fined or losing some TV time) on days the child "forgets" to bring the note home.

• Daily report cards can involve school rewards as well as home rewards. For example, a small school reward such as a sticker or computer time can be given to the child at school on a good day. For a good week, the student can earn a special reward or privilege on Fridays.

• If the family is not able to follow through with monitoring and reinforcement on a consistent and daily basis, it is best to do so at school. If the DRC is likely to get lost coming to and from school daily, then perhaps just a card that simply indicates "yes/no" or "met goal/didn't meet goal" can be sent home or a daily e-mail or phone message for parent notification, and the actual DRC remains at school. In this case, the school needs to be responsible for providing the daily reward when the child was successful (*see checklist 3.5*), but parents should be asked to reward the child on the weekend if it was a "good week." This is manageable in most all homes.

CREATING A DAILY REPORT CARD

• There are many variations of daily report cards. They basically require the following components:

- • Selecting the few goals to be achieved and then defining those goals precisely.

- • Collecting data on how frequently the selected behaviors occur is recommended to determine a baseline and then setting the initial criteria slightly higher than the student currently performs. The criteria for success are slowly raised after the child experiences success in the behavioral program.

- • Deciding on the initial criteria for success—for example, at least twenty yeses out of twenty-eight possible, at least thirty-five points out of a possible fifty-six for the day, or other reasonable criteria.

• A chart is made with time frames broken down by periods of the day, subject areas, or whatever other intervals fit the student's daily schedule and are reasonable for the teacher to monitor consistently.

• Along the other axis of the chart are the designated target behaviors—for example, "has all necessary materials," "on-task/working productively," "cooperating with classmates," "following directions," or others as shown on exhibit charts.

• At the end of each time frame, the teacher marks a simple yes/no, plus or minus sign, thumbs-up/thumbs-down sign, smiley/frowny face, or other such symbol, or rates the student with points earned according to the specific criteria.

• The student's number of points (or yeses, smiley faces) are tallied at the end of the day to determine the net number earned that day, and the student's overall performance (Did the student meet the criteria for success?).

• Rewards are provided accordingly (at home, at school, or both), based on the child's performance on the DRC.

• When defining with the child the target behaviors and what you will be evaluating, be clear. For example, "on task" might be defined as "no more than x number of warnings or redirections during that time interval," "worked all or most of the time frame without bothering others," or "completed at least 80 percent of the assignment."

Exhibit 1.1   Daily Report

STUDENT NAME _____   DATE _____

Teachers: Please write Y (yes) or N (no) by each behavior at end of class, and sign/initial. You may also write comments to student/parents.

First Period   Comments and Signature/Initials
_____ On time to class
_____ Homework turned in
_____ Used class time productively
_____ Followed class rules (no more than 2 warnings)

Second Period   Comments and Signature/Initials
_____ On time to class
_____ Homework turned in
_____ Used class time productively
_____ Followed class rules (no more than 2 warnings)

Third Period   Comments and Signature/Initials
_____ On time to class
_____ Homework turned in
_____ Used class time productively
_____ Followed class rules (no more than 2 warnings)

Fourth Period   Comments and Signature/Initials
_____ On time to class
_____ Homework turned in
_____ Used class time productively
_____ Followed class rules (no more than 2 warnings)

Fifth Period   Comments and Signature/Initials
_____ On time to class
_____ Homework turned in
_____ Used class time productively
_____ Followed class rules (no more than 2 warnings)

Sixth Period   Comments and Signature/Initials
_____ On time to class
_____ Homework turned in
_____ Used class time productively
_____ Followed class rules (no more than 2 warnings)

Seventh Period   Comments and Signature/Initials
_____ On time to class
_____ Homework turned in
_____ Used class time productively
_____ Followed class rules (no more than 2 warnings)

Total number of yeses received today: _____ .

A minimum of ____ yeses are required in order to earn agreed-on reward/privilege.
A successful day of meeting the goal will result in:

Student Signature _____   Parent/Guardian Signature _____

Exhibit 1.2   Individualized Daily Report

_____ 's Daily Report

Date _____

Times or Subjects	Stays Seated No more than ___ warning(s)		On Task No more than ___ warning(s)		Follows Directions No more than ___ warning(s)	
	+	−	+	−	+	−
	+	−	+	−	+	−
	+	−	+	−	+	−
	+	−	+	−	+	−
	+	−	+	−	+	−
	+	−	+	−	+	−
	+	−	+	−	+	−
	+	−	+	−	+	−
	+	−	+	−	+	−
	+	−	+	−	+	−
	+	−	+	−	+	−

My goal is to earn at least _____ pluses (+) by the end of the day (or _____% of the day showing great behavior and effort).

If I meet my goal, I will earn a reward/privilege of:

_____
Teacher signature

_____
Parent/guardian signature

Exhibit 1.3   Daily/Weekly Report Card

Daily/Weekly Report Card

Name: _____   Week of: _____   Daily Goal: _____   Points (total for day)

Period	MONDAY		TUESDAY		WEDNESDAY		THURSDAY		FRIDAY	
	Conduct	Classwork	Conduct	Classwork	Conduct	Classwork	Conduct	Classwork	Conduct	Classwork
1										
2										
3										
4										
5										
6										
7										
Total points										
Any teacher comments										

Conduct:
 – Was respectful to adults and classmates
 – Followed teacher directions
 – Participated in lessons and activities
 – Started on assignments right away

Classwork:
 – Refrained from teasing or bothering others
 – Stayed in assigned place (received permission to leave seat)
 – Came to class prepared (with homework and materials)
 – Stayed on task with little redirection

Teacher Directions: Please enter a conduct score (0–4 points) and a classwork score (0–4 points) at the end of the class period. Base your score on how many of the four specific conduct/classwork behaviors the student demonstrated in your class that day.

Reward/Privilege earned for meeting daily goal: _____

Reward/Privilege earned for a successful week (a minimum of ___ days of meeting the daily goal): _____

Parents: Please sign and return this form to school on Monday. _____

MORE ABOUT DRCS

• It is important that reinforcement is provided consistently and as promised. A well-coordinated system between home and school is the most effective.

• For an excellent source on setting up, implementing, and troubleshooting daily report cards, go to the downloadable section of the Web site of the Center for Children and Families, University of Buffalo, State University of New York: http://ccf.buffalo.edu/resources_downloads.php. This is the site of William Pelham Jr., a researcher and leader in the field of behavioral interventions for children with ADHD and his colleagues.

• It is very important that the child experiences success when beginning these behavioral programs. This can be achieved by starting with goals that are easy to accomplish rather than setting the bar too high and having the child fail.

Token Economies and Token Programs

• Other behavioral programs are also used in the management of children and teens with ADHD such as earning tokens (for example, points, poker chips, stickers on a chart, marbles in a jar, classroom "fake" money, or other immediate reward) that is later cashed in or redeemed for bigger, more motivating, and meaningful rewards. The child can earn a special privilege or other reward of choice by accumulating a prescribed number of those tokens.

• Another option is to design a reward menu together with the child. A list of rewards is created (*see checklists 2.6 and 3.5*) with a price or value attached to each item on the menu. The more desirable and bigger the reward or privilege, the more tokens must be accumulated to earn it.

• As with other behavioral programs, it is important that token programs focus on improving no more than a few clearly defined target behaviors and that expectations for improvement are realistic and achievable for the individual child.

• The program needs to be implemented consistently, and the rewards selected (or choice of rewards from a menu) must be valuable to the child in order to serve as an incentive for behavioral change.

• A fun Web site for designing a behavioral program that is animated and versatile is www.myrewardboard.com.

Contracts

• A commonly used behavioral intervention is a contract, which is usually a two- or three-party agreement that specifies the role each will perform in achieving a certain goal. It is tailored to address the individual student's areas of need.

• Together, the child and key adults identify and select one or more specific goals that the student agrees to work on improving.

• All parties then agree on how the child will demonstrate that improvement and the rewards that will occur for meeting the goals. Sometimes the contract includes a negative consequence that will occur if the child fails to make the improvement.

• All parties sign the contract to show that they agree to its terms.

Response Cost

• *Response cost* refers to when the student loses points or privileges for specific misbehaviors. When implemented correctly and not overused, response costs are an effective disciplinary technique for children and teens with ADHD.

• If a token program is being used that is a combination of positive reinforcement and response cost, there must be far more opportunities for points or tokens to be earned than taken away. Otherwise the child will likely become frustrated and give up. In addition, the child should never be allowed to accumulate negative points.

• As with any other behavioral program, the rewards the child may earn for successful performance must be powerful enough to be an incentive to change behavior. The rewards designated in the program must have meaning and value to that individual child or teen.

• It often helps to change the rewards frequently or provide a menu of different reinforcers the child may choose from in order to maintain interest in the program. *See checklists 2.6 and 3.5.*

• For more details on implementing behavioral programs and examples of charts and forms for home and school use, see my other books listed in *checklist 5.8.*

1.15 WHAT TEACHERS AND PARENTS NEED TO KNOW ABOUT MEDICATION

• Parents do not easily make a decision to medicate their child. Typically they agonize over the decision, and many try avoiding the medical route for years. No parent wants to have their child take a "drug." They often are fearful of the long-term effects. In addition, they are frequently made to feel guilty by well-meaning relatives and friends who are uneducated about proven treatments or biased against the use of medication from misinformation.

• The school's role is to support any child receiving medication treatment and cooperate fully. School personnel need to communicate their observations so the doctor can determine the child's response to the medication, especially during the titration period when the prescription and dosage are being adjusted. This feedback from the school is necessary in helping the physician regulate the dosage and determine if the medication has the desired positive effects on symptoms and functioning and minimal adverse side effects.

• The teacher is an integral part of the therapeutic team because of his or her unique ability to observe the child's performance and functioning (academic, social, behavioral) on medication during most of the day. Teachers need to monitor and observe students on medication carefully and report changes in the child's behavior and functioning, as well as any concerns about possible side effects.

• Teachers should feel free to contact the parent, school nurse, and (if parents provided the school written permission) the doctor directly with their observations and any concerns.

• Generally the school nurse (when there is one) acts as the liaison for the parent, physician, and teacher in helping to manage the medication at school. Coordination and communication among all parties are essential for optimal results.

• Physicians or their office personnel should be initiating contact with the school for feedback on how the treatment plan is working. Some doctors do so through direct contact (for example, phone calls and e-mail), and teachers are asked to share their observations. In most cases, teachers are given follow-up behavioral rating scales or other forms to fill out so the doctor can determine changes in the child's behavior and monitor the medication effects.

Advice for Teachers

• If a student is prescribed a short-acting stimulant medication requiring a dosage to be taken during school hours, the medication must be given on time (it is generally administered just before, during, or right after lunch). Many children and teens have a hard time remembering to go to the office at the designated time for medication because of the very nature of ADHD. It becomes the responsibility of the school staff to help.

• Ways to remind the student (or alert the teacher that the student needs to take a midday dose) may include:

> • Use of a beeper watch or watch alarm for the student (or the teacher).
>
> • Pairing the medication time with a daily activity or natural transition at that time (for example, on the way to the cafeteria). This is a common and effective technique because it helps establish a consistent schedule.
>
> • Rewarding the child for remembering—for example, keeping a sticker chart where the medication is dispensed.

• It is very important to provide these reminders to students discreetly, without breaking confidentiality or discussing medication in front of other students. In the nurse's absence, the office staff should be provided with a list of children who need a midday dose of medication, sending for the child if he or she does not come in to receive it.

• With the intermediate and long-acting formulas that are now available, the need for an afternoon dose is no longer an issue, eliminating the need to keep a prescription at school. For children or teens who are resistant or forgetful in taking their medication at school, an intermediate or long-acting medication is likely a better choice.

• It is important to communicate with parents and report noticeable changes in a student's behaviors. Sometimes parents do not disclose to the school that their child has started taking medication (or has had a change of medication) and are waiting to hear if the teacher notices any difference.

Advice for Parents

• If your child is on medication, it is important that you take responsibility for making sure he or she receives it as prescribed in the morning—on time and consistently. You will need to supervise that your child takes the medication and not leave it as your son or daughter's responsibility to remember.

• Close monitoring and management of the medication are crucial. If the medication is administered haphazardly and inconsistently, your child is better off without it.

• If prescribed a short-acting medication, be sure the school has the permission forms and filled prescriptions needed, or consider using an intermediate or long-acting formula.

• Communicate with the school nurse, principal, and teachers. Obviously the purpose for treating your child with medication is optimal school performance and functioning. This requires teamwork and close communication among the home, school, and physician. If your son or daughter is being treated medically for ADHD, do not keep it a secret from the school.

• Be sure to take your child for all of the follow-up visits scheduled with his or her doctor. These are necessary for monitoring the effects of the treatment plan.

• If there is no follow-up from the doctor in obtaining feedback from you and the school once the child is on medication, that is not appropriate medical care.

• It is very important to educate yourself about the medication treatment or other intervention. There are many excellent resources available. Talk to your physician, and ask all the questions you have.

• Because the commonly prescribed stimulants are classified by the Drug Enforcement Administration as Schedule 2 medications, there are strict laws regarding how they are prescribed and dispensed.

• Children should be counseled about their medication and why they are taking it. There are various resources available that can help children better understand ADHD and why they are taking medication to treat it. Children need to know that the medication is not in control of their behavior; they are. But the medication helps them to put on the brakes and have better self-control and ability to focus, and it therefore enables them to make better choices.

1.16 THE IMPACT OF ADHD ON THE FAMILY

It is important to be aware of the challenges that exist in the home when one or more children (or parent) have ADHD, because this disorder has a significant impact on the entire family. Unfortunately, teachers are generally unaware or underestimate the struggles these families face: typically a much higher degree of stress than in the average family, along with depression or other pathology in one or more family members.

ADHD causes a great deal of stress in families for these reasons:

• There are generally major issues surrounding homework as well as morning and evening routines (getting ready for school and bedtime).

• It is common for parents to disagree about treatment, discipline, management, structure, and other issues.

• Parents may blame one another for the child's problems or be highly critical of one another in their parenting role. This discord causes a great deal of marital stress and a higher rate of divorce than is typical.

• Often it is the mother who must cope with the brunt of the issues throughout the day, which is physically and emotionally exhausting.

• In single-parent homes, dealing with ADHD is far more challenging.

• As any parent of a toddler knows, having a child who needs constant supervision and monitoring is very time-consuming and interferes with the ability to get things done as planned (for example, housework and other chores).

• Parents of children who have ADHD are constantly faced with needing to defend their parenting choices as well as their child. They must listen to negative press about this disorder and reject popular opinion in order to provide their child with necessary interventions and treatment.

• Parents must deal with criticism and advice from relatives, friends, and acquaintances regarding how they should be disciplining and parenting their child. This causes a lot of parental self-doubt and adds to the stress they are already living with day in and day out.

• Frequently the family must deal with such social issues as the exclusion of the child from out-of-school activities. It is painful when your child is not invited to birthday parties or has difficulty finding someone to play with and keeping friends.

• Siblings are often resentful or even jealous of the central role their sibling with ADHD plays in the family's schedule, routines, and activities, as well as the extra time and special treatment this child receives. In addition, siblings are acutely aware of and feel hurt and embarrassed when their brother or sister has acquired a negative reputation in the neighborhood and school.

• Parents have a high degree of responsibility in working with the school and being proactive in the management of their child. Furthermore, they must fully educate themselves about ADHD in order to successfully advocate their child's needs.

Important Points to Keep in Mind

• In many cases, other family members who have ADHD were never diagnosed and have been struggling to cope with their own difficulties without proper treatment and support. That is why the clinicians who specialize in treating children with ADHD say it is important to view treatment in the context of the family. Learning about the family (for example, the ways the members communicate and their disciplinary practices) helps in designing a treatment plan that is most effective for the child.

• Commonly a parent may recognize for the first time that he or she has been suffering with undiagnosed ADHD for years when a son or daughter is diagnosed with the disorder. This realization can result in a positive change in the family dynamics.

• Without question, families of children with ADHD need support and understanding. Fortunately, there are far more supports available now than a decade ago. *See checklists 2.13 and 5.7.*

1.17 THE IMPACT OF ADHD ON SCHOOL SUCCESS

• ADHD generally causes difficulty and impairment in school performance. This disorder can have a significant impact on children and teens in various aspects of school functioning: academic, behavioral, and social.

• Every student has different strengths, weaknesses, and educational needs. Their ADHD symptoms may or may not affect them in the following areas and can do so to varying degrees. For example, while many children with ADHD have social problems, others are quite popular with their peers. Writing difficulties are very common in students with ADHD, but not everyone. Some are gifted, prolific writers. Much of the content in this book addresses specific strategies, techniques, and supports in the following areas, which are problematic for many students with ADHD:

- Organization and study skills
- Planning for short-term assignments
- Planning for long-term projects and assignments
- Various disruptive, aggressive, or annoying behaviors, resulting in a much higher degree of negative attention from and interaction with classmates, teachers, and other school personnel
- Social skills and peer relationships: the ability to work well in cooperative learning groups and get along with peers in work or play activities
- Completing class work to acceptable grade-level standards
- Homework completion, turned in on time and to acceptable grade-level standards
- Listening and following directions
- Following class and school rules
- Memory: remembering instructions, information taught, what they read, math facts, and so forth
- Participating and engaging in classroom instruction and activities
- Working independently (for example, seat work)
- Being prepared with materials for class and homework
- Ability to cope with daily frustrations
- Time awareness and time-management skills
- Issues with low self-esteem
- Building and maintaining friendships
- Written expression and other output
- Handwriting and fine motor skills
- Spelling
- Proofing and editing written work
- Note taking

- Test taking

- Reading comprehension

- Math computation

- Math problem solving

- Anger management

- Problem solving and conflict resolution

• There are numerous strategies that teachers and parents employ to help children build these skills and enhance their school performance. See the checklists in sections 2 through 5.

1.18 CRITICAL ELEMENTS FOR SCHOOL SUCCESS

• Belief in the student
• Clarity of expectations, structure, and follow-through
• Close communication between home and school
• Collaboration and teamwork
• Developing and bringing out students' strengths
• Engaging teaching strategies and motivating instruction
• Effective classroom management and positive discipline
• Environmental modifications and accommodations
• Flexibility and willingness of the teacher to accommodate individual needs
• Help and training in organization, time management, and study skills
• Knowledge and understanding of ADHD (of educators, parents, and the student)
• Limiting the amount of homework and modifying assignments when needed to accommodate the fact that work production often takes students with ADHD significantly longer than it takes other students their age to produce

- More time and more space

- Tolerance and a positive attitude toward the child

- Valuing and respecting learning styles and differences, privacy, confidentiality, and students' feelings

1.19 POSITIVE TRAITS COMMON IN MANY CHILDREN AND ADULTS WITH ADHD

Energetic	Spontaneous
Creative	Persistent
Innovative	Imaginative
Risk taker	Tenacious
Good-hearted	Ingenuity
Accepting and forgiving	Inquisitive
Resilient	Resourceful
Gregarious	Not boring
Humorous	Outgoing
Willing to take a chance and try new things	Good at improvising
Able to find novel solutions	Inventive
Observant	Full of ideas and spunk
Can think on their feet	Good in crisis situations
Make and create fun	Enterprising
Ready for action	Intelligent and bright
Enthusiastic	Know how to enjoy the present

1.20 EDUCATIONAL RIGHTS FOR STUDENTS WITH ADHD

• There are two main laws protecting students with disabilities, including ADHD:

> • Individuals with Disabilities Education Act (known as IDEA, or IDEA 2004)

> • Section 504 of the Rehabilitation Act of 1973 (known as Section 504)

• IDEA is the special education legislation in the United States. It was reauthorized by Congress in 2004, and the final regulations by the U.S. Department of Education clarifying how the law is to be implemented by state and local education agencies were issued in 2006.

• Section 504 is a civil rights statute that prohibits discrimination and is enforced by the U.S. Office of Civil Rights.

• Another law that protects individuals with disabilities is the Americans with Disabilities Act of 1990 (ADA). This overlaps with Section 504 and is not as relevant to school-aged children.

• Both IDEA and Section 504 require school districts to provide students with disabilities:

- A free and appropriate public education in the least restrictive environment with their nondisabled peers to the maximum extent appropriate to their needs
- Supports (adaptations, accommodations, modifications) to enable the student to participate and learn in the general education program
- The opportunity to participate in extracurricular and non-academic activities
- A free, nondiscriminatory evaluation
- Procedural due process

• There are different criteria for eligibility, services and supports available, and procedures and safeguards for implementing the laws. Therefore, it is important for parents, educators, clinicians, and advocates to be well aware of the differences between IDEA and Section 504 and fully informed about their respective advantages and disadvantages.

IDEA

• IDEA applies to students known or suspected of having a disability and specifies what the public school system is required to provide to such students and their parents or guardians.

• IDEA provides special education and related services to students who meet the eligibility criteria under one of thirteen separate disability categories. Students with ADHD most commonly fall under the IDEA disability category of Other Health Impaired.

• Eligibility criteria under this category require that:

- The child has a chronic or acute health problem (ADHD).

- This health problem causes "limited strength, vitality, or alertness" in the educational environment. This includes limited alertness to educational tasks due to heightened alertness to environmental stimuli.

- This disabling condition results in an adverse effect on the child's educational performance to the extent that special education is needed.

• The adverse effect on educational performance is not limited to academics. It can include impairments in other aspects of school functioning, such as behavior, as well.

• Some students with ADHD qualify for special education and related services under the disability categories of Specific Learning Disability or Emotional Disturbance. For example, a child with ADHD who also has coexisting learning disabilities may be eligible under the Specific Learning Disability category.

• Under IDEA, students who qualify for special education and related services receive an individualized education plan (IEP) that is:

- Tailored to meet the unique needs of the student

- Developed by a multidisciplinary team, which includes the child's parents

- The guide for every educational decision made for the student

- Reviewed by the team annually

THE IEP PROCESS

• The IEP process begins when a student is referred for evaluation due to a suspected disability, and a process of formal evaluation is initiated to determine eligibility for special education and related services.

• IDEA 2004 requires that the evaluation obtain accurate information about the student's academic, developmental, and functional skills.

• Children found eligible under IDEA are entitled to the special education programs, related services, modifications, and accommodations the IEP team determines are needed for educational benefit.

• The IEP is a detailed plan. It specifies the programs, supports, services, and supplementary aids that are to be provided and requires measurable annual goals and reports on progress.

• The law requires that the child be reevaluated at least every three years.

• At all stages, parents are an integral part of the process and the team, and the IEP does not go into effect until parents sign and thereby agree to the plan.

KEY FEATURES OF IDEA

• IDEA provides the necessary supports and services to enable students to succeed to the maximum extent possible in the general education curriculum.

• The IEP must incorporate important considerations regarding students' strengths, participation in district and state assessments, and special factors, such as behavioral factors and needs, proficiency in English, and language needs.

• When disciplinary actions are being considered involving removal of the student for more than ten days (through suspension or placement in an alternative placement), there must first be a review to determine if the behavior was related to or was a "manifestation" of the child's disability. If so, that must be taken into consideration in the disciplinary action and consequences the school district is permitted to impose.

• IDEA 2004 makes it clear that eligibility for special education is not based on academic impairment alone. The student is not required to have failing grades or test scores to qualify for special education and related services. Other factors related to the disorder that are impairing the student's educational performance to a significant degree (social, behavioral, and executive function–related difficulties) must be considered as well when determining eligibility.

Section 504

• Section 504 protects the rights of people with disabilities against discrimination and applies to any agency that receives federal funding, which includes all public schools and many private schools.

ELIGIBILITY CRITERIA FOR STUDENTS WITH ADHD

• Children with ADHD who may not be eligible for services under IDEA (and do not qualify for special education) are often able to receive accommodations, supports, and related services in school under a Section 504 plan.

• Section 504 has different criteria for eligibility, procedures, safeguards, and services available to children than IDEA.
• Section 504 protects students if they fit the following criteria:

  • The student is regarded as or has a record of having a physical or mental impairment.

  • The physical or mental impairment substantially limits a major life activity such as learning.

  • As with IDEA, this does not necessarily mean poor grades or academic achievement. Other factors, such as a low rate of work production, significant disorganization, off-task behavior, or social or behavioral issues can indicate the substantial negative impact of the disorder on their learning and school functioning.

• Section 504 entitles eligible students to:

  • Reasonable accommodations in the educational program
  • Commensurate opportunities to learn as nondisabled peers
  • Appropriate interventions within the general education program

ADDITIONAL CONSIDERATIONS

• The implementation of the plan is primarily the responsibility of the general education school staff.
• The 504 plan could also involve modification of nonacademic times, such as the lunchroom, recess, and physical education.
• Supports under Section 504 might also include the provision of such services as counseling, health, and assistive technology.
• In contrast to the IEP, the 504 process:

  • Is simpler, with less bureaucracy and fewer regulations
  • Is generally easier to evaluate and determine eligibility
  • Requires much less with regard to procedures, paperwork, and so forth

• Children who qualify under IDEA eligibility criteria are automatically covered by Section 504 protections. However, the reverse is not true. Many students with ADHD who do not qualify for special education services under IDEA are eligible for accommodations under Section 504, but they are not automatically covered.

504 ACCOMMODATIONS

• Section 504 plans include some accommodations that are deemed most important for the student to have equal opportunity to be successful at school. They do not include everything that might be helpful for the student, just reasonable supports, that generally the teacher is to provide. Following are examples of some possible 504 plan accommodations (also see the academic, behavioral, instructional, and environmental checklists in Sections Three and Four of this book for more classroom accommodations):

- Extended time on tests
- Breaking long-term projects and work assignments into shorter tasks
- Preferential seating (near the teacher or a good role model, away from distractions)
- Use of frequent praise, feedback, and rewards and privileges for appropriate behavior, such as being on task, remembering to raise a hand to speak, and cooperative and nondisruptive behavior
- Receiving a copy of class notes from a designated note taker
- Reduced homework assignments
- Assistance with organization of materials and work space
- Assistive technology, such as access to a computer or portable word processor for written work and to a calculator
- Cueing or prompting before transitions and changes of activity
- Frequent breaks and opportunities for movement
- A peer buddy to clarify directions
- A peer tutor
- Use of daily and weekly notes or a monitoring form between home and school for communication about behavior and work production

Which Is More Advantageous for Students with ADHD: An IEP or 504 Plan?

• This is a decision that the team of parents and school personnel must make considering eligibility criteria and the specific needs of the individual student.

• For students with ADHD who have more significant and complex school difficulties, receiving an IEP is usually preferable for the following reasons:

> • An IEP provides more protections (procedural safeguards, monitoring, accountability, and regulations) with regard to evaluation, frequency of review, parent participation, disciplinary action, and other factors.

> • Specific and measurable goals addressing the student's areas of need are written in the IEP and regularly monitored for progress.

> • A much wider range of program options, services, and supports is available.

> • IDEA provides funding for programs and services. The school district receives funds for students being served with an IEP. Section 504 is not funded, and the school district receives no financial assistance for implementation.

• For students who have milder impairments and do not need special education, a 504 plan is a faster, easier procedure for obtaining accommodations and supports. This plan can be highly effective for students whose educational needs can be addressed through adjustments, modifications, and accommodations in the general curriculum or classroom.

Checklists for Parents

• The high degree of negative feedback and disapproval that children and teens with ADHD receive on a day-to-day basis can take its toll on their self-esteem. Parents have the most important role in providing the loving support and encouragement to enable their child to build resilience for overcoming obstacles and self-confidence needed to achieve success.

• Children and teens need:

- The unconditional love and acceptance of their families
- To know they are not deficient in the eyes of their parents
- Empathy, tolerance, and forgiveness
- Positive attention and feedback
- Support and encouragement
- Clear limits and structure
- Fair, clear, and reasonable rules and expectations
- Supervision and follow-through
- Positive rather than reactive discipline
- Consistency and logical, reasonable consequences
- Predictability of schedules and routines
- Reminders and prompts without nagging, screaming, criticism, or sarcasm

- Praise and recognition for what they are doing right
- To hear the words: "That was a good choice you made." "Thank you for . . ." "I'm proud of you." "I have confidence in you." "I'm here for you."
- To be able to let down their guard at home and express their needs, thoughts, and emotions openly
- To feel they have choices and options and are involved in some decision making
- Help in understanding and labeling their feelings ("I'm frustrated [or disappointed or worried]")
- To have their feelings validated by parents' active listening
- For parents to focus on important issues and downplay less critical ones
- An emphasis on their own personal best efforts and self-improvement
- Help with coping skills and feelings of frustration
- Parent guidance and coaching in appropriate behavior and skills
- Modeling and practicing of calm, rational, problem-solving approaches
- To know that it is okay to make mistakes and for parents to acknowledge when they make mistakes themselves
- To be able to ask for help and know parents will do what they can to provide it
- Buffering from unnecessary stress and frustration
- Preparation for changes and time to adapt and adjust
- Fun and humor
- To hear and feel how much they are loved and appreciated
- Escape valve outlets
- Numerous opportunities to develop their areas of strength (for example, in sports, music, dance, or the arts)
- To be able to pursue their interests and participate in extra-curricular activities
- Special time with parents, not contingent on anything—just time to talk and have fun together, building and strengthening the relationship

- Help with organization, time management, and study skills
- Structuring of their work environment, tasks, and materials
- Help getting started with chores, assignments, and projects
- Help with planning ahead, following schedules, and keeping on target with deadlines and responsibilities
- Parents' involvement and close communication with the school
- Parents to become knowledgeable about ADHD so that they will be well equipped to manage, support, and advocate effectively on their behalf
- To be educated about ADHD: understanding the disorder that affects them, why various treatments and strategies help, and that there are countless highly successful adults with ADHD in every profession and walk of life

2.2 POSITIVE AND EFFECTIVE DISCIPLINE

Discipline, which means teaching responsible behavior, is a key responsibility of parenting. Here are basic guidelines for behavior management, discipline, and helping children learn appropriate, cooperative, and responsible behavior.

• Establish a few specific, important rules and expectations that are clear to all members of the household.

• Plan ahead which behaviors you will work toward increasing in your child through positive reinforcement and which unacceptable behaviors will always result in a punishment.

• Set limits, and let your child know you mean business.

• Enforce your limits with consequences that are logical, reasonable, and fair, and do so consistently.

• Use contingencies in establishing boundaries. This basically involves the age-old Grandma's rule: "First you eat your vegetables; then you get dessert"—for example:

- "As soon as you . . . , you may . . ."
- "Once you have . . . , you will then be able to . . ."
- "You have done your homework. Now you get to go play."

• Children with ADHD receive far more than average negative attention from parents and teachers because misbehavior captures attention. Notice and pay attention to your child when he or she is behaving appropriately.

• Make it a goal to catch your child "being good" at least three times more frequently than when you need to respond to misbehavior.

• Be specific in acknowledging and praising:

> • "I really appreciate how you cleaned up without being reminded."

> • "I noticed how well you were sharing and taking turns when you played with Bobby."

• Always reward or give positive attention to the behaviors you want to increase or continue to occur.

• Immediately reinforce desired behavior with a positive consequence. That means that something your child likes (praise, smiles, hugs, privileges, points or tokens earned toward a reward) follows the behavior.

• Children with ADHD require more external motivation than other children because their internal controls are less mature and they have trouble delaying gratification. Therefore, they need frequent, immediate, and potent rewards for their efforts. Implementing techniques such as a token economy system are effective for children with ADHD. This involves:

> • Rewarding the child with tokens of some kind (poker chips or points, for example) for performing specific, positive behaviors. These include things they are normally expected to do, such as being ready for the school bus on time, clearing the table after dinner, feeding the dog or doing other chores, and remembering to bring home all books and the assignment calendar for homework.

> • A menu of rewards and reinforcers is created with the child, including items and privileges such as those suggested in *checklist 2.6*. A point value is assigned for each of the items on the list. The child then "purchases" the reward from the tokens earned.

> • Children tend to respond best to novelty, so change the choices of rewards frequently to maintain your child's

interest. Negative consequences or punishments are also effective in changing behavior. However, be sure to use far more positives than negatives in your behavioral approach.

• With a token economy system, the child can also be fined by losing tokens for targeted behaviors (for example, each incident of fighting with siblings or talking back). It is crucial in such a system to ensure that the child is earning far more tokens or points than he or she is losing, or the system will not work.

• When punishments are required, they should be enforced as soon as possible following the misbehavior—and usually with one warning, not several.

• The best consequences are those that are logically related to the offense and natural results of the child's actions.

• Some effective punishments include:

  • Ignoring (particularly attention-getting behaviors)

  • Verbal reprimands

  • Removal of privileges

  • Response costs: receiving a "fine" or penalty such as removal of some points or tokens earned

  • Time-out: isolation for a brief amount of time

• When delivering consequences, do so in a calm but firm voice. Try to avoid reacting emotionally. State the consequence without lecturing. Be direct and to the point.

• If using a time-out, choose a location that is boring for your child, as well as safe but away from the reinforcement of other people and activities. It should be clear to your child what behaviors will result in time-out. Typically a reasonable amount of time is one minute per year of age. Use a timer.

• Punishments must have a clear beginning and ending that you are able to control.

• When punishing, be careful to focus on the behavior that is inappropriate. Do not attack the child as "being bad" or criticize his or her character.

• Keep in mind that punishment is reactive: it is a response to misbehavior, but one that does not teach appropriate behaviors to replace the inappropriate ones. So at a different time, work on teaching and practicing alternative desirable behaviors with your child. For example, if your child curses when angry or lashes out by hitting, teach him or her to use another response, such as anger management and calming strategies.

• Anticipate and plan in advance (with your spouse) how to handle challenging behaviors. When parents are able to show a united front in their expectations and how they deal with their child's misbehaviors, it prevents incidences of the child playing one parent against the other. Avoid responding and punishing when you are very angry. You do not want to dole out a punishment you will regret later because it is too harsh, inappropriate, or impossible to enforce.

• Avoid getting pulled into a power struggle or a shouting match with your child. Disengage in this situation. Do not be afraid to say, "I'm too angry to talk about this right now. We will discuss this later." Take time to step back, calm down, and think before you act. When you are calm, discuss the situation.

• Focus on what is important, and then prioritize. You cannot make an issue out of everything.

• No matter how exhausted or frustrated you are, maintain your authority as a parent, and follow through on what you need to do.

• Avoid using sarcasm, ridicule, criticism, nagging, screaming, or physical punishment with your child.

• It is far more difficult to manage the behaviors of children with ADHD than most other children. Be willing to seek professional help to find effective strategies and guidance. Get referrals from other parents of children with similar needs. Find a mental health professional familiar with ADHD and experienced in dealing with hyperactive and impulsive behaviors. Be aware that a high percentage of children with ADHD have coexisting conditions, such as oppositional defiant disorder (ODD). Mental health intervention and training from professionals is essential for parents to manage their children with ADHD/ODD.

• Parents of children with ADHD must become far more skilled in specialized behavior management principles and techniques than other parents in order to cope with and handle the daily challenges and behavioral difficulties resulting from their child's disorder.

• See *checklists 1.7, 1.12, 1.14, 1.16, 2.5, 2.12, 2.13, 5.1, and 5.8* for more information.

2.3 PREVENTING BEHAVIOR PROBLEMS AT HOME

Provide as much structure and predictability in the home as possible. Establish some rules, routines, and schedules to help life run more smoothly.

• With your child, set up routines together: morning routines (getting ready for school), mealtime routines, homework routines, and bedtime routines, for example. Adhere to them as closely as possible.

• The steps of the routines and schedules need to be in a visual format (on a poster, chart, check-off list, or presented on a magnet or dry-erase board). For young children, consider using a picture chart with a clothespin attached to the side of the chart. The child moves the clothespin down to the next picture after completing each task.

• Your child needs to know what is viewed as acceptable and unacceptable behavior at home and the consequences (positive and negative) for both.

• Remind through gentle warnings:

  • "The rule is . . ."

  • "Next time . . ."

  • "Remember to . . ."

• Organize and arrange the home environment in a way that will optimize the chances for success and avoid conflict. For example, remove items or objects you do not want your impulsive or hyperactive child to touch or play with, and child-proof the house.

• Avoid fatigue—your child's and your own. Children with ADHD often have sleep difficulties and a calming bedtime routine can help.

• Be observant. Monitor and supervise. Notice when your child is becoming agitated, overly stimulated, or angry, and intervene. Try redirecting your child's attention to focus on something else. Use calming techniques and strategies such as those in *checklists 2.5, 2.8, and 5.3.*

• It is hard for children with ADHD to disengage from an activity in order to do something else. Calling them to the dinner table or asking them to stop playing to get ready for bed, for example, can be problematic. Use timers to deliver the message that it's time to get ready for something or to stop something they are doing. For example, let the timer tell them when they have ten minutes before dinner is ready or fifteen minutes until they get to take a homework break.

• Prepare your child for changes in the home, such as redecorating, visitors or house guests, and changes in parent work schedules. Talk about the change, and avoid surprises.

• Provide a limited number of choices. Do not allow your child to dump out all of his or her toys or examine all the books before choosing one for you to read with him or her. Allow your child to choose from only a few at one time.

• Provide physical outlets. Your child needs to release energy and participate in physical activities. *See checklist 5.3.*

• Maintain flexibility and a sense of humor!

• Children with ADHD are often immature in social skills and may have a meltdown when losing during competitive games and activities. Teach your child strategies to handle the frustration of losing. Reinforce good sportsmanship, explaining that no one always wins. When playing games, praise and reward behavior that required your child to display self-control.

• If siblings are teasing and provoking your ADHD child, intervene.

• Give your child only the chores and responsibilities that he or she is developmentally able to handle—what he or she is capable of, not necessarily what other kids the same age or other siblings can do.

• Provide the supports to enable your child to follow through with chores and responsibilities. Remember that forgetfulness, procrastination, and disorganization are part of the ADHD picture. Your child will need reminders, help getting started, and so forth.

• Purchase toys, books, and games that are developmentally appropriate for your child.

• Be aware of the conditions and triggers to your child's misbehavior. When you recognize what often precedes your child's negative reactions and misbehavior, you can make efforts to avoid those triggers to prevent problems. Some triggers are:

  • *Environmental:* Uncomfortable conditions in the environment (too noisy and chaotic, over- or understimulating, lacking structure, no space to themselves)

- *Physical:* Overly tired, hungry, medication related (when wearing off, change of prescription or dosage)

- *Related to a specific activity or event:* Change of schedule without warning, math homework, piano lessons, when teased by siblings

- *Related to a performance or skill demand:* Having to wait patiently or remain seated, writing assignments, any task or expectation that is a struggle or frustrating for the child

- *Related to a specific time:* The hour before going to school, late afternoon, evenings

- *Other:* When given no options or choices, when with a particular person, when given no assistance or access to help on difficult, frustrating tasks

• For more information on related topics, *see checklists 2.4, 2.7, 2.8, 5.3, and 5.4.*

2.4 PREVENTING BEHAVIOR PROBLEMS OUTSIDE THE HOME

Many parents of children with ADHD dread taking their son or daughter shopping with them or to other places outside the home where behavior issues often emerge. The behavioral controls expected in some of these environments can be more than a child with ADHD is able to handle. Following are some recommendations for preventing, or at least reducing, potential behavior problems that can occur outside the home.

• Teach, model, and practice appropriate behaviors and manners that you expect your child to display outside the home—for example, following directions, cleaning up after yourself, walking rather than running inside a building, and saying "please" and "thank you."
• Anticipate and prepare for potential problems.
• Remember how any change of routine can be stressful and unnerving, which is why children with ADHD need preparation:

- Give advance notice; avoid catching them off guard.

- Talk about what they should expect.

- Provide your child enough time to get ready.

• Before going into public places (stores, doctor's office, restaurants, church or temple, movie theaters) or visiting other people's homes:

> • Talk to your child about behavioral expectations.
>
> • State the rules simply.
>
> • Have your child repeat the rules back to you.
>
> • Give written directions if appropriate.

• Establish rewards that your child will be able to receive if he or she behaves appropriately and follows the rules. Remind your child of the contingency: "If you . . . , you will be able to earn . . . "

• Try not to put your child in situations that are too taxing on his or her self-control and attention span. Avoid places that you know will be too stimulating or difficult to supervise and manage the behavior.

• If your child is on medication, consider scheduling activities to coincide with the optimal effects of the medication.

• Avoid taking your child out when he or she is tired and needs a nap or some quiet time.

• Let your child know the negative consequences if he or she behaves inappropriately. Be prepared to enforce them. Mean what you say!

• A token economy system can be useful in out-of-the-home situations for behavior management. Let your child know that he or she will earn x number of tokens or points as an incentive for demonstrating self-control and cooperative behavior when you are out together, and inappropriate behavior will result in the loss of x number of tokens.

• When entering a public place such as a department store with your child, scout around for some location that is removed and isolated and can be used for a time-out if necessary.

• Remove your child from the situation when he or she is behaving inappropriately or showing signs of losing control.

• Supervise. Supervise. Supervise. For example, when taking your child to someone else's home, keep aware of where your child is and what he or she is doing—ready to redirect or intervene if necessary.

• Be prepared with a bag of tricks. Knowing the nature of ADHD— that children bore easily and need to be kept busy—do not leave the house without toys, books, MP3 player, handheld electronics, games, a pad of paper and colored pencils, and so forth that can occupy and keep your child entertained. Keep the bag of tricks replenished to maintain novelty and interest.

• If your hyperactive or impulsive child will be expected to sit quietly (such as in a doctor's office, church or synagogue, or movie theater), provide a quiet fidget toy. This keeps his or her hands busy and can help regulate behavior. Try giving a piece of Wikki Stix (a piece of twine with a nontoxic wax covering, available at www.wikkistix.com) or some other item to fidget with silently. For companies that carry a variety of such products, *see checklist 5.8.*

• Give your child feedback when you are with him or her outside the home: "I'm proud of how well you are . . . It looks like you'll probably earn the reward we talked about."

• If your child is beginning to lose control, prompt him or her to use previously taught self-regulation techniques—for example, "Let's calm down. Take three deep breaths. Now count to ten slowly."

• If your child is showing signs of losing control in a public place, prompt him or her to use self-talk or other self-regulation strategy—for example, taking a few deep breaths, pushing an imaginary stop button, or repeating to himself or herself, "I need to calm down . . . put on the brakes."

• Talk with your child about the natural consequences of inappropriate behavior: friends or their parents will not want to invite him or her to their house again; other children will get angry and not want to play.

• Provide your child with social skills training and practice skills for interacting positively with others. *See checklist 5.4.*

2.5 COPING AND DEALING WITH YOUR CHILD'S CHALLENGING BEHAVIORS

• Make a conscious effort to pay attention to, compliment, and reinforce your child when he or she is behaving appropriately, and try to provide at least three times more positive interactions and feedback than negative. This is not easy to do, but it is very important.

• Children with ADHD seek stimulation. When your child is misbehaving, avoid an explosive and emotional response, which is very stimulating. You do not want your highly charged response to be rewarding and reinforcing your child's misbehavior.

• A child who also has oppositional defiant disorder (ODD) has a need for power and control. If your son or daughter knows how to provoke you to the point where you lose control, your response will be rewarding and reinforcing the inappropriate behavior, because your child will have effectively gained power and control over you.

• Do not feel compelled to give an immediate response in dealing with situations until you are in a calm, thinking state. You might say, "I'm upset right now. I need time to think about this before we discuss the consequence of your behavior. I'll get back to you." Then walk away.

• Realize that you cannot control your child's behavior. Change what you can control: yourself (your attitude, body language, tone and volume of voice, strategies, consistency and follow-through, and the nature of the interaction).

• Physically relax your body before dealing with challenging situations. Take a few deep breaths, unfold your arms, relax your jaw, and cue yourself to be calm.

• Disengage from power struggles. Remember that you cannot be forced into an argument or power struggle. You enter into one only if you choose to do so (it takes two). Say calmly, for example, "I am not willing to argue about this now. I will be free to discuss it later if you wish, after dinner."

• Affirm and acknowledge your child's feelings: "I see you're upset." "I understand that you are angry now." "I can see why you would be frustrated."

• Express your confidence in your child's ability to make good choices.

• Avoid *why* questions, for example, "Why did you do that?"

• Use *what* questions, for example, "What are you supposed to be doing right now?" "What do you want?" "What is your plan to solve the problem?" "What can I do to help you?" "What would you like to see happen?" "What are you risking by doing that?"

• Try your best to remain calm (relax your body, uncross your arms, and lower your voice), communicating your hope that your son or daughter will choose to cooperate.

• Remind your child of the rules.

• Try to maintain your sense of humor.

• Send "I messages": "I feel . . . when you . . . because . . ." "I want [or need] you to . . .")

• Avoid nagging, scolding, lecturing, and threatening.

• Do not take the bait.

• Use the "broken record" technique: respond by repeating your directions with the same words in a calm, neutral voice. Use the words *however* and *nevertheless*—for example, "I understand you are feeling ... However ..." or "That may be .... Nevertheless ..."

• Avoid being judgmental in your interactions.

• Take time to actively listen to your child: Be attentive, listen without interjecting your opinions, ask a lot of open and clarifying questions, and rephrase and restate what was said.

• Provide choices: "I can't make you ... But your choices are either ... or ..."

• It is okay to call for a break. Go to a different room, take an exercise break, or do something away from each other.

• Discuss, problem-solve, and negotiate solutions when you both have had time to cool down and are in a calm, thinking mode.

• Teach your child problem-solving strategies: identify the problem, brainstorm possible solutions, evaluate pros and cons, choose one and try it, review its effectiveness, and try another if it was not working.

• If your child appears on the verge of losing control, try prompting him or her to use self-calming, self-regulation techniques such as visualization, deep breathing, counting slowly, or progressive muscle relaxation, as described in *checklist 5.3.*

• Teach your child to use self-talk as a self-regulation strategy and then prompt him or her to do so when needed—for example: "I am calm and in control." "I need to chill out." "I can handle this. I'll relax and stay calm."

• There is a wonderful book (Copeland, 2005) that teaches children self-regulation strategies through the concrete example of a remote control that has different buttons: channel changer, pause, fast forward, rewind, slow motion, coach, zapper, and way to go! For example, instead of saying to a child, "Pay attention," one would say, "What channel are you on?" or "Put your channel on me."

• Some recommended resources for discipline and behavior management of children who are a challenge to handle include *1, 2, 3 Magic* (Phelan, 2004), *SOS! Help for Parents* (Clark, 2003), *Taking Charge of ADHD* (Barkley, 2000), *From Defiance to Cooperation* (Taylor, 2001), *From Chaos to Calm* (Heininger and Weiss, 2001), *Setting Limits with Your Strong Willed Child* (MacKenzie, 2001), and *The Explosive Child* (Greene, 2001).

References

Barkley, R. (2001). *Taking charge of ADHD* (Rev. ed.). New York: The Guilford Press.

Clark, L. (2003). *SOS! Help for parents: A practical guide for handling common everyday behavior problems* (2nd. ed.). Bowling Green, KY: Parents Press & SOS Programs.

Copeland, L. (2005). *Hunter and his amazing remote control: A fun, hands-on way to teach self-control to ADHD children.* Chapin, S.C.: Youth-Light.

Greene, R. (2001). *The explosive child* (2nd ed.). New York: Quill.

Heininger, J., & Weiss, S. (2001). *From chaos to calm.* New York: Perigee Books.

MacKenzie, R. (2001). *Setting limits with your strong-willed child: Eliminating conflict by establishing clear, firm, and respectful boundaries.* Roseville, CA: Prima Publishing.

Phelan, T. (2004). *1, 2, 3 magic* (3rd. ed.). Glen Ellyn, IL: Child Management.

Taylor, J. (2001). *From defiance to cooperation.* Roseville, CA: Prima Publishing.

2.6 REWARDS AND POSITIVE REINFORCERS FOR HOME

It is important to catch your child being good, that is, demonstrating appropriate behavior. Be particularly generous with praise, attention, and other social reinforcers during that time.

Social Reinforcers

- Positive attention from parents—preferably your undivided attention for even a short amount of time
- Parents' physical signs of affection (hugs, kisses, cuddles)
- Smiles, thumbs-up, high five, cheers
- Playful attention (piggyback ride, sharing jokes)
- Relaxed time together (talking, playing)
- Specific, sincere praise and recognition, such as:
    - "That sure was grown up of you when . . ."
    - "That was great the way you . . ."

- "I appreciate the good choice you made when . . ."
- "It makes me so happy to see you . . ."
- "I'm so proud of how you . . ."
- "That was so helpful when you . . . Thank you!"
- "I can really tell you worked hard on . . ."
- "I noticed how well you . . ."
- "I see the effort you put into that . . ."
- "Let's make a copy of this for Grandma . . ."
- "Let's hang this up somewhere special . . ."
- "Great job on how you . . ."
- "I can't wait to tell Dad how you . . ."
- "I knew you could do it!"

• A key behavioral approach for children with ADHD is to reinforce their positive behavior and reward their success in meeting goals. Find out what privileges, items, and activities your child finds valuable and would be motivated to work toward earning. You might develop a reward menu together with your child. Be sure to change that menu as often as necessary to maintain your son or daughter's interest.

Activity Reinforcers

- Playing a special indoor or outdoor game
- An outing to a park, restaurant, arcade, or beach or a camping trip, for example
- Extended bedtime
- Extended curfew
- Earning extra time (for watching TV, computer or Internet access, playing games, riding bikes, listening to music, talking on the phone)
- Special time alone with a parent (out for breakfast, shopping, ice cream, ball game, building something together)
- Freedom from chores
- Craft project

- Drawing or painting
- Selecting a meal or restaurant for lunch or dinner
- Baking cupcakes, cookies, or another treat
- Extra story or reading time with a parent
- Going to the theater, a sporting event, or another special outing
- Participating in a school activity that costs money, such as a dance or ski trip
- Participating in sports activity or lessons of choice (for example, skating, bowling, martial arts, tennis)
- Gym membership
- Going shopping
- Driving privileges (the parent drives to a place of the child's choice or gives the car keys to a teen with a driver's license)
- Playing musical instruments
- Gymnastics or dance
- Club participation
- Going to a movie or watching a DVD at home
- Playing computer games
- Spending time with a special person (grandparent or a favorite aunt or uncle, for instance)
- Staying overnight at a friend's or relative's house
- Inviting a friend over to play, stay for lunch or dinner, or sleep over
- Some of these activities can also be considered social reinforcers.

Material Reinforcers

- Toys
- Arts or crafts supplies
- Collectibles such as baseball cards
- Snacks
- Books or magazines
- Games
- CDs and DVDs

- Clothing or accessories
- Puzzles
- Pets
- Tickets to movies or events
- Gift certificates
- Sports equipment
- Wanted items for the child's room
- Electronics (various types)
- Money
- A purchase of the child's choice within a specified price range

• Some reinforcers may be used for daily rewards or privileges, such as needing to earn their TV or Internet time; some for weekly rewards (a movie rental or special activity on the weekend); and others for a privilege or item the child is working toward earning or saving up to purchase.

2.7 FOLLOWING DIRECTIONS AND INCREASING COMPLIANCE: TIPS FOR PARENTS

When you are communicating what you want your child to do, you can increase the likelihood that your son or daughter will listen and comply.

• Get your child's attention directly before giving directions. This means face-to-face and direct eye contact, not just calling out what you expect your child to do.

• You may need to touch or physically cue your child prior to giving directions.

• Do not attempt to give directions or instructions if you are competing with the distraction of TV, music, or video games. Turn those off to gain your child's attention and focus.

• Show your child what you want him or her to do. Model and walk through the steps.

• Depending on the developmental level of your child, one direction at a time may be all he or she is capable of remembering and following through on. Do not give a series of directions.

• Break down tasks into smaller steps that you want to get done. Give one step at a time.

• Use a visual chart of tasks or chores your child is expected to do.

• A helpful technique for young children is to make a picture chart depicting the steps or sequence of morning or evening tasks and responsibilities, such as a morning routine chart showing pictures of (1) clothing (getting dressed), (2) a cereal bowl (eating breakfast), and (3) a hairbrush and toothbrush (for grooming). A clothespin is attached to the side of the chart that your child moves down to the next picture when completing each task.

• For older children, in addition to giving the directions orally, write them down, highlighting key words in color.

• Always check for understanding of directions. Have your child repeat or rephrase what you asked him or her to do.

• Write down the task you want done (in words or pictures), and give that written direction or task card to your child for easy reference.

• Keep verbal directions clear, brief, and to the point. Eliminate unnecessary talking and elaboration.

• Be sure to give immediate praise and positive feedback when your child follows directions or is making a good effort to do so.

• Provide follow-up when you give directions; for example, inspect or check your child's work, and praise a job well done.

• Reward your child for following directions, as appropriate—for example: "You did a great job straightening up your room. You get to [choose a game, have a snack]."

• Try not to lose your temper when your child fails to follow directions. Remember that it is characteristic of children with ADHD to have difficulty:

- Disengaging from activities (especially fun ones) that they are in the middle of and have not completed

- Responding and following through without structuring, adult prompting, and cueing

- With recall and memory

• Examine what you asked your son or daughter to do, and see if you provided enough structure and assistance to enable him or her to follow through with the directions given. It is easy to forget that even though they are at an age where they should remember and be able to do a task independently, children with ADHD developmentally may not be able to do so. They need some of the supports that a younger child would normally require.

• Avoid vague directions that your child can interpret differently from you, such as: "Clean up your room." Be specific in defining just what you mean and expect done: clothes hung in closet or folded and placed in drawers, bed made, toys in storage bins. What you may perceive as noncompliance when your child does not listen to you may actually be a matter of poor communication on your part.

• Try turning unpleasant chores and tasks into more pleasant or motivating experiences by making a game of it when possible. Try beat-the-clock challenges such as, "Let's see if you can finish picking up your toys and get in your pajamas while the commercials are on [or before the alarm goes off or by the end of the song]."

• You may need to work alongside your child on a task to get started. Once you have provided the necessary support and guidance, it is important that your child work independently to the best of his or her ability. You do not want to establish codependent behaviors that can be disabling to both you and your child.

2.8 ENVIRONMENTAL MODIFICATIONS AT HOME

• Help your child organize his or her room for ease in locating, using, and cleaning up his or her belongings and creating a sense of order.

• Provide your child with his or her own space for doing homework and studying that is as removed as possible from constant distractions and interference.

• Design your child's work space with easy access to necessary supplies and materials.

• Use color strategically to organize.

• Post calendars, and use master schedules. Write each family member's name and activities in different colors.

• Write down and post all chores in a visible place.

• Remember to use as many visuals as possible. Pointing to a picture of a routine or poster of expectations is a better way to remind your child and reduce conflicts than talking about it or nagging.

• Place sticky notes on mirrors, doors, and other visible places as reminders.

• Establish in your home specific locations that will be used for homework, time-out (if you use it as a discipline technique), and the

Internet (if you wish to be able to monitor your child's access and its use).

• *See checklists 2.9 and 2.11* for more ideas on how to establish a home environment conducive to studying.

• Experiment with the use of timers or other types of sounds as an auditory cue to get ready for dinner and time to come in the house, for example.

• Some children have difficulty concentrating and are uncomfortable and overstimulated in noisy environments. Find ways to reduce the noise level, especially during homework and study times and before bedtime if possible.

• Some children find it difficult to study or concentrate in complete quiet because they are distracted by all the sounds in the environment that most other people never notice (household appliances, electronics, and lights and traffic and other outside noises, for example). If this is the case for your child, music or radio playing in the background may help them filter out those annoying sounds that are distracting to them.

• Experiment with music for a variety of purposes besides enjoyment. Different kinds of music have been found to increase productivity and stimulate our ability to think and be creative. Having your child listen to such music may be helpful when doing homework. Music can be calming, relaxing, mood changing, and healing. It may be worth experimenting with calming music before bedtime or other times when you wish to add peace and quiet to your home environment. See Eric Jenson's resources available at www.corwinpress.com, Gary Lamb's Music for the Mind at www.garylamb.com, and *checklist 5.8.*

• We all have our own learning styles and preferences. Some of us do not like to work at a desk and are more comfortable and productive sitting on the carpet or propped up against a back rest, writing with paper attached to a clipboard or on a laptop. Have your child experiment with doing homework using different types of seating options; round therapeutic balls, T-stools, and the kind of computer seat that is meant to be knelt on may be helpful alternatives to a hard chair. Also, seat cushions such as Move 'N Sit and Disc 'O' Sit Jr. are inflatable dynamic seat cushions that may be able to accommodate your child's need to squirm and wiggle in the chair. For Web sites of companies that carry such products, *see checklist 5.8.*

• We all need a time and place for quiet. Children with ADHD particularly need to be able to have a quiet space to be able to go to, regroup, and calm down. Design, if possible, an area with quiet, calming colors (blues, aqua, light green, and pale tones are recommended, as opposed to bold colors). If you have an aquarium in your home, that might be a good spot; watching the fish swim around can be calming. Any member of the family should be able to escape to that quiet spot when needed.

• If your child tends to be accident prone or destructive, make purchases with this in mind, and place furniture and items strategically.

• Consider covering a desk or table top with butcher paper for doodling and drawing.

• If possible, design an area of the house, such as the basement, with furniture (or none at all) where rambunctious behavior is tolerated.

• If your child and other family members do not have allergies to fragrances, you might want to experiment with aromatherapy. Various scents are believed to have certain effects. For example, the scents of peppermint, spearmint, lemon, orange, and pine are believed to enhance alertness or attention. Perhaps your child may be more attentive when doing homework with one of those scents in the environment.

• Many children with ADHD are skilled at and love to construct, build things and take them apart, and do arts and crafts and other hands-on activities. These activities should be encouraged, although they can be messy. Supply the necessary materials, tools, and storage containers.

• Many working parents with late schedules restrict their children to the house after school because it is unsafe to let them play outside unsupervised. Children with ADHD need to be able to release their energy with vigorous activity: playing outside, riding bikes, and participating in organized sports, for example. Explore ways for your child to have this opportunity, such as after-school programs at a recreation center.

• *See checklist 5.3 for more on related topics.*

2.9 WHAT PARENTS CAN DO TO HELP WITH ORGANIZATION

Supplies and Materials

• Provide your child with a backpack and notebook or binder according to the teacher's specifications.

• It is recommended that beginning in third grade, your child should use a three-ring binder with colored subject dividers and a plastic pouch for pencils and other small supplies. Students in kindergarten through second grade should use a soft pocket folder for storing their papers.

• Provide a spelling dictionary or list of common and frequently misspelled words, a multiplication chart, and any other useful reference materials for your child's notebook.

• Provide your child with plastic sleeves that can be inserted into the notebook for storing important papers that are not three-hole-punched.

• Colored folders that are three-hole-punched and can be inserted into the notebook are recommended for storing and easily locating papers. For example, a red pocket folder can be labeled "homework" and contain all homework, and a different colored folder may be for graded and returned papers or anything to leave at home.

• Another technique is to use large laminated envelopes that are hole-punched and inserted in the binder for homework and assorted project papers.

• An accordion folder is an alternative to a three-ring binder for children who find it easier to manage at school. The tabs of the accordion folder are labeled for homework assignments, work to turn in, and each subject. At school during the day, papers can be quickly placed behind the tab for that subject. Nevertheless, I recommend that papers be refiled into the three-ring binder maintained at home in the evening.

• Your child's planner, monthly calendar, or assignment sheet should be hole-punched and kept in the front of the notebook (or in the front or back file of an accordion folder if used instead of the three-ring binder at school).

• Provide the necessary supplies to help your child be organized at school. You will likely have to replace and replenish school supplies often. Have your child take inventory of what needs replacement, or ask the teacher.

• Use of a specific bag for organizing and keeping each of your child's extracurricular activity supplies is helpful. Provide a laminated list, or place the list inside a transparent plastic sleeve that itemizes what needs to be inside the bag (for example, specific equipment, shoes and other clothing, and books and notebooks).

The Homework Supply Kit

• You can help significantly reduce wasted time searching the house for homework supplies and materials. This is a frustrating waste of precious minutes that also causes a major break in productivity, unnecessarily pulling your child off-task.

• This homework supply kit can be stored in anything portable—preferably a lightweight container with a lid. With this system, it does not matter where your son or daughter chooses to study. The necessary supplies can accompany your child anywhere.

• These are recommended supplies (depending on the age of your child):

Plenty of paper	Paper clips
Sharpened pencils with erasers	Single-hole punch
Pencil sharpener	Three-hole punch
Ruler	Dictionary
Crayons	Thesaurus
Paper hole reinforcers	Electronic spell checker
Glue stick	Self-stick notepads
Colored pencils	Highlighter pens
Colored pens and markers (thick and thin points)	Index cards
Stapler with box of staples	Calculator
Clipboard	

Work Area

• Together with your child, choose a place in the home that has adequate lighting, is comfortable for working, and is as free from distractions as possible.

• Carefully examine your child's work space. Make sure there is a large working surface (desktop) that is free from clutter.

• Have your child clear out desk drawers and shelves of work, projects, and papers from previous school years. Together, decide on what you would like to keep and store out of the way (in colored boxes, portfolios, or large plastic zipped bags) in order to make room for current papers and projects.

• Take digital pictures of school projects, copy school work your child did on the computer, and scan other important documents of your child's work each semester or school year. Burn to a clearly labeled CD for safe keeping.

• Burn CDs of important school work files stored on the computer each semester or school year.

• Provide your child with a corkboard and pins to hang up important papers.

• Keep trays and bins for storing supplies and materials that will remove some of the clutter from the desktop.

• Provide the necessary storage space for organizing your child's room efficiently: shelves, closet space, bins, trays, and drawers.

• Label shelves and storage bins.

• Keep a three-hole punch and electric pencil sharpener easily accessible.

• Besides a master family calendar, provide your child with a desk calendar that serves as an overview of important dates, activities, and events.

Visual Reminders and Memory Cues

• Dry-erase boards are helpful to hang in a central location of the home for all phone messages and notes to family members. In addition, hang one in your child's room for important reminders and messages.

• Write notes and reminders on colored sticky notes, and place them on mirrors, doors, and other places where your child is likely to see them.

• Encourage your child to write himself or herself notes and leave them on the pillow, by the backpack, by car keys, and so forth.

• Use electronic reminders and organizers.

• Use color strategically:

  • Provide a file with color-coded folders in which your child can keep papers stored categorically.

  • Color-coordinate by subject area—for example, a history notebook and book cover for the history textbook in green, a schedule with the time and room number of the history class highlighted in green, and the tab of the subject divider in the notebook for history in green.

• Color-code entries on a calendar according to category: school related, sports, and social activities, for example.

More Organizational Tips

• Take the time to help your child clean and organize his or her backpack, notebook, desk, and room. Help with sorting and discarding.

• Assist your child with cleaning and organizing by at least starting the job together.

• Offer a reward or incentive for straightening and organizing materials, putting away belongings, and so forth.

• If you are using a token economy system or behavior modification at home, give points or tokens for meeting an organizational or cleanup goal.

• Label your child's materials and possessions with his or her name.

• To avoid early-morning rush and stress, have your child get as much as possible organized and ready for school the night before; for example, set out the next day's outfit, prepare lunch, and load everything into the backpack. Shower or bathe in the evening.

• Have your child place his or her loaded backpack in the same spot every night.

• *See checklist 3.13* for recommended supports and accommodations that teachers can provide to help your disorganized child.

2.10 WHAT PARENTS CAN DO TO HELP WITH TIME MANAGEMENT

Difficulty with adequately budgeting and managing time is certainly not unique to children, teens, or adults with ADHD. But for those with ADHD, time awareness and time management are often exceedingly difficult and problematic.

Tools, Schedules, and Supports

• Make sure your child knows how to tell time and read a nondigital (analog) clock.

• Check that your child knows how to read calendars and schedules.

• Make sure clocks in the home are accurate.

• Watches or alarms that can be set to vibrate and cue your child to be on-task, be somewhere, call home, or take medication, for example, are helpful.

• Other electronic devices with timers to help remember appointments, curfews, and keep on schedule are also beneficial.

• Teach and model how to use to-do lists by writing down things that need to be done and then crossing off accomplished tasks.

• Help your child schedule the evening, and estimate how long each homework assignment or other activity should take.

• Developing the habit of using a personal planner or agenda is essential. Your child should be expected to record assignments in a planner, calendar, agenda, or assignment log of some sort by the mid- to upper-elementary grades.

• Expect your child to record assignments, and monitor that this is being done. Ask to see your son or daughter's assignment calendars, sheets, and planners every day. See the teacher for help in ensuring that assignments are recorded. Your child may need direct assistance from a classmate or buddy or the teacher to be sure assignments are recorded. *See checklist 3.14.*

• Post a large calendar or wall chart in a central location of the home for scheduling family activities and events. Encourage everyone to refer to it daily. Each family member may have his or her own color pen for recording on the calendar.

• Help transfer important extracurricular activities and scheduling to your child's personal calendar or planner.

• Phone calls and electronic messages can easily interfere with staying on schedule and pull your child off-task. If your child has a cell phone, have him or her turn it off and remove it from the room while doing homework. Checking messages and returning phone calls can be done at homework breaks.

• Help your child create a weekly schedule.

• For older children, a recommended time management strategy is to take a few days to track and record how they spend their time over the course of twenty-four hours. After a few days, your child should have better awareness of how much time is typically spent on routine activities: meals, sleeping, grooming, walking to class, screen time (watching television, on the computer), talking on the phone, recreational and social activities, and study and homework time.

• With your child, schedule a time for homework. This is a priority. Some children like to come home and immediately get part or all of their homework done and out of the way. Others need a break before tackling any homework. The homework schedule should be adhered to as consistently as possible. *See checklist 2.1.*

Managing Routines

• Morning and evening routines and rituals for getting ready for school and preparing to go to bed at night are very helpful. Clear reminders of the routine (for example, through the use of a checklist of sequential tasks to complete) reduce the nagging, rushing around, and negative interactions at these times of the day.

• Checklists are great tools for time management and staying on schedule. Each task that is completed on the list or chart is crossed off.

• Combine checklists and routines with a positive reinforcement system. If your child has all items completed and checked off by a certain time, he or she earns extra points or tokens as a reward.

• Help your child establish a routine for extracurricular activities as well. Include scheduled time for practice and gathering needed items (with the aid of a checklist) for that extracurricular activity.

Long-Term Projects

• Your assistance with time management and structuring of long-term school assignments such as book reports and science and research projects is critical to your child's success. Build in plenty of time. When scheduling, allow for unforeseen glitches and delays.

• Help your child break down longer assignments into smaller, manageable chunks with deadlines marked on the calendar for completing incremental steps of the project.

• Pay close attention to due dates, and post the project requirements. Together with your child, record on a master calendar the due date of the final project, and plan when to do the steps along the way (for example, going to the library and getting resources and materials).

• Ask the teacher for feedback and help monitoring that your child is on track with the project. Do not assume your child is working on projects at school, even if he or she is given some time in class to do so.

• Large and long-term projects can be easily overwhelming and discouraging for your child (and you too). Your son or daughter will likely need your assistance, as well as help at school, with pacing and monitoring time lines toward project completion.

• *See checklists 2.9 and 2.11.* Also look at the recommendations to teachers for helping with organization, time management, and homework in *checklists 3.12, 3.13, and 3.14.*

2.11 HOMEWORK TIPS FOR PARENTS

In most homes of children and teens with ADHD, homework is problematic and a source of frustration for both the student and parents. This challenge stems from the core symptoms and executive function difficulties associated with ADHD, which affect organization, time management, and study skills.

Creating the Work Environment

• Make sure your child has a quiet work space with minimal distractions, and where it is easy for you to supervise and monitor work production.

• Provide your child the necessary supplies, materials, and organized work area as described in *checklist 2.9.*

• Experiment with music softly playing while your child is doing homework. Music may help block auditory distractions in the environment. The right music stimulates the brain and can be helpful for studying. Try various types of classical and instrumental music and other selections of your child's choice that may make studying more pleasant and increase productivity. *See checklists 2.8 and 5.3.*

Developing a Homework Routine and Schedule

• Together with your child, establish a specific time and place for homework. In order to develop a homework habit, it is important to adhere to a schedule as closely and consistently as possible.

• Consider a variety of factors when scheduling homework: extracurricular activities, medication effects at that time, mealtimes and bedtimes, other chores and responsibilities, your availability to supervise and monitor, and your child's individual preferences and learning styles.

• Some children prefer and are more productive if they start homework shortly after they come home from school. Others need time to play, relax first, and then start homework later. However, they should not wait until the evening to get started.

• Encourage and help your child get in the habit of putting all books, notebooks, signed notes, and other necessary materials inside the backpack before bedtime.

• Place the backpack in a consistent location (for example, by the front door) that your child cannot miss seeing or tripping over when leaving the house in the morning.

• *See checklist 2.9.*

Preparation and Structuring

• Expect your child to have all assignments recorded. Request the teacher's help in making sure all assignments are recorded daily, perhaps by initialing or signing the student's calendar or assignment sheet or other system.

• Be sure to follow through by reviewing the recorded assignments with your child.

• Emphasize to your child the importance of not leaving school without double-checking the assignment sheet or calendar and making sure all necessary books and materials to do the homework are in the backpack.

• Have your child take the phone numbers of a few responsible classmates to call if there is a question about school work. Many schools help in this regard with homework hotlines, recording daily assignments on teachers' voice mail, or classroom Web sites where teachers post assignments online.

• Help your child look over all homework assignments for the evening and organize materials needed before beginning.

• If your child frequently forgets to bring textbooks home, ask if you can borrow another set for home. If not, consider purchasing a set.

• Assist your child with structuring long-range homework assignments such as reports and projects, and be vigilant in monitoring and supporting him or her through the process. *See checklist 2.10* for more on this topic.

Help During Homework

• The amount of direct assistance required during homework will depend on your child's age and specific needs.

• Assist your child in getting started on assignments, perhaps by reading the directions together, color-highlighting the key words in the directions, doing the first few items together, observing as your child does the next problem or item independently, and offering feedback and help if needed. Then get up and leave.

• Monitor and give feedback without doing all the work together. You want your child to attempt as much as possible independently.

• Even with younger children, try to get your child started, and then check and give feedback on small segments of his or her independent work (for example, after every few problems or one row completed). Being available to help and assist as needed is wonderful, but try not to get in the habit of having your child rely on your overseeing every minute.

• As tempting as it may be, even when homework time is dragging on, do not do the work for your child.

• Have your child work a certain amount of time and then stop. Do not force him or her to spend an excessive and inappropriate amount of time on homework. If you feel your child worked enough for one night, write a note to the teacher and attach it to the homework.

• If your child struggles in writing, he or she may dictate as you write and record the responses. These accommodations to help bypass writing difficulties are reasonable for children with ADHD. Speak to the teacher.

• It is not your responsibility to correct all of your child's errors on homework or make him or her complete and turn in a perfect paper.

• As homework supervisor and coach, praise your child for being on task, getting to work, and taking responsibility. Give extra praise for accomplishment and progress.

Increasing Motivation and Work Production

• Use a kitchen timer to challenge your child to stay on task, and reward work completed with relative accuracy during that time frame. Tell your child that you will come back to check his or her progress on homework when the timer rings.

• A beat-the-clock system is often effective in motivating children to complete a task before the timer goes off.

• Ask to see what your child has accomplished after a certain amount of time or to show you when a particular assignment is done. Praise and reward work on completion.

• Help your child in setting up mini-goals of work completion (read a specified number of pages, finish writing one paragraph, complete a row of problems). When accomplishing the goal or task, your child is rewarded with a break and perhaps points or tokens or other reinforcers.

• Remind your child to do homework and offer incentives: "When you finish your homework, you can do . . ."

• Allow your child a break between homework assignments. In fact, your child can reward him- or herself with a snack and a play or exercise break after completing each assignment or two.

• A contract for a larger incentive or reinforcer may be worked out as part of a plan to motivate your child to persist and follow through with homework—for example, "If you have no missing or late homework assignments this next week, you will earn . . ."

• Avoid nagging and threatening. Instead use incentives to support and motivate your child through the difficult task of doing homework.

• Enforce consequences such as loss of points on a token economy or behavior modification system when your child fails to bring home needed assignments or materials to do the homework.

• Withhold privileges (for example, no TV or other screen time or access to the phone) until a reasonable amount of homework has been accomplished.

Communicating with Teachers About Homework Issues

• If the homework is too confusing or difficult for your child to do (or for you to understand from the directions what is expected), let the teacher know.

• If homework is a frequent cause of battles, tears, and frustration in your home, seek help. Make an appointment with the teacher to discuss the homework problems, and request reasonable modifications and adjustments in homework assignments.

• Communicate with the teacher and try to come to a reasonable agreement about daily homework expectations. Remind the teacher that children with ADHD often take two to three times longer (or more) to complete the same amount of work as their peers, and some of the homework demands might exceed your child's capacity without enormous stress.

• Let the teacher know your child's frustration and tolerance level in the evening. The teacher needs to be aware of the amount of time it takes your child to complete tasks and what efforts you are making to help at home.

• Ask for progress notes or use of a daily or weekly report card that keep you appraised as to how your child is doing. *See checklist 1.14.*

Other Ways to Help

• If your child is on medication during the school day but cannot get through the homework once the medication effects wear off, consult with your doctor. Many children with ADHD are more successful with homework when given a small dose of medication in the late afternoon or switching to a prescription with a long-acting formula.

• Many students with ADHD need homework accommodations written into a 504 Plan or IEP. *See checklist 5.7.*

• It is common for students with ADHD to fail to turn in their finished work. Naturally, it is frustrating to know your child struggled to do the work and then never got credit for having done it. Supervise that completed work leaves the home and is in the notebook and backpack. You may want to arrange with the teacher a system for collecting your child's work as soon as your child arrives at school.

• Help your child study for tests. Use memory strategies to increase recall and retention of material. Practice and study using a variety of multisensory formats and memory techniques. *See checklists 4.2, 4.4, 4.9, and 5.2.*

• If your child struggles with reading, math, or writing, see the academic strategies and supports found in *checklists 3.15, 3.16, 3.17, 4.2, 4.4, 4.6, 4.7, 4.8, 4.9, 4.10, and 4.11.*

• Many parents find it difficult to help their own child with schoolwork. If that is the case, find someone who can. Consider hiring a tutor. Often a junior or senior high school student is ideal, depending on the need and age of your child. Every community has a variety of tutorial services available. Of course, check references.

• Encourage your child, and emphasize effort as the most important criterion when doing his or her homework.

• For recommended strategies teachers can use to teach skills and support students with organization, time management, and homework, *see checklists 3.12, 3.13, and 3.14.*

2.12 PARENTING YOUR CHILD WITH ADHD: RECOMMENDED DO'S AND DON'TS

Understand, Appreciate, and Enjoy Your Child

• *Do not* be confused by your child's inconsistent performance.

• *Do* understand that variability of performance is a key symptom of ADHD, and it is to be expected. It can be frustrating and puzzling to see your child able to perform a task with ease one day or minute, and be unable or struggle to perform that same task at a different time.

• *Do not* assume your child is lazy or apathetic.

• *Do* realize that your son or daughter may be working as hard as or much harder than the average child of his or her age or grade.

• *Do not* forget the importance of time for your family to enjoy each other's company; laugh and have fun together.

• *Do* play games and enjoy recreational activities together. Spend time listening and talking to each other, and appreciate the joyful moments and memories that you build together.

• *Do not* focus on your child's weaknesses, or overlook how essential it is to cultivate and nurture your son or daughter's areas of strength.

• *Do* involve your child in opportunities to build on his or her talents, interests, and passions. Help your son or daughter gain confidence and competence through activities in life that give him or her joy.

Work for a Positive, Collaborative Relationship with the School

• *Do not* be adversarial, accusatory, or hostile with school personnel.

• *Do* remain polite and diplomatic, and always try to build and maintain a positive rapport with teachers and other school staff. Casting blame and being confrontational is almost always counterproductive.

• *Do not* be unrealistic or overly demanding of teachers with regard to the individual attention and degree of accommodations you expect for your child.

• *Do* understand the teacher's responsibility to all students in the classroom, and keep in mind what is reasonable when making requests of teachers.

• *Do not* bypass the classroom teacher by going directly to the administrator with issues or concerns.

• *Do* grant the teacher the courtesy and professional respect to first meet, share concerns, and try to resolve problems directly with him or her.

• *Do not* feel you must accept the school's proposed plan of intervention if you are not comfortable with that plan or feel it is not addressing your child's needs.

• *Do* know that your input is welcome and generally requested by the school. No plans are set in stone, and they can always be reviewed and changed if they are not working. Also, be assured that any special programs or placements recommended for your child cannot go into effect without your agreement and written consent.

Be the Leader of Your Child's Team and His or Her Strongest Advocate

• *Do not* accept an evaluation or diagnosis by any clinician who does not adhere to the diagnostic and treatment guidelines for ADHD set forth by the American Academy of Pediatrics and the American Psychiatric Association. *See checklists 1.11, 2.15, and 2.17.*

• *Do* make sure that that the person who evaluates your child is qualified to do so and is familiar with accepted clinical diagnostic and treatment protocol. Ask questions regarding their diagnostic process. Check their background and experience with diagnosing and treating ADHD.

• *Do not* act on the advice from others (as well intentioned as they may be) who are not truly knowledgeable about ADHD.

• *Do* have the confidence to follow your own best judgment. After learning from expert sources, then make an informed decision on how to best treat, educate, and manage your child with ADHD.

• *Do not* isolate yourself or try to deal with the ADHD-related challenges without support from others.

• *Do* know that many other parents are in the same situation as you are. It helps to connect with those parents, for example, through organizations such as CHADD (Children and Adults with Attention Deficit/Hyperactivity Disorder) and other support groups. Build a team of support for your child and yourself.

• *Do not* keep your child's ADHD a secret from those who spend much time with your son or daughter, such as babysitters, teachers, coaches, relatives, and close family friends.

• *Do* inform those people who will benefit from having a better understanding of ADHD and what is driving some of your child's behaviors that are difficult to understand and cope with. It is also helpful to share some key strategies you find effective in preventing or minimizing some of the challenging behaviors.

• *Do not* believe what you hear or read about ADHD (the various myths and alternative treatments) if they do not come from reputable, knowledgeable sources.

• *Do* ask for and seek out information that is based on evidence from the scientific research.

• *Do not* stop learning all you can about ADHD.

• *Do* educate yourself through a number of avenues: books, seminars and conferences, ADHD-related Web sites, parent support groups and organizations, and training from specialists in the field. Knowledge about ADHD and treatments that are proven to work will empower you with the confidence, hope, and skills you need.

Be Kind to Yourself

• *Do not* neglect yourself or your own needs: your own physical and mental health, nurturing, respite, and support.

• *Do* take time for yourself, seek help, and find ways to recharge and fulfill your own personal needs. This is important for everyone, especially parents who live with the daily stress that is so common in families of children with ADHD. You are best able to parent and care for your family when you are happy and healthy.

• *Do not* doubt your parenting abilities, or be hard on yourself for what might have or have not taken place so far.

• *Do* know that it is never too late to learn, make changes, and move ahead. You are not to blame for your child's ADHD or for not acting on what you did not yet know.

2.13 SUPPORTS AND TRAINING PARENTS NEED

Parenting a child with ADHD can be far more challenging and stressful than parenting a child without the disorder. Many people make the assumption that the child's poor self-control and behavior problems are a result of poor parenting and lack of discipline. Anyone making such unfair judgments needs to be more aware of the difficulties and empathetic. Teachers need to be sensitive to the struggles that may be occurring at home as the child and family try to cope with ADHD-related behaviors and issues. To better help their child and cope with the challenges, parents of children with ADHD need support and training.

• Educate yourself about ADHD. Fortunately, a wealth of resources is available about ADHD, with reliable information and expert advice. The more you know and understand about the disorder, school laws and educational rights, research-validated treatments, and practical strategies for success, the better off you and your child will be. This knowledge will give you the confidence, hope, and skills to make life easier for your child and your family.

• Learn about ADHD by attending conferences or purchasing the audio recordings of speaker sessions from CHADD (Children and Adults with Attention Deficit/Hyperactivity Disorder) or Attention Deficit Disorder Association conferences, read (books, magazines, online articles) about ADHD and related topics, or work with a professional specializing in ADHD.

• Seek counseling if you are having individual or personal problems with stress and coping. Families of children with ADHD commonly need counseling at some point as there is an impact on the on the family when a child is struggling, and often parenting conflicts involved as well. *See checklist 1.17.* Parents need to support each other and do everything they can to function as a team, which means getting professional help when needed. Family counseling may be needed to work out problems.

• Join support groups for parents of children with ADHD. Find out information about the local chapter of CHADD. Many communities have other support groups for parents through schools, agencies, and hospitals. CHADD, a grassroots organization that developed from parent need and advocacy, is well recognized and respected for the quality and amount of up-to-date research-based information and support it provides to parents and professionals interested in ADHD. It has also established a parent-to-parent training program in communities and online that is very beneficial. For more information, go to the CHADD Web site at www.chadd.org.

• Support groups are very helpful in that parents can network with other parents of children with ADHD and learn from each other. Just hearing that you are not alone—that many others are dealing with the same struggles that you are—can be reassuring, comforting, and empowering.

• Often parents become good friends with other parents of children with ADHD, and they understand and help each other.

• Other parents are often the best sources for referrals to professionals in the community as well. Most of the support groups have meetings with guest speakers who address topics of interest to parents of children with ADHD.

• You need to share the load with household responsibilities, as well as all of the parenting issues: homework, monitoring, discipline, and so on. Find ways to simplify and reduce some of the additional demands on your time that may take away from your ability to support each other and parent effectively.

• Single parents need to find support wherever possible: friends, relatives, neighbors, and after-school tutoring programs, for example.

• Providing parents with some respite by volunteering to babysit or inviting the child to your home for a weekend is a wonderful gift from a relative or good friend.

• It may be necessary to hire help in the home: for housekeeping, to assist with driving carpools, or assisting with homework.

• You need to ask for help when needed. If you are on physical or emotional overload and need a break, try to find someone who can help you.

• You need the support of teachers: their accessibility and willingness to communicate clearly and regularly, monitor your child's daily and weekly performance, and give feedback; their sensitivity and responsiveness to struggles with social difficulties, homework, and other key issues; and their flexibility and follow-through in providing agreed-on accommodations and modifications your child needs for school success.

• You need the support of other school staff members—counselors, administrators, special education personnel, the school nurse—who interact with or provide services and interventions to your child. Regular communication and teamwork are important.

• It is important that any clinical professionals with whom you choose to work (counselors, physicians, psychologists) have a solid understanding of and expertise in treating ADHD and are responsive and communicative with you.

2.14 BUILDING A POSITIVE RELATIONSHIP WITH THE SCHOOL

As a parent of a child with ADHD, you will need to communicate with school staff to a far greater degree than is necessary for most children. Your level of involvement with the school significantly increases when you have a child with any disability or special needs.

• At the beginning of the school year, meet with your child's teachers, share information about your child, and establish the best means of communication (phone, e-mail, home-to-school notes, or a journal).

• Let teachers know you are interested, available, and accessible and want to support their efforts.

• Keep in mind what is reasonable when making requests.

• Cooperate in reinforcing appropriate behavior and work production goals.

• Communicate closely, openly, and frequently with classroom teachers. Find out as much as you can about how your child is functioning at school and ways you can support him or her at home.

• Ensure that your son or daughter is coming to school ready to learn: adequate sleep; prepared with books, materials, and homework; and having received medication if it is prescribed.

• Often the best way to establish a positive relationship with the school is to be a helpful, involved parent who volunteers time and service to the school. There are countless ways that schools can use the direct or indirect services of parents. All schools seek parent involvement in the classroom or on various school committees, programs, and projects. Become more involved in the school community, and get to know staff members.

• Let teachers or other staff members who are making a strong effort on behalf of your child know that you are appreciative. It is generally the little things that make a difference: a thank-you note, a positive comment or a message to the teacher or administrator, a positive e-mail to the teacher with a copy to the principal.

• You might wish to provide the teacher or school professional library with a donation of a book or other resources and information about ADHD. Much of the teacher training and public awareness regarding ADHD during the past years has been a direct result of parents' strong efforts, individually and through organizations such as CHADD, to educate others about the needs of their children.

• Your child's school success may require the use of tools (such as timers and assignment notebooks) and purchase of items to be used as rewards for achieving goals in a behavioral plan. This can be expensive for a teacher, so consider offering to purchase such items the teacher needs to help your child.

2.15 ADVOCACY TIPS FOR PARENTS

Know Your Child's Educational Rights

• Learn about your child's rights under the law to a free, appropriate public education and to accommodations or direct special services if the ADHD is affecting your child's ability to learn or perform successfully at school.

• Your son or daughter might be eligible for either an individualized education program (IEP) or a 504 accommodation plan under federal laws protecting the rights of children with disabilities. *See checklist 5.7.*

• You have a right to have your child's educational needs assessed by the school district. Speak with the classroom teacher, special education teacher, school psychologist, the principal, or director of special education if you wish to pursue an evaluation.

• Submit to the school a written, dated letter requesting an evaluation expressing concern about your child's educational performance and including the specific reasons you feel an evaluation is necessary. This will begin the IEP process. The evaluation will determine whether your child qualifies for special education or related services based on an identified area of disability.

• Schools generally request that parents proceed through the school's multidisciplinary student support team (SST) process before requesting formal testing. (The SST, which goes by various other names and acronyms in districts around the country, is a forum for discussing the student and planning supports and interventions.) However, it is not a requirement to do so.

• When the IEP process is initiated, you will receive paperwork from the school district regarding procedures, the assessment plan, and your due process rights under the law. If you have any questions, ask before signing.

• After testing, there will be an IEP meeting at which time the results of the evaluation will be shared with you and other members of the team. Ask for clarification on any of the test data, interpretations, or recommendations you have questions about.

• If your child qualifies for special education or related services, an IEP will be written with specific goals and objectives to address his or her areas of need. You are an integral part of the team in planning your child's special education program and goals. Be prepared for that IEP meeting, and ensure your satisfaction with the goals, objectives, and accommodations designed to address your child's needs.

• Most students with ADHD who qualify for special education will be in the general education classroom with special supports and services. But, if the team's recommendation is to place your child outside the general education classroom, ask to observe those special education classes or placements. As your child's advocate, make sure the program or placement is appropriate. You do not have to accept any services, programs, or placements.

• Your child might not qualify or need special education programs or services but may be eligible for and benefit from a 504 accommodation plan.

• If your child receives a 504 plan, be prepared to share the accommodations and supports that you feel are necessary for your child to learn and succeed in school.

• To be an effective advocate for your child, regularly monitor your child's school programs and plans, as well as his or her progress. Keep in mind that if something is not working, it can always be changed. Communicate your concerns, and attempt to solve problems using a cooperative team approach. The best way is to maintain close communication with the school to monitor your child's growth and progress and implement changes and modifications as needed.

Be an Effective Advocate at Team Meetings

• Parents can feel uncomfortable at school team meetings to discuss their child. These team meetings may involve several members of the school or district staff, and they can feel intimidating. It can also be painful to hear and talk about your child's difficulties.

• Try to enter such meetings with an open mind, cooperative attitude, and problem-solving approach. Be willing to share your opinions, feelings, observations, suggestions, and any information about your child or the rest of the family that may help with planning and intervention.

• Do not be afraid to ask questions and request that any unfamiliar language (educational jargon) be explained. Ask for clarification on anything you do not understand.

• Take notes during meetings. In addition, it is helpful if you come to meetings prepared with a few notes to yourself regarding items you wish to share, discuss, or ask about.

• You are welcome to bring someone with you to meetings. It is most helpful if both parents can attend school meetings together, even if parents are divorced but share custody. Schools frequently work with sensitive family situations and do what they can to communicate and work effectively with parents and guardians.

• To be an effective advocate for your child, prepare for meetings by trying to learn:

- • How your child is functioning in the classroom and other school settings

- • In what areas your child is struggling—academic, social-emotional, and behavioral

- • The kinds of supports and accommodations that may be helpful and available

Ensure the Right Care from Doctors and Other Professionals

• If through your health care plan you are limited as to which doctors your child may see for an ADHD evaluation, be sure that the physician is aware of and follows American Psychiatric Association and American Academy of Pediatrics guidelines in the diagnostic and treatment process. *See checklists 1.11 and 2.1.*

• When seeking a professional in your community, be assertive in checking qualifications. Look for experience and expertise in treating children with ADHD and common coexisting conditions.

• Be sure you feel comfortable and confident with the clinicians treating your child. They should take the time to listen, address your concerns, and answer your questions and those of your child. If the doctor or other clinician does not appear committed to a team approach and communicating with you and the school, you will be better off finding someone else.

• You will be the case manager among your child's team of support and professionals. It is in your hands to be sure that the treatment plan is being followed and monitored by all parties. For example, if your child is receiving medication, be sure that the doctor obtains feedback from the school as to the effects on symptoms, functioning, and any apparent side effects.

Maintain Good Records

• Keep a file on your child that includes all copies of testing, reports, IEPs and 504 plans, report cards, health records, immunizations, and other important data.

• Include in the file a log of communication with the school and other professionals working with your child including:

- • Dates of doctor appointments and medication logs

- • Summaries of conversations and meetings, notification of disciplinary actions and referrals your child received at school, interventions promised to be put into effect, and so forth

- • Having the information in a file that is readily accessible will likely come in handy at some time.

2.16 PLANNING AHEAD FOR THE NEXT SCHOOL YEAR

As the current school year winds down, there are things that can be done to help get the next school year off to a good start.

Classroom Placements

• Many schools go to great efforts to place students in classes so that they are balanced by the number of boys and girls, the range of academic levels, children who have learning or behavioral difficulties, and other factors.

• Most schools cannot accommodate requests for a specific teacher. School administrators making placement decisions do, however, typically take into consideration parents' requests for a particular type of teaching style or environment, such as one that:

- • Is well structured

- • Provides clear directions

- • Is inclusive and understands and accepts children with ADHD

- • Is willing to communicate with and work closely with parents

- • Will follow through with implementing IEPs, 504 plans, or other recommended supports and interventions

- Uses and provides access to technology
- Engages and motivates students through a lot of hands-on activities and experiential learning experiences

• Communicate in writing to the principal and also share with the current classroom teacher the factors you want considered when decisions are being made about next year's placement for your child.

• It is hard to know and predict which classroom may be best suited or who may turn out to be the best teacher for a child any particular year. Just because a certain teacher has a fine reputation does not mean that he or she will be the best for your child.

• It is often surprising how well a student performs with a teacher who may not appear to be a good match and how sometimes a class placement that one would assume would be perfect turns out to be a disaster for a particular student. Be flexible and reasonable, and trust that the school staff also want to place your child in a class with the best chances for success.

• If you wish to provide information and make any requests regarding your child's placement the following school year, ask the school when you may do so. Some schools communicate that information to parents; others do not.

Moving to a New School

• During the last couple of months of the school year, parents of children who will be moving from elementary to middle school or middle school to high school should prepare for the transition.

• Be sure that the strategies and interventions that have been successful for your child are documented. Many elementary schools do a very good job of accommodating children's needs and providing supportive strategies without a 504 plan or anything formal in place. At the middle school level, however, this might not happen.

• If your fifth-grade child with ADHD has needed and received informal accommodations but does not currently have a 504 accommodation plan, discuss this situation with the school immediately. If your child qualifies for a 504 plan, it is wise to put one into effect before moving to middle school.

• If your child is moving to another school, arrange for a visit. A chance to walk through the building and meet with some key school staff such as the counselor or resource teacher (if your child is in special education) is helpful. Before the new school year begins, take advantage of any such opportunities to familiarize your child with the layout of the school campus, use of lockers, and so forth to ease your child's anxiety about what to expect.

• It is recommended that you contact the school your child will be attending and set up an appointment to discuss his or her needs and ask for information.

2.17 PURSUING AN EVALUATION FOR ADHD: RECOMMENDATIONS FOR PARENTS

If your son or daughter is displaying symptoms and characteristics of ADHD that are affecting his or her successful functioning academically, socially, or behaviorally in daily life, you may wish to pursue an evaluation.

• Many symptoms associated with ADHD are common in and of themselves. They do not mean the child has a disorder. But when your child displays a significant number of those symptoms or behaviors, much more so than other children that age, and they cause problems for your child at school, at home, and in other settings, you have cause for concern and should pursue an evaluation.

• It is common for parents to become aware and concerned about their child's problematic behaviors when the child starts school and faces the demands of an academic environment. For many children, it is not until third or fourth grade that they start to struggle in school as the academic work and expectations for independent learning, on-task behavior, and self-control intensify.

• Some children have great difficulty functioning from as young as preschool and kindergarten. *See checklist 5.5.*

• Sometimes the student manages to function adequately in an elementary school setting but falls apart in middle school or even higher. A look at the student's elementary school history will probably reveal that the behaviors or symptoms were evident but under control. Now clearly something needs to be done to help the child.

• At whatever stage you may become concerned about your child's functioning and suspect that it may be the result of ADHD, there are several steps you may take in pursuing an evaluation:

• Communicate your concerns with your child's primary care physician and teachers.

- Speak to the classroom teachers. Ask for their observations regarding your child's performance, production, achievement, and behavior. Ask them to implement a few reasonable interventions to help with any of these concerns, and find out how you can assist them and support your child at home.

- Let the teacher know you want to have your child evaluated and why. Then speak to the school counselor, principal, school nurse, or school psychologist.

- At many schools, the first step is scheduling a team meeting. Many schools call this team the student support team (SST) or other such name. During this meeting, information and concerns are reviewed with the teachers, parents, support staff, and administrator working as a team. This is recommended protocol, particularly if your child has never been referred before and the school has not implemented an intervention plan to address some of his or her needs.

- It is especially helpful to have an SST meeting when considering a clinical or school evaluation for the following reasons:

  - The school can share with you its role in the assessment of ADHD and obtain your parental permission (in writing) to begin gathering data from the school that will be needed in the evaluation.

  - It is likely to ensure better coordination and communication if parents and school staff meet prior to initiating the diagnostic process.

- A school-based evaluation for educational purposes may be initiated at the time of the SST meeting if a review of information indicates it is appropriate.

- The school evaluation team has the responsibility of determining if a child has a disability under federal law impairing his or her educational performance and whether a child meets eligibility criteria for special education and related services or a 504 accommodation plan. *See checklist 5.7.*

- As long as the school arranges to meet with the parents in a reasonable time frame, it is often best if parents channel their concerns and request for testing through the SST (if one exists at the school). However, parents may choose not to go through this process and may request school testing at any time.

• When a parent submits to the school a request for evaluation, a right under IDEA, it formally opens an individualized education program—also called individualized education plan (IEP) time line to begin the assessment and special education process. *See checklist 2.15.*

• If your child is experiencing problems with learning and is underachieving, a school evaluation is recommended. There is a very high rate of children who have both ADHD and a coexisting learning disability that can be identified through a psychoeducational evaluation at school.

• The actual label of *ADHD* is a medical or clinical diagnosis, generally obtained outside the school through a medical or mental health professional.

• For any appropriate clinical evaluation of ADHD, the school will be called on to supply the necessary data (records, reports, observation forms, rating scales, work samples) to the physician or other licensed medical or mental health professional conducting the evaluation.

• For details on a comprehensive evaluation for ADHD and what is involved in the diagnostic process, *see checklist 1.1.*

• A school-based assessment is for the purpose of determining if the student qualifies as having a disability and meeting the other specific eligibility criteria for special education, related services, or accommodations according to the law.

• Seek referrals when looking for professionals in your community who have expertise and experience assessing and treating children and adolescents with ADHD. Local support groups for parents of children with ADHD such as CHADD (Children and Adults with Attention Deficit/Hyperactivity Disorder; www.chadd.org) can be very helpful. School nurses and school psychologists are also excellent resources and often knowledgeable about health care providers in the community who have expertise in ADHD and coexisting conditions.

Checklists for Teachers

3.1 PROACTIVE CLASSROOM MANAGEMENT

The best classroom management is to anticipate potential problems and avoid them through careful planning and prevention.

Create a Good Classroom Climate and Environment

• Create a respectful, supportive, well-structured, and well-organized learning environment.

• Many behavioral problems are triggered by environmental factors: the classroom is too noisy, too crowded, lacks structure, or is uncomfortable for any number of other reasons. Set up the classroom environment to prevent problems. Provide the environmental supports and accommodations addressed in *checklist 3.6.*

• Impose the necessary structure—rules, expectations, limits and boundaries, positive and negative consequences, organization—that is critical to the management and success of all students, especially those with ADHD.

Establish Rules and Behavioral Expectations

• Establish no more than four or five well-defined rules and behavioral standards. Make sure they address observable behaviors—for example, "Keep your hands, feet, and objects to yourself" and "Be on time and prepared for class."

• Define concretely what the behaviors should look like and sound like. Discuss, model, role-play, and practice those desired behaviors and expectations. Post them in words or pictures, and refer to them frequently.

• Reward students for rule-following behavior (for example, with praise and privileges).

• Remind students of your expectations with established visual or auditory prompts and signals.

• Enforce your rules and expectations, but take into consideration factors that may require flexibility and handling some situations differently.

Teach Procedures and Routines

Smooth classroom management is dependent on the teaching of specific and consistent procedures and routines.

• Decide on your classroom procedures, and write those down for clarity.

• Teach, model, role-play, and practice procedures until they become so well established and automatic that they become routine for all students. Plan procedures for the start of the school day or class period all the way through dismissal at the end of class or day.

• Monitor, review, and reteach the procedures and routines as needed throughout the year.

• Particularly practice procedures requiring movement of materials, furniture, and students themselves, and positively reinforce students for following the procedures quickly and quietly.

• Use songs, chants, timers or other noisemakers, and verbal and nonverbal signals to teach and cue various procedures and routines.

Use Your Proximity and Movement

• Circulate and move around the room frequently.

• Use your physical movement, proximity, and positioning for managing disruptive students. Seat them closer to you or in a location that you can reach quickly and easily to be able to make eye contact and provide discrete cues, signals, or warnings, like placing a hand on a shoulder or pointing to a visual reminder on the desk.

• Walk or stand near students prone to misbehaving.

• Create a floor plan for desks and other furniture that enables easy access to all students and paths for walking by and among students without obstruction.

Develop Signals and Visual Prompts

• Provide a visual reminder of rules and behavioral expectations (for example, proper seating and learning position, cooperative group rules and behaviors) that are posted on the wall or taped to students' desks, or both.

• Use pictures or icons of behavioral expectations, and point to or tap on picture prompts as a reminder. You can also use an actual picture that you have taken of the student engaged in the appropriate behavior (in seat, on-task working productively) as the visual reminder of expected behavior.

• Establish visual and auditory signals for getting students to stop what they are doing and give you their attention for moving from one activity to the next. For example, you could flash the lights, use a clapping pattern, play a bar of music, call out a signal word, or hold up your hand.

• Set up some signals and cues that will serve as warnings and private communication between you and the student so as not to embarrass him or her in front of peers. Consider using American Sign Language hand signals or other nonverbal signals.

• Establish a private signal that the student can use to indicate he or she needs a break, and assign a brief task or errand that will enable the student to have a short break.

• Provide students with some form of nonverbal signal to cue they need help when they are working independently.

• Post a time on the board or set a timer to signal when work time has started and will end.

Monitor Student Behavior

• Scan the room frequently, and stay alert as to what students are engaged in at all times. Provide positive feedback to reinforce on-task behavior: "I see Karen and Alicia busy on their assignment. Thank you."

• Develop the teacher skill of having eyes in the back of your head. Monitor and be aware of what students are doing in all parts of the room.

• Provide close supervision and more frequent direction and redirection to students with ADHD.

• Address inappropriate behavior when scanning by signaling, giving a gentle reminder or warning, or giving the student "the teacher look."

• Redirect students by mentioning their name, getting eye contact, and using a calm but firm voice.

Provide Positive Attention and Reward Appropriate Behavior

• Increase the immediacy and frequency of positive feedback and encouragement to students—particularly those with ADHD.

• Focus your attention on the student when he or she is engaged in appropriate behavior rather than caught in a rule violation. Remind yourself frequently to catch them being good. Call attention to the behavior, and reinforce it at that time through praise. Reward in other ways, such as earned tokens, to students who demonstrate good self-control by remembering to raise their hand before speaking or leaving their seat, for example.

• Give at least three times more positive attention and comments to students than negative or corrective feedback. Make a particular effort to do so with students who have ADHD. They receive more than their fair share of negative attention and feedback and need a much heavier dose of positive comments.

• Use positive verbal reinforcement and sincere praise that is descriptive and specific about the behavior exhibited—for example: "Great job cooperating with your group"; "Nice job staying focused and finishing the assignment on time"; "I noticed the effort you put into that assignment. Well done"; "I'm glad you chose to . . . That will help you . . ."; or "I see Michael is standing in line quietly, with his hands and feet to himself. Thank you, Michael."

• Frequently acknowledge and recognize good work, behavior, and social performance.

• Many older students would be humiliated if teachers praised them openly in front of peers. However, they still need and appreciate positive feedback. Provide this through notes and quiet statements before or after class. Try using a sticky note pad to jot down positive comments and place a note on the student's desk. Also, use nonverbal signals such as a thumbs up or a nod and smile.

• Use incentive systems to increase motivation, such as table or team points, marbles in a jar, or chart moves for demonstrating appropriate behavior. There are various types of charts that can be used (sticker charts, dot-to-dot charts, moving a marker or object to the next space, coloring in the next square, and so on). Students advance on their chart as a reward, and on completion or reaching a point on the chart such as the last square, a bigger reward is earned. These can be done by the whole group, a small group, or individually. For example, when the class or group has accumulated a certain number of points or reached the top of the marble jar or end of chart, there is a group reward. Students can earn class money or currency, points, or other tokens of some type and later redeem them for prizes or privileges.

• There are several varieties of class reinforcement systems teachers may choose to use to fit their style of teaching, comfort level, and particular group of students.

• The best incentives in a classroom are generally those involving activity reinforcers. Students are motivated to earn time or opportunity to participate in activities of their choice, such as games, high-interest centers, and time to work on special projects.

• Together with the class, create a menu of possible rewards that can be earned.

• For ideas of possible reinforcers or rewards for the classroom, *see checklist 3.5.*

Accommodate the Need to Move

• Assign tasks such as passing out papers or taking something to the office so students with ADHD have opportunities to move around.

• Build in "brain breaks" and stretch or exercise breaks, particularly after sustained work periods or being seated a lengthy period of time.

• Hyperactive students particularly need the chance to release their energy, so avoid using loss of recess time as a consequence for misbehavior or incomplete work if possible.

Provide Academic Support

• For students with impulsive work habits that can result in the frustration of redoing assignments or making a lot of corrections, provide support such as editing assistance, extra time for checking over work, and use of rewards or incentives for neatness, completing tasks, and accuracy.

• Require impulsive students to repeat directions (to a peer, an aide, or a teacher) before being allowed to start a task.

Other Important Strategies and Tips

• Position yourself at the classroom door, and greet students as they enter each morning.

• As students enter the room, immediately direct them to routine warm-up activities. Writing journal entries, interpreting a brief quotation on board, writing sentences using vocabulary words, or solving two or three math problems avoids having students wait undirected for instruction to begin.

• Prepare for and provide procedures, structure, and supervision for transitional times of the day. These change-of-activity times tend to be the most problematic. For transition strategies, *see checklist 3.2.*

• Use contingency management: students must do the less desirable task or activity first in order to get, do, or participate in something they want. Say, for example, "When you finish . . . , you may then . . ."; or "First . . . needs to be done, and then you may . . ."; or "You may . . . as long as you . . ."

• Effective classroom management goes hand in hand with good teaching and instruction. Students generally demonstrate appropriate behavior when teachers provide:

- Differentiated instruction with engaging, meaningful, high-interest learning activities

- Effective pacing to avoid frustration or boredom

- Lessons that are well planned to maximize student engagement and minimize lag time, when students are unoccupied and waiting to find out what they are expected to do next

• Students with ADHD are often penalized for their difficulties with work production by missing out on their art, physical education, music, or other specials or enrichment classes when they have not completed their class work. Avoid doing this when possible. Find ways to provide more support and accommodations to help them get caught up with their work.

• The key to effective classroom management is building positive relationships and rapport with students and making a connection on a personal level. This requires teachers to be understanding, flexible, patient, and empathetic. Children typically work hard and want to cooperate and please adults whom they like, trust, and respect.

• Smile, laugh, and communicate through your daily interactions that you sincerely care about and expect the best from all of your students and would never give up on any of them.

• Consider creating a "take a break" area in the classroom. This is not a punitive time-out area, but a place designed to be calming and to change the child's brain state, preventing escalation in negative behaviors. For example, set a desk near a fish tank or lava lamp that the student can look at and be distracted from negative thoughts and emotions. You might equip this area with sensory toys to hold (a stuffed toy, a stress ball), or perhaps headphones with soft, low-tempo music. A student can request a couple of minutes in this area, or the teacher may direct the child to this area to take a break.

• Some children are better able to remain seated and control their behavior if they are permitted to doodle or color or are allowed to touch or hold objects in their hand while listening in class. Objects might actually be provided to the student as a "fidget toy," such as a piece of Wikki Stix (www.wikkistix.com), a stress ball, or something else that can be held and manipulated quietly. For Web sites of companies that are good sources of fidget toys, *see checklist 5.7.*

• Teach and model positive strategies for anger management, conflict resolution, dealing with frustration, and stopping, thinking, and planning before acting.

Address Misbehavior

Effective behavior management requires a focus on positive incentives and reinforcement opportunities in the classroom. However, teachers also need to implement mild corrective consequences for addressing student misbehavior and enforcing their behavioral expectations.

• Choose to ignore minor inappropriate behavior that is not intentional. Not every behavior warrants teacher intervention.

• Back up behavioral limits with fair and reasonable consequences for misbehavior.

• Enforce with consistency and predictability and in a calm, unemotional manner.

• Handle inappropriate behavior as simply and promptly as possible.

• Deliver consequences using as few words as possible. Act without lecturing or scolding. Discussions about behavior can occur later.

• There are a number of corrective consequences or punishments that can be used, such as the following:

  • Last person to line up or be dismissed.

  • Loss of time from participation in a desired activity.

  • Owing time (for example, one minute of time owed for each incident of interrupting instructional time). Time owed can be paid back prior to being able to participate in a desired activity or before being dismissed at the end of the day.

  • Time out from class participation within the room at a designated area or in another classroom or other location under supervision in the school.

  • Restriction or removal of privilege or desired materials for a period of time.

  • Playground restriction from certain games or areas.

  • Undesirable task or chore assigned.

  • Filling out a think-about-it (problem-solving) sheet or behavioral improvement form.

  • Being "fined" or losing points or tokens of some kind

• For additional behavior management strategies, supports, and interventions, *see checklists 3.2, 3.3, 3.4, 3.10, 1.14, 5.5, and* recommended strategies for parents in *checklists 2.2, 2.3, 2.4, and 2.5.*

3.2 PREVENTING BEHAVIOR PROBLEMS DURING TRANSITIONS AND CHALLENGING TIMES OF THE SCHOOL DAY

Students with ADHD typically have the greatest behavioral difficulties in the classroom during transition times of the day and changes of activity. They also frequently have problems in settings outside the classroom that have less structure and supervision, such as the playground, cafeteria, hallways, and bathrooms.

Classroom Transitions

• Communicate clearly when activities will begin and when they will end, and give specific instructions about how students are to switch to the next activity.

• Clearly teach, model, and have students repeatedly practice transition procedures. This includes such things as quick and quiet movement from their desks to the carpet area, putting away and taking out materials, and moving to the next learning station.

• Use signals for transitions to alert students that an activity is coming to an end and they need to finish whatever they are doing.

• Train students to respond to specific auditory signals (a musical sound or novel noise, a clap pattern, a word or phrase) and visual signals (hand signals, flashing lights). These signals get their attention and aid the transition during changes of activity.

• Get creative in finding tools for the classroom that make unusual auditory signals—for example, timers, and children's or pets' toys that make various noises, musical instruments such as chimes, xylophone, a bar of music on a keyboard, bells, and so forth.

• Some teachers signal and tell students they will have a brief amount of time (three to five minutes) to finish what they are working on before the next activity or to clean up. They then set a timer.

• Primary grade teachers typically use songs or chants for transitions such as cleaning up and moving to the rug.

• Use songs that you have recorded, and play them during certain procedures and transitions. You can use songs of various lengths (two or three minutes) depending on how long you expect it to take for students to perform that procedure or transition (line up to leave room or get materials out for the next activity, for example). Using a specific song or part of a song during transitions is motivating and cues students to what they need to do and how much time they have to do it.

• Set the timer and reward students for a quick, quiet transition. If they are ready for the next activity when the timer goes off, praise and reinforce. This can be done for the whole class (with, say, marbles in a jar, move-on class chart, class points earned, or bonus time earned toward a fun activity at the end of the week) or by rewarding successful tables or teams of students or individuals with tickets, points, or other tokens.

• Visual timers are helpful for alerting students as to how much time they have remaining. Some recommended visual timers are TimeTimer (www.timetimer.com), Time Tracker (www.learningresources.com), and Teach Timer, an overhead timer (www.stokespublishing.com).

• Provide direct teacher guidance and prompting to students who need more assistance.

• Reward smooth transitions. Many teachers use individual or table points to reward students or rows or table clusters of students who are ready for the next activity. The reward is typically something simple, like being the first row or table to line up for recess, lunch, or dismissal.

• Prepare for changes in routine such as assemblies, substitute teachers, and field trips through discussion and modeling expectations. Avoid catching students off guard.

• Maintain a visual schedule that is reviewed and referred to frequently. Point out any changes in the schedule.

Transition from Out-of-Classroom Activities to the Classroom

• It is helpful for teachers to meet their students after lunch, physical education, recess, and other activities outside the classroom and walk with them quietly back to the classroom.

• Provide and structure clear expectations for classroom entry procedures.

• Greet students at the door as they enter the classroom.

• Set a goal for the class—for example, that everyone enters class after lunch or recess and is quiet and ready to work by a certain time. On successful days of meeting that goal, the class is rewarded with a token, class point, chart move, or something else.

• Use relaxation and imagery activities or exercises for calming after recess, lunch, and physical education. Playing slow-tempo quiet music and assigning a silent, calm activity such as journaling or reading to students at these times is also effective.

Out-of-Classroom School Settings

• Teach, model, and practice appropriate behaviors and expectations for out-of-classroom activities in the cafeteria, passing in hallways, and during assemblies, for example.

• Assign a buddy or peer helper to assist students who have self-management difficulties during these transitional periods and out-of-classroom times.

• It is important to have schoolwide rules and behavioral expectations so that all staff members calmly and consistently enforce appropriate behavior in all school environments through positive and negative consequences.

• Schoolwide incentives and positive reinforcers (for example, "caught being good tickets" redeemable for school prizes) are helpful in teaching and motivating appropriate behaviors outside the classroom.

• Provide plenty of practice and rehearsing of behavioral expectations in all school environments. See the Web site of Positive Behavioral Interventions and Supports (www.pbis.org) for recommended schoolwide practices to prevent behavioral problems.

• Special contracts or some type of individualized behavior plan with incentives for appropriate behavior may need to be arranged for the playground, cafeteria, or other such times of the day. *See checklists 1.14 and 3.4.*

• For students who have behavioral difficulty on the bus, create an individual contract or include safe bus behavior as a target goal on a daily report card. Enlist the cooperative efforts of the school, bus driver, and parent.

• If you are using a daily report card or other monitoring form, a student who has had no reports of behavioral referrals in out-of-classroom settings for the day can get bonus points on his or her card or chart. *See checklist 1.14* and examples of DRCs in that list.

• Provide more equipment and choices of activities during recess to avoid boredom and keep all students engaged. Some ideas are hula hoops, jump ropes, board games, and supervised games.

• Students with ADHD often have great difficulty in environments that are noisy, overly stimulating, unstructured, or undersupervised. Awareness training of the nature of ADHD and strategies to help should be provided to all school personnel, including those involved with supervision outside the classroom.

• Schools should identify and positively target students in need of extra support, assistance, and careful monitoring outside the classroom.

• Increase supervision in all environments outside the classroom: the playground, the cafeteria, bathrooms, hallways and stairwells during passing periods, lunch, recess, and school arrival and dismissal.

• It is helpful to have organized clubs and choices for students before and after school, and during the break before and after lunch.

• One of the biggest transitions students face is the move from one grade level to the next, particularly the change from elementary to middle school and middle school to high school. It is very helpful to prepare students, especially those with ADHD, by visiting the new school, meeting with counselors and teachers, practicing the locker combination, receiving the schedule of classes in advance, and practicing the walk from class to class.

3.3 TIPS FOR GIVING DIRECTIONS AND INCREASING STUDENT COMPLIANCE

• Wait until it is quiet and you have students' attention before giving instructions. Do not talk over students' voices.

• You may need to walk over to touch or physically cue certain students for their focus prior to giving directions.

• Face students when you talk.

• Use an auditory signal, such as an attention-getting sound like a bell or chimes or verbal cue like "1, 2, 3 . . . eyes on me," to indicate students are to stop what they are doing and pay attention to the instructions.

• Give concise, clear verbal directions that are to the point. Avoid unnecessary talk.

• Provide multisensory instructions—visual cues and graphics along with simple verbal explanations. Write on the board key words, picture cues, phrases, and page numbers.

• Avoid multiple-step instructions. Whenever possible, provide one instruction at a time.

• Break down tasks into smaller steps, simplifying directions for each phase of the task or assignment.

• If multistep directions are used, always clearly delineate the steps and sequence (1, 2, 3) of the directions in writing.

• Write assignments and directions needed on the board in a consistent spot, and leave them there for reference.

• Always check for understanding of directions by having individual students volunteer to repeat or rephrase your directions to the whole class.

• It is helpful to use a partner for clarification of directions: "Tell your partner what we are going to be doing on page 247."

• Provide a discrete means of clarifying directions without calling attention to and embarrassing individual students who need extra help. One way is to use private signals.

• Model what to do by showing the class. Leave visual models in the classroom as reference.

• Read written directions to the class, and have students color-highlight, circle, or underline key words in the directions.

• Give frequent praise and positive feedback when students are following directions or making a good attempt to do so.

• Provide follow-up after you give directions by checking the student's work and praising a job well done.

• Make sure to give complete directions to students, including what you expect them to do if they have any questions and when they are finished with the task or assignment.

• For students who have difficulty following directions, make eye contact, and give directions from a closer proximity.

• Focus on what behavior you want started, rather than stopped, and be specific—for example, "Desks cleared except for a pencil" or "Books open to page 21, please."

• What may be misinterpreted in children as noncompliant behavior—deliberately disobeying an adult—is often due to the adult's poorly stated directions, such as being vague or giving a string or chain of multiple directions that the student didn't understand or promptly forgot.

• Keep in mind that students with ADHD often need more assistance and support because they tend to have difficulty:

  • With transitions and changes of activity, particularly disengaging from a fun activity they are involved in when given a direction to do something else

  • Remembering and following through with the direction without a prompt or cue

3.4 MANAGING CHALLENGING BEHAVIOR

This checklist provides recommended strategies and tips for working with students whose behaviors require intervention and for dealing with disruptive and challenging behaviors effectively.

Checklists 3.1 and 3.2 and others in this section address strategies for preventing or minimizing behavior problems.

Behavioral Interventions

• Use preferential seating and proximity control for students with ADHD (close to you, in a location where you can easily make eye contact and cue or signal the student).

• Take action and enforce negative consequences when needed through time-out, loss of privilege, or some other response as found in *checklist 3.1.*

• Prioritize your focus. Be tolerant and willing to ignore some minor behaviors that are basically annoying and irritating. But clearly deal with behaviors that interfere with learning in the classroom and any behaviors that are a matter of safety and infringement on the rights of others.

• Watch for warning signs that a student is becoming overly stimulated, upset, frustrated, agitated, or restless, and intervene at once. For example, you can provide warning cues or signals, divert the student's attention and redirect, change the activity or expectations, remind the student about rewards and consequences, and lend direct support.

• Provide time and a place for an agitated student to be able to regain control, calm down, and avoid escalation of emotions or conflict. Consider creating a "take a break" area in the classroom for this purpose. For example, setting a desk near a fish tank or lava lamp, which is calming to watch, can distract the student out of his or her negative emotional state. This area might be equipped with such things as a stuffed toy or stress ball to hold, headphones with soft, low-tempo music to listen to, or picture books or magazines to thumb through. The teacher can signal the student to go to that area for a few minutes when needed, or the student may make the request. Some teachers call this spot a name, such as *Hawaii* or *Tahiti.* A short time in this relaxing area can prevent escalation of problem behavior. Remember that this is not designed to be punitive. It is not meant as a time-out area. Time-out is supposed to be a punishment or negative consequence, which means time out from positive reinforcement.

• Impulsive students may have more success following rules with a combination of reward (for example, earning points when remembering to raise their hand to get permission before leaving their seat) along with a response cost (being fined by losing a token or point for wandering around the classroom without permission).

• Children with ADHD seek stimulation. When they are misbehaving, avoid any explosive and emotional response, which is very stimulating to the child. You do not want your highly charged response to be rewarding and reinforcing the student's misbehavior.

• An individualized behavioral program is often needed for students with ADHD in addition to the class management system. Initiate a daily report card, token economy plan, contract, or other chart and monitoring system that enables the student to receive frequent feedback and stronger incentives. *See checklist 1.14.*

• Set up behavioral charts or contracts specifically focused on just a few behaviors that you want the student to improve, such as raising a hand to speak, staying in his or her seat, and completing assignments. Determine the baseline behavior: How frequently does the student typically disrupt by blurting or talking without permission? How long can he or she generally stay seated? What percentage of work assigned is typically done and turned in? Set your goals for gradual and reasonable improvement so the student can achieve the goal if motivated to try his or her best. *See checklist 1.14.*

• Be sensitive to social issues and difficulties that are occurring in and out of the classroom. Facilitate friendships when possible. Set up situations that increase the chances of success by pairing students with ADHD with other children who tend to be kind, patient, and tolerant. Seek assistance from the school counselor or administrator to help with problem solving, and keeping an eye on social situations and interactions on the playground, in the lunchroom, and in other areas. *See checklist 5.4.*

• Use humor to deescalate potential problems.

Managing Argumentative, Oppositional, Emotionally Reactive Student Behavior

• Avoid lecturing, nagging, criticism, and sarcasm, and do not take the child's inappropriate behavior personally.

• If the student appears on the verge of losing control, try prompting him or her to use relaxation and self-regulation techniques such as visualization, deep breathing, counting slowly, and self-talk ("I am calm and in control." "I need to chill out."). These strategies must have been taught and practiced before the student can be prompted to use them. *See checklist 5.3.*

• Be very careful of *your* response and behavior with this student. Remain professional, keep calm, and watch your voice level, words, and body language. Lower your voice, and speak in a calm, unemotional, matter-of-fact manner.

• Students with oppositional defiant disorder seek power and control. That is the function behind many of their behaviors. If they know how to get an emotional reaction out of you, they have succeeded in having power over you; the student is controlling *your* behavior. Hard as it is, do not yell or provide that emotional response.

• Do not feel compelled to give an immediate response in dealing with situations until you are in a calm, thinking state. You might say to the student, "I'm upset right now. I need time to think about this before we discuss the consequence of your behavior. I'll get back to you." Then walk away.

• Affirm and acknowledge the student's feelings: "I see you're upset." "I understand that you are angry now." "I can see why you would be frustrated."

• Avoid *why* questions: "Why did you do that?"

• Use *what* questions: "What are you supposed to be doing right now?" "What do you want?" "What is your plan to solve the problem?" "What can I do to help you?" "What would you like to see happen?" "What are you risking by continuing with that behavior?"

• Send "I messages": "I feel . . . when you . . . because . . ."; "I'm concerned about you because . . ."; "I want/need you to . . ."

• Use the broken-record technique: respond by repeating your directions with the same words and in a calm, neutral voice. Use the words *however* and *nevertheless*—for example, "I understand you are feeling. . . . However . . ." or "That may be . . . . Nevertheless . . ."

• Provide choices: "I can't make you do *x*. But your choices are either . . . or . . ."

• After students have been trained in anger management, conflict resolution, positive self-talk, or other such techniques through counseling or in some other way, encourage and prompt the student to employ those strategies, and then provide reinforcement and feedback.

• Alert administrators or the school counselor or nurse if a student arrives at school angry or exhibiting behaviors that clearly predict he or she will need intervention early. If the child takes medication at home before leaving for school, the parents might be called to see if it was administered that morning. Perhaps the student can talk to the counselor or other designated support person in this situation, or someone can follow the child into class and stay there a while until he or she has settled down.

Other Things to Keep in Mind

• Dealing effectively with the behaviors of children with ADHD takes flexibility, a sense of humor, and a good deal of tolerance on your part.

• Understanding the nature of the disorder—that children with ADHD lack the inhibition and self-regulation to control many of their disruptive behaviors due to neurobiological factors—is important. Knowing that the behaviors are not deliberate helps us maintain a positive attitude and mind-set.

• Children with ADHD are developmentally delayed (approximately 30 percent) in their ability for self-management, self-control, and executive functioning. They cannot act their age, so adjust your expectations to be reasonable.

• Establish a close partnership with the parents of students with ADHD. Win their trust that you are going to do your best to help their children be successful. Encourage frequent communication and mutual support. Talk about and plan strategies that can be used at home and school. *See checklist 3.11.*

• Let the student know that you care about him or her and are willing to provide help and support to enable his or her success. The more challenging the student is, the more important it is to find ways to build a positive relationship.

• The Individuals with Disabilities Education Act (IDEA) provides protections for students with disabilities so that they are not unfairly disciplined when their misbehavior stems from the disability itself. This safeguard is particularly important to students with ADHD whose behavior frequently results in disciplinary action such as suspension. It is important to know about manifestation determination reviews and other aspects of the law, particularly before school districts impose a change of placement by removing a student from school. *See checklist 5.7.*

• If you have a student with ADHD who has significant behavioral problems, speak to the school psychologist or administrator about a functional behavioral assessment and behavioral intervention plan for the student.

- Many students with ADHD have coexisting medical or mental health conditions such as oppositional defiant disorder, depression, anxiety disorder, or sleep disorders. The school needs to communicate and work closely with parents and other treatment providers. *See checklists 1.7, 1.12, and 5.1.*

3.5 REWARDS AND POSITIVE REINFORCERS FOR SCHOOL

The possible rewards listed here may be used with classroom (group) and individual behavior management and modification programs. For any social, activity, or material reward to be effective in motivating a child, it must have meaning and value to that student. When you use them for behavior modification and incentive programs, you will need to discover (through inventory or questioning) what the child likes. A menu can be created of possible rewards for an individual student, or a class menu of rewards and reinforcers can be developed with input from the class.

Social Reinforcers

- Positive teacher attention (verbal praise, smiles, thumbs-up, high fives)
- Written praise and acknowledgment (attached to a student's papers, on a sticky note placed on the student's desk, or an e-mail, for example)
- Positive notes, e-mail, and phone calls or voice messages to parents
- A form or certificate given to a student recognizing his or her accomplishment or success
- Class applause or cheering of student, high fives, and compliments
- Earning a class privilege of social status, such as being a team captain or class messenger
- Name being called on the school intercom or at school assembly recognizing something positive the student accomplished
- Posting the student's name and photo on the wall or a bulletin board
- Being named "Star of the Day" or "Student of the Week"
- An object symbolizing success, such as a trophy or stuffed animal, placed on student's desk for the day

Activity Reinforcers and Privileges

- Playing a game, studying, or working on an activity with a friend
- First in line for dismissal at lunch, recess, or the end of the day
- Early dismissal of one to two minutes for lunch, recess, or passing to the next class
- Special activity: a field trip, party, assembly, movie, dance, or school performance, for example
- Lunchtime activities or privileges: a choice of seating or eating in a special location, games, passing to go to the front of cafeteria line, or an extended lunch period
- Earning time in class to catch up on work with teacher or peer assistance available if needed
- Extra time or access to the gym, library/media center, music room, or playground
- Responsibilities or privileges that are desirable: tutoring or mentoring a younger student, ball monitor, sharpening pencils, taking care of the class pet, assistant to the teacher or other staff member, operating audiovisual equipment, taking attendance
- Opportunities to access and use special material and tools such as art supplies, the computer to make a PowerPoint presentation or do an Internet search, or certain sports equipment not generally available
- Selecting a book to be read to the class
- Listening to music of choice
- A special game of choice in class, at recess, or during physical education
- Breakfast or lunch with the teacher, a vice principal, the principal, or another staff member
- An ice cream, popcorn, or pizza party for the class or group of students who have achieved a certain goal
- Getting awarded a "no homework" pass for the evening, a "good for removing two or three items from an assignment" coupon, "one late assignment accepted as on time," or "removing one bad grade from the daily recorded assignments" coupon

- Earned time for a physical break, such as running a few laps, dancing to a song, or playing an outdoor game
- Free or earned time (individual or class) for activities of choice such as games, listening to music, drawing, working on special projects, or accessing learning or interest centers
- Decorating a bulletin board or a corner of the room
- Sharing a joke in class
- Listening post access to hear a story or book on tape
- Time for free reading, including books of choice, magazines, or comic books
- Work on school projects, such as painting a school mural or gardening

Material Reinforcers

- School supplies (special pencils, pens, erasers, folders)
- Stickers, stars, badges, and certificates
- Food (various treats—preferably healthy snacks)
- Cold drinks
- Magazines and books
- Class or school fake money used for purchases in the class or school store
- Tickets, points, or other tokens redeemable at auctions or lotteries or in class or school stores
- Items of choice from a treasure chest (small toys, school supplies, trinkets)
- Free tickets for school dances, concerts, plays, and sporting events
- Coupons from businesses in the community for discounts toward purchases or free items

3.6 ENVIRONMENTAL SUPPORTS AND ACCOMMODATIONS IN THE CLASSROOM

Environmental considerations are essential for classroom management and accommodating individual learning styles.

• Establish a classroom environment that:

- Is calm, predictable, and well structured, with a clear schedule, routines, and rules and behavioral guidelines.
- Is well organized (materials, furniture, physical space).
- Builds a sense of community, teamwork, and interdependence.
- Is flexible enough to accommodate the individual needs of students.
- Is safe physically and emotionally. Students are not fearful of making a mistake or looking or sounding foolish, and they are willing to take the risk of participation.

Student Seating

• Physically arrange the classroom with options for seating. More optimal desk formations for students with ADHD are single-desk options instead of two-person desks or tables, U-shapes, E-shapes, and straight or staggered rows rather than table formations with desk clusters facing each other.

• Students with ADHD are usually best seated:

- Close to the center of instruction
- Surrounded by positive role models and well-focused, on-task students
- Within teacher cueing and prompting distance
- With their desks positioned so the teacher can easily make eye contact
- Away from high traffic areas and distracters such as noisy heaters or air-conditioners, learning centers, doors, windows, and pencil sharpeners

• The key to furniture arrangement is the ability to easily access (with as few steps as possible) each student without obstruction. The best classroom management strategy is teacher proximity: moving among students to monitor, cue, and give feedback.

• Be open, flexible, and willing to make changes in seating when needed.

• Consider other alternatives to sitting in one's desk chair to work. This often increases productivity and motivation and is an accommodation for a child who has discomfort sitting in a hard chair for any length of time.

> • Allow the child to work on the carpet or a beanbag chair if he or she is more productive than at a desk, with papers attached to a clipboard.

> • Establish some standing work stations—desks or table at which a student can do work standing up rather than seated. Place these in the back of the room where they will not obstruct other students' vision.

> • Consider assigning two desks to a student with ADHD, with the option of doing his or her work at desk A or desk B. This allows for the need to get up and move, but within boundaries. The student must be at either desk A or B, not roaming around the room.

> • Try seat cushions such as the Move 'N Sit Cushion or the Disc 'O' Sit Jr. Both are inflatable "dynamic" seat cushions that accommodate a child's need for squirming and wiggling in the chair. *See checklist 5.7* for Web sites of companies that carry such products. You might also buy soft beach balls and blow them up partially as an alternative seat cushion.

> • Experiment with other kinds of seats such as a round therapeutic ball, a T-stool, or the kind of computer seat that is meant to be knelt on.

Space, Materials, and Adjusting for Environmental Distractions

• Students with ADHD are often spilling into or intruding in others' space. Designate physical boundaries within which the student is supposed to stay. For example, use a strip of colored duct tape on the carpet, floor, or tables. The student is asked to try not moving his or her desk, chair, or body past the line.

• Store materials in clearly labeled bins, shelves, tubs, trays, or folders.

• Reduce clutter and visual distractions, such as unnecessary writing on the board.

• Be aware of noises in the classroom environment that can be auditory distractions, and find ways to mask or minimize those sounds. Some students are highly sensitive to environmental sounds like clocks ticking and air conditioners running that most people do not notice.

• Permit students to use earphones to block out noise during seat work, test taking, or other times of the day.

• If the room is not carpeted, insert old tennis balls on the tips of each chair leg to reduce the noise when chairs are moved. Of course, tips on chair and desk legs can also be purchased at hardware stores.

• Provide "office areas" or "study carrels" for seating options during certain times of the day (such as independent seat work time) as needed. They are set apart from the other desks and designed to reduce distractions. It is important that they are not viewed as punitive locations or meant for students with special needs only. The class should know they may be used by any student who feels more productive working in an office area.

• Purchase or construct privacy boards to place on tables during test taking or at other times to block out visual distractions and limit the visual field.

• Turn off the classroom lights at various times of the day for calming, particularly after physical education and recess.

• Allow students to work in or move to a quiet corner or designated area of the room when they need a respite.

Visual and Auditory Cues to the Environment

• Use color cues (such as red, yellow, and green cards) to indicate the noise and movement levels permitted in the class at different times of the day. A red sign posted means "no talking; stay in your seat." Yellow can designate limited movement and talking permitted, and the teacher would need to be explicit and clear in precisely what that means. For example, during small-group activities, talking only to your table partners, using inside voices, and not leaving your table unless to pick up or turn in your group's materials.

• Use private visual cues that the student understands mean various things (for example, no talking, wait your turn, make a good choice).

• Provide a lot of visual prompts, models, and displays—visual depictions of procedures, routines, and behavioral expectations.

• Use auditory tools such as timers, bells, chimes, and other devices that make a noise so a particular sound signals students about an expectation. For example, a sound can be used that means students need to line up quietly and according to class procedure. A different sound indicates students must stop what they are doing and look immediately at the teacher.

Using Music

• Music in the classroom, another environmental support, can be used during transitions (for example, to clean up and be finished by the end of the song) and to calm and settle a class with soothing, quiet music after recess, physical education, and lunch.

• For some students, music acts as a filter to other environmental noises and helps block out auditory distractions.

• Music can be played quietly during work periods to motivate and stimulate thinking and increase productivity.

• Music is beneficial for energizing the class, such as playing a lively, upbeat tune in the afternoon.

• Try a variety of music, including classical music, show tunes, and environmental sounds of nature (such as a rain forest or the ocean). Good resources for recommended music for different purposes in the classroom can be found at www.thebrainstore.com.

• For more on supports and considerations in creating a classroom environment conducive to learning and behavioral and social success, *see checklists 3.1, 3.2, 3.7, 3.8, 3.9, and 3.10.*

3.7 GETTING AND FOCUSING STUDENTS' ATTENTION

Before beginning instruction, teachers need to obtain students' attention and direct their focus to the task at hand. The following are classroom strategies and techniques to do so.

Auditory Techniques

• Signal auditorily through the use of sound or music: chimes, xylophone, playing a bar or chord on a keyboard, or a few seconds of music on a CD.

• There are various toys and noisemakers that make a novel sound that may be an interesting auditory signal. Beepers or timers may also be used.

• Use a clap pattern. You clap a particular pattern (for example, two slow and three fast claps), and students repeat the clap pattern back to you.

• Use a clear verbal signal: "Popsicles . . . Freeze!" or "Everybody . . . Ready," or "1, 2, 3, eyes on me").

Visual Techniques

• Use visual signals such as flashing the lights or raising your hand, which signals the students to raise their hands and stop talking until everyone is silent and attentive.

• Teach specific hand signals such as American Sign Language to signal students.

• Use pictures and other graphics, gestures, manipulatives, and other interesting visuals to engage students' attention and interest. If using a projector (overhead or document camera), placing a novel object or colored shape that is shown on the screen is a visual attention getter.

• Use a dowel, stick, or other pointer or a laser pointer to point to written material you want students to focus on.

• Use visual timers such as Time Timer (www.timetimer.com), Time Tracker (www.learningresources.com), or Teach Timer (www.stokespublishing.com).

• Cover or remove visual distractions. Erase unnecessary information from the board, and remove visual clutter.

• Color is highly effective in getting attention. Use colored pens and bold colors to write or frame important information. Use color highlighting pens or tape and colored sticky notes. Write, circle, or underline in color key words (particularly when giving directions).

The Tech Advantage

• Overhead projectors have traditionally been useful tools for focusing students' attention in the classroom because they enable the teacher to:

- • Model and frame important information
- • Block unnecessary information by covering part of the transparency

- Face students and not have to turn their back on the class in order to write on the board
- Avoid instructional lag time while writing on the board and erasing
- Prepare transparencies in advance, saving instructional time
- Project novel items such as math manipulatives
- Motivate students by allowing them to write on the overhead or share their work with the class

- There are now far more engaging and sophisticated technologies in classrooms, such as document cameras and interactive whiteboards. Document cameras can project any object on the screen without the need for making transparencies and enable students from all areas of the classroom to see objects or teacher demonstrations clearly.

- PowerPoint presentations and other multimedia tools are enhancing instruction in many classrooms. They are wonderful for getting and maintaining students' attention and interest.

Arousing Students' Curiosity and Anticipation

- Ask an interesting, speculative question; show a picture; tell a little story; or read a related poem or passage to generate discussion and interest in the upcoming lesson.

- Add a bit of mystery by bringing in one or more objects relevant to the upcoming lesson in a box, bag, pillowcase, or draped with a cloth that you later reveal. This is a wonderful way to generate predictions and can lead to excellent discussions or writing activities.

Livening It Up

- Try playfulness, silliness, humor, the use of props, and a bit of theatrics to get attention and peak interest.

- Use storytelling, real-life examples, and anecdotes, particularly personal ones, such as something that happened to you as a child.

- Be an animated, enthusiastic presenter. Model excitement about the upcoming lesson.

Making It Personal

- When giving examples, use students' names or other people they know (only in a positive, unembarrassing way). Make the examples interesting and relevant to them.

- Activate students' prior knowledge and draw on their experiences.

Organizing Students' Thinking

• Provide an overview of the major points the students will be studying and their relationship to prior learning.

• Explain the lesson's purpose and importance. Identify the objectives, content standards being addressed, and ultimate goals or outcomes to be achieved by the end of the session or unit.

• Graphic organizers (there are numerous kinds) are excellent tools to focus attention, as well as help students organize and comprehend ideas and information.

• Post a few key points for students to be attentive to, listening for, and thinking about during the lesson.

Management Tips

• Walk by or stand near a distractible student. Place a hand on the student's shoulder, tap the desk, or use another cue to get his or her attention.

• Position or seat the student in a location that enables you to easily make eye contact and provide prompts and cues to get his or her attention when needed.

• For more on this topic, *see checklists 3.1, 3.3, 3.8, 3.9, and 3.10.*

3.8 MAINTAINING STUDENTS' ATTENTION AND PARTICIPATION

Sustaining students' attention requires active, not passive, learning. It also requires that teachers incorporate a variety of formats and activities throughout the lesson. Within a fifty-minute period of time, for example, the lesson may be formatted to include a mix of whole group instruction and end-of-lesson closure (with engaging ways for students to respond and participate), predominantly small group and partner structures for maximum involvement in learning activities, and some time to work on a particular task independently.

Tips for Keeping Students Engaged

• Move around in the classroom, maintaining your visibility, as well as providing individual assistance (clarification, cueing and prompting, redirection) and feedback as needed.

• Use high-interest materials, and teach to students' varied learning styles.

• Write key words or draw pictures on the board or projector while presenting.

• Use technology in your instruction—document cameras, interactive whiteboards, video-streaming, PowerPoint, interactive software, and the Internet.

• Illustrate throughout your presentation, even if you lack the skill or talent to draw well. Drawings do not have to be sophisticated or accurate. In fact, generally the sillier they are, the better, and stick figures are fine. Your efforts to illustrate vocabulary, concepts, and so forth not only focus students' attention but help in their retention of information.

• Incorporate demonstrations, role playing, hands-on activities, anecdotes and storytelling, and multimedia presentations into your teaching whenever possible.

• Build in several movement opportunities during the lesson.

• Reduce lag time by being prepared.

• Monitor and vary your rate, volume, and tone of voice.

• Have students write brief notes or illustrate key points during instruction.

• Endeavor to greatly increase student responses by saying and doing something with the information being taught throughout the lesson. This can be done, for example, through frequent pair shares: "Turn to your partner and summarize [or paraphrase or share] your understanding," or "With your partner, clarify any questions you still have about what we just discussed."

• Supplement verbal presentations with visuals, graphics, and demonstrations.

• Use a variety of graphic organizers and techniques, such as webbing, graphing, clustering, mapping, and outlining.

• Increase the amount of teacher modeling, guided practice, and immediate feedback you provide to students.

• Use study guides, partial outlines, or other graphic tools to accompany your verbal presentation. While you are presenting a lesson or giving a lecture, students fill in the missing words based on what you are saying or writing on the board or overhead. Jotting down a few words or filling in missing information in a guided format is helpful in maintaining their attention.

• Cooperative learning formats (partners or small groups) are highly effective in keeping students engaged and participating during lessons. Teachers need to follow the proper structure for cooperative learning groups concerning assignment of roles, individual accountability, and other matters. This is not just group work. Many students with ADHD do not function well in groups without clearly defined structure and expectations.

• Use motivating computer programs for specific skill building and practice (programs that provide frequent feedback and self-correction) and games for skill practice, whenever possible.

• Differentiating instruction is necessary for keeping students motivated and engaged. Offer students a choice of activities, projects, and assignments and options in how they demonstrate their learning—oral or written reports, demonstrations, or creative designs, for example.

• Differentiate instruction through the use of learning centers, flexible grouping, interest groups, independent projects and study, and a variety of other instructional strategies, structures, and accommodations.

Questioning Techniques to Increase Student Engagement and Response Opportunities

• Teachers who have the most success in engaging students are those who are skilled in the art of questioning. They know how to design instruction and provide high student response opportunities, accountability, critical and divergent thinking, and active participation, with everyone having a voice that is heard and respected.

• Format lessons to include a variety of questioning techniques that involve whole class, small group, partner, and individual responses.

• Before asking for a verbal response to a question, have all students jot down their best-guess answer. Then call for volunteers to answer the question.

• Provide at least five seconds of wait time when asking a student to respond to a question.

• Structure the lesson so that it includes the opportunity to work in pairs or small groups for maximum student involvement and attention. Use alternatives to simply calling on students one at a time. Instead, have students respond by telling their partner, writing down or drawing their response, and so forth.

• Ask questions that are open-ended, require reasoning, and stimulate critical thinking and discussion.

• Use questioning strategies that encourage student success—for example, probing techniques, providing clues, or asking students if they would like more time to think about the question.

• Expand on students' partial answers: "Tell me more." "How did you arrive at that answer?"

• Pose a question, ask for volunteers, and wait until several hands are raised before calling on individual students to respond.

• Make use of a set of individual student cards or popsicle sticks with the names of each student written on them. Draw a card from the deck or pull a stick from the can to call on students randomly and fairly. Draw names from the discard pile as well, or use two sets of class cards that you pull from. That way, students who have already been called on must remain attentive, because they know their name may be drawn again.

• It is important for teachers to incorporate many techniques that enable students to have frequent response opportunities throughout instruction. Following are some suggestions for whole group (full class), small group, and partner responses that require active involvement of students.

WHOLE GROUP AND UNISON RESPONSES

• *Use choral responses.* Have students recite poems or share reading of short passages or lines from the text chorally (in unison). Singing songs or chants, reviewing such material as irregular and sight words or math facts, and whole class response to flash cards are examples of choral responses.

• *Hand signals for whole group responses.* Unison responses can also be obtained by having students use various hand signals—for example: thumbs up/thumbs down or open hand/closed hand responses from students indicating "yes/no," "I agree/I disagree," or any other "either/or" response.

• *Write-on tools (other than paper and pencil).* Most students (particularly those with ADHD or learning disabilities who often resist paper-and-pencil work) are motivated to work with colored pens and markers on dry-erase boards. Another way of eliciting unison responses is to ask the class a question, pause for thinking time, and ask students to write their answer on an individual dry-erase board, individual chalkboard, or other write-on tool.

• Premade response cards. Elicit unison responses through premade response cards—for example: (1) a small set of cards with a single-hole punch that are held together by a metal ring, (2) four or five cards that are held together by a brass fastener and opened up like a fan, and (3) a single card made of card stock or construction paper that is divided into sections (halves, thirds, or quarters), preprinted with a choice of answers in each section of the card. Each student indicates his or her answer by placing a clothespin on the box of the card containing that choice or holding up his or her answer choice on the ringed card set. When the teacher poses the question and provides a signal ("Ready . . . show"), students select their answer by holding up their response card so the teacher can see. Premade response cards are very useful at any grade level or content area to integrate into whole-class questioning strategies.

METHODS FOR SMALL-GROUP AND PARTNER RESPONSES

• Much of classroom instruction involves small groups of students working together. Small-group active responses take place in any cooperative learning group structure. There are countless activities, learning tasks, and projects that are best accomplished in small groups: creating a product together, solving a problem, brainstorming, analyzing, summarizing, conducting an experiment, studying and reviewing, reading and discussing, and others.

• Use of partners (pair shares) is perhaps the most effective method for maximizing student engagement. Students turn to their partner for short interactions: predicting, clarifying directions, summarizing information, drilling and practicing (vocabulary, spelling words, math facts), combining ideas and resources for a joint project, taking turns reading aloud or questioning and discussing a reading passage together, listening to and providing feedback on each other's writing, working out math problems together, checking that each other correctly recorded homework assignments in his or her daily planner, and numerous other tasks.

• Partner activities are an excellent format for keeping students with ADHD engaged and productive. When these students are partnered with well-focused, cooperative, and tolerant classmates, there is also less likelihood of behavioral or social problems than in a whole or small group. Try building in some opportunities for "standing partner" activities—enabling students to get out of their seats to work and share with their partner.

• Here are some more partner-structured examples:

> • "Pair up with your neighbor, and share your ideas about . . ."
>
> • "Turn to your partner [or neighbor] and . . ." After giving partners a chance to respond, ask for volunteers to share with the whole class: "Who would be willing to share what you or your partner thought about . . . ?"
>
> • "Turn to your partner [or the person across from you or behind you], and discuss . . . for a few minutes" or "Write down with your partner all the things you can think of that . . ."
>
> • "Help each other figure out how to do . . ."
>
> • "Try answering your partner's three selected questions about this reading material."

3.9 KEEPING STUDENTS ON TASK DURING SEAT WORK

Due to their inattention and distractibility, students with ADHD often have significant difficulty remaining focused and productive during seat work. The following strategies are beneficial for all students, but are particularly important for those with ADHD.

• Provide sufficient guided practice before having students work independently on seat work activities.

• Be aware that if the student was not paying attention when you taught something necessary for understanding the seat work assignment, the child will not be able to do the work without being retaught or without assistance.

• Check for clarity. Make sure your directions are clear and students understand them before beginning their seat work.

• Give students a manageable amount of work that they are capable of doing independently.

• Make sure necessary supplies are available so students can work during independent time without excuses. Have extra (but less desirable) materials available for unprepared students. For example, rather than providing new pencils, have a can of old pencils or golf pencils they may borrow from.

• Keeping a small plastic pencil sharpener at their desk eliminates the excuse for students to get up and sharpen their pencil when they should be seated and working.

• Send students to their seats with a written task card or checklist of things to do. Instruct them to cross out or make a checkmark as they complete each task.

• Be sure that the independent seat work assigned is developmentally appropriate and within the student's capability of doing successfully without assistance. Nevertheless, provide access to peer or adult assistance as needed.

• Assign study buddies or partners for clarification purposes during seat work. When part of the class has a seat work assignment to do while you are working with other students (say, during a guided reading group), set the expectation that students who have a question during seat work must first ask their partner or classmates in their table group. Only if no one in the group can answer the question may the teacher be interrupted. Some teachers also assign one or more "experts" of the day for students to go to in need of help.

• Scan the classroom frequently, praising students specifically whom you observe to be on task. All students need this positive reinforcement, and it also serves as a reminder to students who tend to have difficulty in this area.

• Monitor students with ADHD frequently during seat work time. Ask them periodically to show you what they have accomplished. Redirect them when they are off task.

• Prepare a signal to be used from the child's desk to indicate he or she needs help. One method is to provide a red card to prop up or a red plastic cup that can be placed on the desk when the student needs to signal the teacher for assistance. When scanning the room, the teacher can spot the cup or card to see who needs help.

• Give other fail-proof work that the student can do in the meantime if he or she is stumped on an assignment and needs to wait for teacher attention or assistance.

• Try using a timer and beat-the-clock system to motivate completion of a reasonable amount of work for students with ADHD. Set short time intervals for each timing. For example, if it is a twenty-minute seat work period, provide for two ten-minute timings or four five-minute timings with mini-goals set in advance (how much work must be completed during that time frame). Reward for on-task behavior and having met the work completion goal during that time interval.

• Accommodate the need for quiet, less distracting work areas during independent work through the use of study carrels, privacy boards, and an optional seat or table away from the student's regular assigned desk.

• Permit the use of headphones or earplugs or other tools during seat work as an accommodation for students who are easily distracted by sounds in the classroom environment.

• Many students with ADHD need help getting activated. Once they do get started, they are often able to do the work independently. Try to offer support getting them started on the assignment.

> • Provide examples of problems or other references at their desk to help with the assigned task.
>
> • Block or mask some pages of assigned seat work by covering up part of the page or folding the page under so smaller amounts are visible at one time.
>
> • Cut worksheet assignments in half or smaller segments, and pass out one part at a time. Blocking or cutting into segments pages of work may help reduce the frustration a student feels on seeing a paper that appears lengthy and overwhelming.

3.10 STRATEGIES FOR INATTENTIVE, DISTRACTIBLE STUDENTS

Environmental Factors and Accommodations

• Provide preferential seating: up front, within cueing distance of the teacher, and away from as many environmental distractions as possible, such as doors, windows, high-traffic areas of the room, enticing learning centers, and visual displays.

• Seat distractible students near well-focused peers who are good role models.

• Provide options for a less distracting work area through the use of study carrels, office areas, partitions, and privacy boards. These should not be used if they are viewed by the students in the class as punitive measures or as accommodations for students with special needs only.

• Be aware of and try to reduce unnecessary environmental noises in the classroom.

• Allow the use of earphones or earplugs for distractible students at certain times of the day, for example, during seat work time. Keep a few sets available for students to access, as well as requiring use of earphones when working on classroom computers or listening centers.

• For more environmental strategies and accommodations, *see checklist 3.6.*

Management Factors and Accommodations

• Increase visual, auditory, and physical cues and prompts to gain attention and help refocus inattentive, distractible students:

- Place a hand on the student's shoulder or back.

- Private, prearranged visual signals (for example, when you point to and tap your chin, you mean, "Watch my face and pay attention") or teaching some American Sign Language hand signals for nonverbal cueing and communication.

- Use picture prompts and cues at the student's desk—for example, a prompt card showing picture icons or words indicating behaviors such as sitting properly in the seat, book open, pencil in hand, eyes on paper, busy working. As you walk around the room, tap on the picture icon of the card as a prompt or reminder to demonstrate the appropriate on-task behavior.

- Nonverbal signals such as flashing lights or a ringing bell

- Private, prearranged signal words to redirect off-task students verbally

• Frequently make direct eye contact with inattentive students.

• Increase teacher proximity in order to facilitate attentiveness (standing near or seated close by).

• Have students clear their desks of distracters, allowing only essential items for the current task on the desk.

• Children with ADHD often have the need to touch or have an object in their hands. For many children, this helps with self-regulation and staying alert while required to sit and listen. Consider providing certain students with access to "fidget toys"—something to hold and manipulate while seated and listening, as long as it stays within their hands and is not bothering others. Examples are a small squishy ball, a piece of Wikki Stix (www.wikkistix.com), or a key chain with a small object at one end that the child can attach to his or her belt loop and touch. Companies that sell sensory toys, such as those that provide resources for occupational therapists, are good sources of such products. A few such companies are www.childtherapytoys.com, www.sensorycomfort.com, and www.theraproducts.com. Others can also be found in *checklist 5.7.*

Instructional Factors and Accommodations

• Make lessons fun, interesting, and relevant to engage students' attention.

• Use a lot of multisensory teaching strategies: color, movement, graphics, demonstrations, and music, among others.

• Incorporate variety and novelty into lesson presentations.

• Address students' learning style differences and preferences, providing auditory, visual, and tactile-kinesthetic input, and letting students demonstrate their learning through a variety of methods: role play, hands-on or experiential, performances, multimedia, artistic, and written expression.

• Significantly increase opportunities for active student involvement in the lesson, and use questioning techniques that engage all students.

• Be an enthusiastic, animated presenter, and incorporate into your teaching style a variety of techniques to capture and hold the attention of students.

• For a host of instructional strategies to obtain attention, engage participation, and accommodate the learning needs of distractible, inattentive students, *see checklists 3.7, 3.8, and 3.9.*

• Increase students' motivation to focus and attend to task better. Use behavior modification techniques with positive reinforcement and incentives for motivating and reinforcing attentive, on-task behavior; examples are table points, individual charts for teacher initials, stickers, points, and contracts.

• Use an individual contract for on-task behavior with positive incentives.

• Call positive attention to the student when he or she is focused: "I like the way Nick is following along and is on the right page."; "See how nicely Sarah is sitting up and looking at the board."

• Reward students for meeting work production goals that are reasonable and realistic for the student.

• Include a target behavior such as "seat work completed within the designated time" for monitoring and reinforcement of on-task behavior on a daily report card (or other form of monitoring or incentive plan). *See checklist 1.14* and examples of such forms in that checklist.

• Use a self-monitoring program such as *Listen, Look and Think: A Self-Regulation Program for Children* (available at www.addwarehouse. com). This is an audiotape that has nothing recorded on it except intermittent beeps. Whenever there is a beep, students mark a recording form at their desk with a plus sign if they were paying attention or are on task and a minus sign if not. This can be done as a whole group or individually (with headphones). It helps self-awareness and regulation and can also motivate on-task performance.

3.11 COMMUNICATING WITH PARENTS: TIPS FOR TEACHERS

Establishing open lines of communication between home and school is critical to the success of students with ADHD.

• To build rapport and a positive relationship with parents, make every effort to learn about and recognize the student's individual strengths, interests, and positive characteristics.

• Be able to speak to parents about their child's areas of strength and competence, as well as concerns.

• Much closer, frequent, ongoing communication is needed with parents of students with ADHD than is generally necessary with other parents. Determine with parents what system will work best: phone calls, e-mail, home-to-school notes, logs, or something else.

• Make yourself easily accessible, and let parents know when and how they can best reach you.

• When contacting parents, be prepared to describe how the student is functioning academically, behaviorally, and socially.

• If you are calling a parent to share concerns, always try to have something positive to share with them as well, and end the conversation on a positive note.

• Be careful not to judge or blame parents, and never make assumptions.

• State your observations objectively about the student's performance without labeling the behavior (as, say, "lazy" or "apathetic").

• Ask parents about strategies that have been effective in the past, what they have found to be helpful at home, and their suggestions.

• Show empathy, and listen carefully.

• Never recommend to parents that they should medicate their child. Redirect medication questions to their child's physician or the school nurse. If the student has been diagnosed with ADHD and is taking medication, your observations and feedback about the child's functioning during the school day is very important.

• If you note positive or negative changes in a student's behavior and performance—for example, better able to stay on task and complete work, more attentive, notably better self-control, increase in outbursts and emotional responses, or lethargy—report these observations to parents. Parents need your feedback to share with treating physicians. *See checklists 1.13, 1.15, and 5.1.*

• You may suspect that a student has been placed on medication, had a change of prescription, or did not take his or her medication (based on the child's change in behavior, positive or negative). Do not wait for the student's parents to inform you of changes in treatment; they may be waiting to see if you noticed anything different or significant enough to contact them.

• When observing such changes, communicate with parents—for example, "I noticed that Jared had three really good days so far this week. He has been very focused and completed 90 percent of his work. I'm so pleased," or "I don't know why, but Kelli has been weepy and not wanting to participate in class the past two days. She didn't want to go out for recess either, which is very unusual for her."

• To build a positive relationship with parents, communicate:

  • In a manner that is respectful and nonjudgmental

  • That you welcome their partnership and all collaborative efforts (school, home, other professionals at school and in the community)

  • Your acknowledgment that they are the experts on their son or daughter

  • That you value any information or insights they can share with you

  • Your sincere interest in doing what is possible to help their child be successful

• *See checklist 3.18* on how to communicate with parents if you suspect the student has ADHD (not as yet diagnosed), *checklists 1.13 and 1.15* if a student is on medication, and *checklists 1.11, 2.17, and 3.18* if you or the parent feels an evaluation is indicated.

3.12 HOMEWORK TIPS FOR TEACHERS

Homework time is often a nightmare in homes of children with ADHD. There are many ways teachers can be supportive and build a good relationship between home and school in the process.

• Keep in mind how much longer it typically takes for a student with ADHD to do the work. What takes an average child about fifteen to twenty minutes to complete often takes three to four times that long for those with ADHD, even with parental supervision and direct assistance.

• Be responsive to parents who are reporting great frustration surrounding homework. Be willing to make adjustments so that students with ADHD or learning disabilities spend a reasonable amount of time doing their homework. For example, shorten the assignment or reduce the amount of writing required.

• Students with ADHD who receive medication during the school day to help them focus and stay on task are often not receiving medication benefits after school or in the evening hours. It is an unreasonable expectation that parents be able to get their child to produce at home what you were not able to get them to produce all day at school.

• Many teachers have a practice of sending home unfinished class work. Avoid this if possible. Of course, some in-class assignments will need to be completed at home, but try to find alternatives for your students with ADHD when possible. Provide the necessary modifications and supports so that in-school work is in-school work, and homework is homework.

• Remember that homework should be a time for reviewing and practicing what students have been taught in class. Do not give assignments involving new information that parents are expected to teach their children.

• Homework should not be busywork. Make the homework relevant and purposeful so that time spent is not on obscure assignments that are not helping in reinforcing skills or concepts you have taught.

• Do not add on homework as a punishment or negative consequence for misbehavior at school.

• Avoid unnecessary copying, recopying, or expectations for high standards of neatness with your ADHD and learning disabled students.

• Visually post homework assignments as well as explaining them. Write the assignments in a consistent location of the classroom (in a corner of the board or on a chart stand, for example).

• Modify the homework for students with ADHD or learning disabilities, particularly reducing the written output required. Ask yourself: "What is the goal?" "What do I want the students to learn from the assignment?" "Can they get the concepts without having to do all the writing?" "Can they practice the skills in an easier, more motivating format?" "Can they practice the skills doing fewer problems?"

• If you have extra copies of textbooks to lend parents, do so for students who are forgetful and frequently leave the books they need at home or school.

Communicating Clearly

• Make sure you have explained the homework carefully and clarified students' questions.

• If your school has modernized communication between home and school, for example, by providing homework hotlines or classroom Web sites, use them regularly. Keep information to parents and students up-to-date.

• Consider assigning homework when possible at the beginning of the period rather than at the end.

• Communicate regularly with parents of students who are falling behind in homework. Do not wait until the student is so far behind in completing work that catching up is almost impossible. For example, use a monitoring form indicating missing assignments, or notify parents by phone or e-mail every x number of missing or incomplete assignments.

• When you assign a long-term major project or report, consider calling the parents of some students. Just because you have talked about the assignment a lot in class and provided written information does not mean the parents know a thing about it. You may call to ask parents to check the notebook for the written information about the project, or volunteer to send another copy to post at home. A "heads up" phone call or e-mail to parents about the assignment and letting parents know you are available for support and assistance if needed is appreciated and can make a big difference in how the student does the assignment.

• Communicate with other teachers on your team. Students who have several teachers are often assigned a number of tests, large projects, and reading assignments all at the same time from their different classes. Be sensitive to scheduling. Stagger due dates, and coordinate whenever possible with other teachers to avoid the heavy stress of everything being due at the same time.

Monitoring and Support

• Supervise your students with ADHD before they walk out the door at the end of the day. Make sure they have their materials, books, and assignments recorded and in their backpacks.

• Assign a study buddy (or two) to your students with ADHD, responsible and willing classmates they can phone or e-mail in the evening regarding homework questions or to find out what they missed on days they were absent.

• One of the most important ways you can help all students (and their parents) keep on top of homework, tests, and long-term projects is to require students to use an assignment sheet, calendar, or planner. Then guide, walk through, and monitor the recording of assignments. If this is a daily expectation and routine, everyone in the class will benefit.

• With some students you will need to check and initial their assignment calendar, sheet, or planner.

• Also have parents initial the assignment planner, calendar, or sheet daily. There can be a place for parents and teacher to write notes to each other as well, an excellent communication system between home and school.

• Establish a system for directly collecting homework from your students with ADHD. Even when they have spent hours on homework assignments, it is very common for students with ADHD to forget to turn them in and get credit for the work they did.

• Work with your school about the possibility of having supervised study halls, homework labs or clubs, tutorials, and other assistance available for students who need it.

• Be sure to collect homework, and give some feedback when you return it. It is frustrating to students and parents to spend a lot of time on assignments that the teacher never bothers to collect.

• Allow the student to e-mail homework to you to avoid lost assignments, a common problem of students with ADHD.

Keeping Things in Perspective

• It is critical for students with ADHD or learning disabilities to participate in extracurricular activities. They need every opportunity to develop areas of strength and interest (athletics, dance, arts and crafts, music) that will be their source of self-esteem and motivation. These nonacademic, after-school activities are important to their development, and the child should have the time to participate.

Be flexible and willing to make adjustments in the homework load, differentiating homework assignments as needed.

• Keep in mind that many students with learning and attention difficulties have tutors, work with other professionals in the community such as counselors, and participate in additional academic training programs outside school. Factor that in when assigning homework to these students as well.

Increasing Motivation

• Try to make the homework assignments interesting. One way to add interest and increase motivation to work on homework is to build in the component of student choice. For example, you can tell students to select three of the five questions to answer or choose one of the three topics offered.

• Include some homework that incorporates an element of play or fun, such as a learning game to reinforce or practice a skill.

• Write a goal for improvement in homework performance together with the student (and the parent if possible). If, for example, the child turns in less than 50 percent of homework assignments during the typical week, the initial goal might be to turn in 60 or 70 percent of weekly assignments, gradually raising the goal or performance standard to 80 percent and then 90 percent as the student achieves success.

• Write the goal into a contract or daily report card with rewards for achieving the goal. *See checklist 1.14* and sample DRCs in that list.

• Reward students for completing and turning in homework with extra points, tangible treats, "one free homework" pass, "one late homework without penalty" pass, special privileges, or whatever else students find positively reinforcing. *See checklist 3.5.*

• See the Web site www.homeworkopoly.com for a tool and method to motivate students to turn in their homework.

• *See checklists 3.14 and 3.15* for more related information and *checklists 2.10 and 2.11* for recommendations to parents on this topic.

3.13 WHAT TEACHERS CAN DO TO HELP WITH ORGANIZATION

Students with ADHD often have significant difficulty with organization, a common impairment due to their poor executive functioning skills. *See checklist 1.5.* Fortunately, there are many strategies that both teachers and parents can use to help.

Organize Students' Work Space and Materials

• Require the use of a three-ring binder or notebook starting in the third grade (fourth grade at the latest).

• Students in kindergarten through second grade should use a pocket folder for carrying their papers daily.

• Require all students to carry a backpack or book bag and to bring the notebook, binder, or pocket folder to and from school in their backpack every day. Starting at an early age with this expectation builds the habit by training both students and their parents to use these organizational tools daily.

• Require the use of colored subject dividers and a pencil pouch for the notebook for a few sharpened pencils with erasers, a plastic pencil sharpener, and other small supplies and essentials.

• Teach students how to keep their papers organized by placing them in the appropriate subject section of their notebooks.

• Require the use of a monthly assignment calendar or planner or a daily or weekly assignment sheet to be kept at all times at the front of the notebook. Whichever is used (calendar, student planner, or assignment sheet) it should be three-hole-punched for storage in the notebook. Students should use it consistently for recording all classroom assignments, and the teacher should model and monitor its use.

• Students should have a consistent location in their notebook for storing homework assignments (or work to do and work to turn in). There are a variety of ways for doing so:

> • Use colored pocket folders (single pocket or double) that are three-hole-punched and inserted in the notebook. For example, a red pocket folder can be labeled "homework" and contain all homework; a different colored folder may be for graded and returned papers or anything to leave at home.

> • Use large laminated envelopes that are three-hole-punched and inserted into the notebook for homework, assorted project papers, and so forth.

• Encourage students to keep a supply of notebook paper handy in a consistent location of their binder.

• Provide handouts to students that are always three-hole-punched in advance.

• Give students a clipboard for anchoring papers on the desk.

• Consider attaching a pencil to the child's desk (with either string or Velcro).

• Provide bins, cans, boxes, buckets, trays, baskets, and other containers for storing materials and supplies and having them easily accessible at desks and tables or nearby when needed.

• To help students keep papers stored appropriately in the notebook, provide adhesive hole reinforcers for ripped-out papers and plastic sleeves for papers that you do not want to three-hole-punch.

• Encourage students who need such daily reference tools as the times tables chart, or lists of frequently misspelled words, to keep them in a section of their notebook.

• Some students have difficulty managing the three-ring notebook system and may do better using an accordion folder. Students who are using the accordion folder should color-code and label the tabs of each section or pocket of the folder: the subject, homework to do, papers to turn in and for storing the assignment sheet or planner and sheets of notebook paper, for example.

• Limit the amount of materials or clutter on the student's desk or work area.

• Some students do better with a large envelope attached to the side of the desk for their papers or a tote bag on back of the chair for their books. This enables them to keep materials near them and accessible without needing to place them in a desk. A basket or box on the floor or shelf is another alternative to keeping things on or in their desk.

• Organize the classroom with clearly labeled shelves, files, and bins so that you and the students know precisely where things belong and can easily locate (and replace) them.

Visual Reminders and Memory Cues

• Use visual or pictorial cues for showing expected materials, daily routines, and schedule.

• Encourage students to use sticky notes for reminders to themselves. Have them stick the notes to book covers, on their lockers and planners, and other useful places.

• Use color strategically for help organizing:

  • Color-coordinate by subject area to make locating subject materials quick and easy. For example, the science text is covered in yellow paper or has a yellow adhesive dot on the binding, the science notebook or lab book or folder is yellow, the schedule with the science class period and room number is highlighted in yellow, and so is the tab or divider for science in the three-ring notebook or accordion folder.

- Use one specific colored box, tray, or folder for students to place completed assignments they are turning in and another colored box, tray, or folder for unfinished work.

- Prepare important notices and handouts on colored paper, preferably color-coded for certain categories. For example, weekly or monthly newsletters could be in blue and spelling lists in pink.

- Use brightly colored paper for project assignments, providing details and due dates. Give the student two copies: one for the notebook and one to be posted at home.

Monitoring, Supports, and Incentives

• Have periodic desk and notebook organization checks—perhaps every other week. Prior to the desk or notebook inspection by the teacher, students would be encouraged clean out unnecessary papers and items from their desks, make sure they have all needed supplies, and file papers in the proper sections of their notebooks.

• Positively reinforce using prizes, certificates, and privileges such as "no homework tonight passes" for passing inspection of notebook and work space checks.

• Provide bonus points or some other reward for improved organization, and reward your disorganized students who, on request, are able to quickly locate a certain book or paper in their desk or notebook.

• Provide time and assistance as needed for cleaning and organizing desks, notebooks, and lockers. It helps, for example, to have another organized student or adult supervise as desk contents are dumped into a shopping bag and brought to another area with a larger table while working on this. Recycle unnecessary papers, apply adhesive paper reinforcers to ripped-out papers, refile miscellaneous papers in the appropriate section of the notebook, throw away dried-up pens and markers, and so forth. Ask parents to help their child clean out their backpack contents from time to time.

• At the end of the day, check that students have the necessary books and materials in their backpack to take home.

• Provide in-school help and adult assistance as needed for putting together projects. Many students with ADHD or learning disabilities have a hard time laying out the pieces of projects and impulsively glue papers to boards without first planning for the amount of space they have. Help with the little extras, such as nice lettering on the computer and cutting papers straight with a paper cutter rather than scissors, to make projects look much better.

Organizational Assistance in Planning and Thinking

• Provide advanced organizers and study guides to help organize thinking about key topics of the lesson.

• Use graphic organizers. Model and guide through the use of all graphic organizers that aid comprehension and planning: sequence charts, story maps, webs, clusters, flowcharts, and Venn diagrams, for example. Structure writing assignments of various genres. *See checklists 4.6 and 4.7.*

• Provide framed outlines for filling in missing words and phrases during instruction.

• Help students organize their ideas (prewriting, preplanning) with the use of sticky notes, whiteboards and dry-erase pens, tape or digital recorders, and questioning and prompting. *See checklist 4.6.*

• Encourage the use of software that helps students plan and organize their written work. For example, the programs Inspiration and Kidspiration enable children to easily web and organize ideas and outline them. See www.inspiration.com.

• With all writing assignments, provide a scoring rubric to help the student in planning, organizing, and producing work at standard with grade-level expectations. *See checklist 4.7.*

More Organizational Tips

• Encourage students to organize materials when they arrive at class each day and before dismissal at the end of the school day.

• Teach and provide models of how to organize and structure (1) their papers (headings, margins, spacing), (2) display boards for science and other research projects, (3) writing genres and formats (paragraph, essay, business letter), (4) their notebooks and desks, and (5) their portfolios.

• If the student has trouble remembering to bring books to and from school, consider loaning an extra set of books to keep at home.

• Require that materials and supplies be labeled with students' names.

• Keep spare supplies available so that no time is wasted as students search or ask around to borrow from classmates. Consider "charging" students (for example, they must pay you from their class money or tokens) or fining them in some way (points) for not being prepared and needing to borrow supplies.

• Allow for natural consequences of not having materials. Do not positively reinforce students who are unprepared by giving them new, desirable materials and supplies. Instead, let students borrow only your less desirable materials. For example, many teachers keep a box of golf pencils and old pencils and erasers for this purpose.

3.14 WHAT TEACHERS CAN DO TO HELP WITH TIME MANAGEMENT

Students with ADHD often have significant difficulty with time awareness and time management, which is related to their weakness in executive functioning. *See checklist 1.5.* There are many ways teachers can help.

Time Awareness

• Lack of time awareness is common among individuals with ADHD. They often underestimate how much time they have to complete a task or to arrive somewhere on time. They also tend to be oblivious to deadlines and due dates. This is a part of the child's disorder (it is related to executive functioning weaknesses), not apathy or deliberate irresponsibility.

• Any opportunity to practice time estimation is helpful in increasing such awareness. For example, challenge your students to estimate how long it takes to walk to the office and back without running or any other task. Make a game out of predicting, timing, and checking the students' time estimates for various activities.

• Encourage self-monitoring during independent seat work time by recording the start time on the paper. When the work period is over, record the time, regardless of how much work the student actually produced. This is helpful documentation as well with regard to how well the student is able to stay on task and work productively.

Assignment Sheets and Student Planners, Calendars, and Agendas

• Communicate and maintain the clear expectation that all assignments are to be recorded on whatever tool is used in your classroom: a planner, calendar, or assignment sheet. For students to build this important study skill habit, it is important that you are consistent and make recording assignments a priority.

• Model and walk students through the process of recording assignments by writing down and projecting a copy of the filled-in planner or calendar or the assignment sheet. Allow time at the beginning or end of the subject period or school day to do so.

• Provide extra assistance to students who have difficulty recording assignments.

• Assign study buddies so students can help each other. Partners can be responsible for checking each other to make sure assignments are recorded on planners and calendars. And when a student is absent from school for any reason, his or her partner can collect all handouts, notices, and assignments.

• Be sure to select tolerant, helpful partners or study buddies for students with ADHD.

• Partners should exchange phone numbers and e-mail addresses to call each other when the other is absent and communicate about what was missed that day in class.

• Routinely ask table partners or buddies (or groups seated together) to check each other and make sure everyone has recorded the information accurately. Some teachers have partners initial each other's planner after doing so.

• Keep a master monthly calendar posted in the classroom, recording special activities and events that are scheduled and assignments due.

• If students are using a daily planner or assignment sheet, also provide them with a single- or double-page monthly calendar for important dates they can see at a glance. Help them record due dates of projects, tests, class trips, and other important activities and events for the month onto the monthly calendar.

Schedules

• Post all schedules, and refer to them throughout the day.

• Walk through the schedule each day, and point out any changes in the daily or weekly schedule or routine that will be taking place.

• With younger students, use a pictorial schedule depicting the daily routine.

• For students receiving special education or related services, write down their weekly schedule, and have copies for their easy reference that they can tape to their desk, place in their notebook, or attach to the inside of their locker door.

• Keep each student's special schedule accessible so that you know the days and times they are pulled out of class or when service providers are coming to the classroom to work with the student.

Long-Term Projects

• Structure any long-term assignments such as book reports, research projects, or science fair projects by breaking them into smaller, manageable increments.

• Make sure students have access to needed materials.

• Assign incremental due dates to help structure the time line toward project completion. For example, assign separate due dates for each stage of the project: getting a topic approved, submitting an outline, listing research notes and resources, turning in the first draft, and so on to completing the assignment.

• Call close attention to due dates. Post those due dates, and frequently refer to them as reminders.

• Make sure that parents of students with ADHD are aware of the project and due dates. Besides sending home a hard copy of the handout explaining project guidelines, time line, and scoring rubric, consider also calling home and sending an e-mail attachment with the important information. You may want to have parents sign a form to return to school indicating that they are aware of the assignment. Keep project information and reminders posted on your school or class Web site if you have one.

• Suggest to parents that they closely monitor time lines and help with pacing. They can help their child start promptly with research on the Internet and in the library and gathering resources and note taking, for example.

• Monitor the student's progress by asking to see what he or she has accomplished so far and provide feedback along the way.

• Consider providing some parents of students with ADHD advanced notice about upcoming projects and reports, enabling them to have a head start, especially with planning and research.

Other Ways to Help with Time Management

• Provide students with a course outline or syllabus.

• Assist with prioritization of activities and workload.

• Teach students how to tell time and read a nondigital clock.

• Teach students how to read calendars and schedules.

• Make sure that all assignments, page numbers, due dates, and so forth are presented to students verbally and visually.

• Post all assignments in a consistent place in the room, such as a corner of the board or on a separate assignment board.

• Use to-do lists, modeling for the class and teaching the students how to write down and cross off accomplished tasks.

• Provide enough time during transitions for students to put material away and get organized for the next activity.

• Set timers for transitions. First state: "You have five minutes to finish what you are working on and put away your materials." Then set the timer.

• Include "seated by beginning bell time" or some other similar behavior to indicate the student's punctuality on any home-to-school monitoring system such as a daily report card or monitoring form. *See checklist 1.14.*

• If tardiness is an issue with the student, try an individual contract to motivate the student to improve this behavior.

• As an accommodation, provide extended time as needed, and consider more flexibility with regard to accepting late work.

• Provide praise and positive reinforcement. Reward the student for meeting deadlines, finishing in-school assignments, and other responsible behavior.

• Suggest to parents the recommendations and tips for homework and time management in *checklists 2.10 and 2.11.*

• For more on this topic, *see checklist 3.12.*

3.15 ADAPTATIONS AND MODIFICATIONS OF ASSIGNMENTS

Students with ADHD may need various accommodations and modifications, as well as extra support or tools to help them with assignments. Consider trying the following suggestions.

• Reduce the number of paper-and-pencil tasks. Provide accommodations to bypass written output difficulties, and allow students to show their mastery or understanding of subject matter through means other than writing; possibilities are demonstrations, verbal responses, oral exams, and projects.

• Modify or otherwise adjust the length of tasks. Shorten assignments.

• For written tasks, allow students to use cursive handwriting or printing (whichever is easier for the student and more legible to read) or the computer.

• Allow student to dictate responses while someone else records or transcribes them.

• Reduce the amount of required copying from the board or books. Provide a photocopy or copying assistance instead.

• Record assignments clearly for students to see and in a consistent location, such as a designated area of the board.

• Back up oral directions with written instructions.

• Provide directions or instructions that are clear and listed step-by-step with a few words and pictures if appropriate.

• Simplify complex directions.

• Block sections of the work. For example:

  • Fold under part of the page or cover it partially.

  • Cut the page into parts, with rows of math problems handed out one or two rows at a time, for example.

• Monitor the student closely as he or she begins assignments to ensure understanding.

• Assist students in getting started on assignments.

• Many students with ADHD have a hard time organizing their ideas and getting started writing. With a sentence starter or topic sentence provided as a scaffold to begin their paragraph, they are often able to continue writing the rest of the paragraph without a problem.

• Structure assignments so that they are broken down into a series of smaller segments. Assign one part at a time.

• Check assignments midway through (or sooner) for corrective feedback.

• Break long-term assignments into segments. Provide interim due dates and help with time management and monitoring of project time lines.

• Use an individual contract or other incentive system with positive reinforcement for work completion.

• Initiate a daily report card or other individualized monitoring form between home and school. Indicate work production and completion of assignments as one of the behaviors to be monitored, evaluated, and reinforced at home and school.

• Provide extended time for completion of assignments as needed.

• Use digitized texts.

• Provide more direct and guided instruction, with lots of support and scaffolding, before the student works on the assignment independently.

• Differentiate the assignment by modifying the level of difficulty or complexity, offering choice in how students work (independently or with a partner or small group), and offering project and assignment options that draw on a range of student learning style preferences, strengths, and interests.

• When providing options to choose from, limit the number of choices in tasks, topics, and activities so as not to overwhelm the student.

• Assist the student in determining the amount of time the assignment should take to complete.

• Get the student started on assignments in class, and monitor his or her progress.

• Keep in mind that it typically takes students with ADHD significantly longer than other students (often two to four times as long) to produce work. Factor that in when giving assignments for in-class work and homework.

• Modify homework as needed, being responsive to parent feedback about the battle and stress in homes surrounding homework issues.

• Provide in-school assistance in getting started on homework assignments.

• Allow students different ways to get the assignment done. For example, instead of having to write, the student may type or dictate to a scribe or record the work on a tape or digital recorder.

• Provide an assignment sheet, planner, or calendar, as well as teacher or peer assistance, to ensure that assignments are recorded daily and taken home.

• Provide samples and models of "at standard" and exemplary work.

• Provide a rubric or scoring guide detailing your guidelines and expectations, including the specific criteria that will be used to evaluate students on the assignment.

• Increase the novelty of the task by turning it into a game or providing different materials for student use, for example, dry-erase boards or colored markers rather than paper and pencil.

• Provide handouts that have fewer items on a page than usual and are easy to read.

• Reduce the number of problems on the page.

• Enlarge the type size and spacing on the page.

• Increase direct assistance and support. This includes peers and cross-age tutors.

• For more information and strategies related to this topic, *see checklists 1.14, 3.7, 3.8, 3.9, 3.12, 3.13, 3.14, 4.2, 4.4, 4.6, 4.7, 4.8, 4.9, 4.10, and 4.11.*

3.16 ADAPTATIONS AND MODIFICATIONS OF MATERIALS

Use Materials That Increase the Rate and Immediacy of Feedback

• Make answer keys accessible for immediate self-correction.

• Use flash cards with answers on the back for immediate checking and correction.

• Use interactive educational software and online programs for teaching and reinforcing academic skills.

• Use computer programs for drilling and practicing basic skills: spelling, word recognition, math facts, grammar, and vocabulary.

• Provide access to information and to other resources available through computers and other engaging technologies.

• The element of self-correction, self-pacing, and competition against oneself or the computer (not another peer) is much less threatening for children with learning difficulties and low self-esteem. The immediate feedback and reward, color and sound, graphics, and novelty in the programming are highly motivational—perfect for holding the interest of children with ADHD.

Use a Digital or Tape Recorder as an Adaptive Device

• Record directions and specific instructions for tasks, so students may listen as many times as necessary.

• Record text chapters and literature that students may listen to, preferably while following along with the text.

• Record test questions for students to respond to verbally or in writing.

• Record lectures, assignments, and class reviews prior to exams.

• Download digital recordings of your lectures, and organize them by date or subject matter so students may easily access important points you presented in class.

• Allow students with ADHD to use a recorder to give self-reminders. One inexpensive tool for recording a brief (ten-second) personal reminder is the "Please Remember" memory card available at www .childtherapytoys.com.

• Recommend that students use a recorder as a study tool for verbalizing information and rehearsing before performance tasks.

Structure Materials to Enhance Students' Attention and Focus

• Block the page or fold it in such a way that only part of the material is shown at one time.

• Frame the material.

• Highlight, underline, circle, and draw arrows and boxes in vivid colors.

• Provide clear, clean copies of handouts that are well organized and easy to read.

• Use illustrations and graphics.

• Enlarge the type size and spacing on the page.

• Provide markers (strips of cardboard, window box frames, or index cards) to students who lose their place frequently when reading. When attention drifts, so do eyes from the page, and a tool of some type that is placed on the page can help.

• Provide an outline of the lesson.

• Rearrange the page format to simplify and reduce visual distractions.

Compensate for Writing Difficulties

• Permit writing directly on the page or test booklet rather than having to copy answers onto another page or answer sheet.

• Experiment with a variety of pencil grips to find one that is comfortable for the student's use.

• Have the student experiment with the use of a mechanical pencil. For some children who exert so much pressure while writing that the lead frequently breaks it might be a better option.

• Provide a clipboard to anchor papers.

• Provide access to the computer or to a portable word processor such as AlphaSmart. *See checklist 4.11.*

• Experiment with different-sized graph paper and lined paper. Some children with writing difficulties can write more neatly and easily within smaller or narrower lines; others do better with wider lines.

• Provide photocopied pages rather than requiring students to copy from the board or book onto paper.

• If it is easier and faster for an upper-grade student to write in print rather than cursive, allow him or her to do so.

• There is excellent assistive technology available, such as programs with word prediction and speech recognition, that some students with significant writing difficulties may be eligible for according to their individualized education program or may be recommended to parents for purchase.

• For more related writing strategies, *see checklists 4.5 through 4.11.*

Use Math Material Supports and Adaptations

• Reduce the number of problems on the page.

• Use frames, boxes, or windows to separate and space problems.

• Use graph paper to structure the placement of numerals and help with alignment and organization of problems.

• Use an assortment of colorful, concrete, manipulative materials (pattern blocks, tiles, cubes, counters, number lines, more/less than spinners, dice, beans, or cups) to teach and reinforce number concepts of whole numbers, fractions, geometry, quantity, patterning, and so forth.

• Use calculators for problem solving and checking work after paper-and-pencil calculations.

• Allow the use of and provide students with multiplication tables and charts, a chart of formulas, and lists of measurements and conversions.

• For more related strategies, *see checklist 4.4.*

Additional Suggestions

• Use creative learning center activities with hands-on, motivating materials for students to work on independently, with partners, or in small groups. My books listed in *checklist 5.8* contain a host of such activities.

• Organize classroom materials by placing them in tubs and bins, self-locking plastic bags, or colored boxes, and clearly label them using words or pictures.

• Turn assignments into a game format whenever possible to practice skills in a fun, motivating way.

• Have an array of learning materials and books that span the range of developmental levels of students in order to differentiate instruction. For example, if the class is studying inventors, have an assortment of biographies and resources on inventors available at an easy reading level through more challenging levels. Regardless of their readability level, students can learn the same general concepts and information.

• Use word walls of vocabulary.

• Adapt a few textbooks to have available that are color-highlighted for key words and information (main ideas and important vocabulary).

• Use tactile materials and opportunities to use their sense of touch, such as math manipulatives or writing with fingers in a tray of colored sand or in pudding on a paper plate.

• Use lots of games.

• Use high-interest supplemental reading materials.

3.17 TESTING ADAPTATIONS AND SUPPORTS

This checklist contains an extensive list of possible adaptations to consider when trying to provide a fair assessment of students' learning. Included are recommendations to keep in mind when preparing exams for all students. Others should be considered as accommodations or modifications for students who are unable to demonstrate their comprehension or mastery of the content material under normal testing conditions and criteria.

• Prior to testing, conduct extensive reviews.

• Provide students with handouts and test copies that are easy to read: typed, written in clear language, at least double-spaced, clean copies, and with ample margins.

• Avoid handwritten tests.

• Eliminate unnecessary words and confusing language in the test.

• State directions in clear terms and simple sentences.

• Underline or color-highlight directions or key words in the directions.

• Provide many opportunities for short-answer assessment: multiple choice, matching, and other similar questions.

• On vocabulary tests, give the definition and have the student supply the word, rather than providing the word and requiring the student to write out the definition.

• For fill-in-the-blank tests, provide a word bank for students to select the correct word for the blanks.

• Provide students with examples of different types of test questions they will be responsible for on the exam.

• Administer frequent short quizzes throughout the teaching unit, reviewing the next day, and thus providing feedback to students on their understanding of the material. These short quizzes do not need to be graded; their purpose is to help students in their learning and confidence prior to the exam.

• Read aloud the directions for the different parts of the test before students begin the exam.

• Teach students the strategies and skills for taking a variety of tests: true/false, multiple choice, fill-in-the-blank, essay, fill-in-the-bubble, and others.

• Give students the opportunity to write their own test questions in a variety of formats.

• Practice all types of testing formats, sharing and discussing test-taking strategies.

• Use more short-answer testing formats (fill-in-the-blank, matching, multiple choice).

• Test only what has been taught.

• Provide generous work space on the test, particularly for math tests.

• Avoid questions that are worded in a way to deliberately trick students.

• Write multiple-choice questions with choices listed vertically rather than horizontally, as it is easier to read that way.

• Use portfolio assessment: progress evaluated on individual performance and improvement as opposed to comparing with other students.

• For a change of routine, assign take-home tests on occasion.

• Reduce the weight of a single test grade. Have several shorter and more frequent quizzes rather than a lengthy unit test.

• Allow students to use graph paper or other paper to solve math problems and attach to the test rather than requiring that computation be done on the limited work space directly on the math test.

• Divide a test into parts, administering each part on different days rather than rushing students to complete lengthy tests in one class period.

• Allow students with writing disabilities to retake the test orally after taking it in written form to add points to their score if they are able to demonstrate greater knowledge and mastery than shown on the written test (especially for essay questions).

• Do not penalize students for spelling, grammar, or other mechanics on tests that are measuring mastery of content in other areas.

• Color the processing signs on math tests for students who do not focus well on details and make careless errors due to inattention; for example, highlight yellow for addition, green for subtraction, and blue for multiplication.

• Use privacy boards at desks during test-taking time, or find other means of reducing distractions when students are tested.

Individualized Testing Accommodations and Modifications

• Administer the test in a different location, such as a resource room, individually or in a small group.

• Administer the test at a different time of the day.

• Administer the test in shorter intervals in a few different sessions.

• Provide extended time for testing: one and a half or twice the amount of time, for example.

• Take the exam in the classroom and again in a small group or with a special education teacher. Average the two grades.

• Substitute an oral for a written test as appropriate.

• Permit the student to verbally record his or her answers to essay questions on tape or digital recorder rather than write them or in addition to writing the response. For students with writing disabilities, this alternative will provide a more accurate assessment of their understanding.

• Read test items orally to students.

• Read the directions again to students who need additional clarification.

• Provide audio-recorded test questions so the student can go back and listen to the questions as many times as needed.

• Before providing the final grade on a test, point out some test items you spot as incorrect, and allow the student to try self-correcting careless errors before the scoring.

• Give reduced spelling lists for students who struggle with spelling (for example, ten to fifteen words rather than twenty). When dictating the words on the test, dictate those ten to fifteen words in any order first; then continue with the other words for the rest of the class. The students who are tested on reduced spelling lists have the option of trying the additional words being dictated for bonus points. But misspelling any of those additional words will not be counted against them on their test grade.

• Score tests for number correct out of the total number assigned per student (which can be shortened for individual students).

• Eliminate the need for students with writing difficulties to copy test questions from the board or book before answering. Allow students to directly write in the test booklet if needed.

• Seat the student near the teacher or in an optimal location for teacher monitoring and focusing.

• Permit an adult to serve as a scribe and record the student's answers if needed.

• Allow calculator and multiplication charts and tables on math tests that are assessing problem-solving skills, not computation.

• Revise the test format as needed for certain students depending on their special needs; you can reduce the number of items on a page, increase the spacing between items, use a simplified vocabulary, or use a larger type size. Collaborate with special educators in making the changes.

• Permit brief breaks during testing if needed.

• Permit the use of earplugs or some other device to block out auditory distractions during testing.

3.18 IF YOU SUSPECT A STUDENT HAS ADHD

When you observe a student displaying inattentive, hyperactive, and impulsive behavior in the classroom, you should automatically attempt to deal with those behaviors by using strategies proven to be effective: environmental structuring, cueing and prompting, study skills assistance, and behavior modification techniques. Obviously, this is simply good teaching practice of providing behavioral and academic interventions for any student displaying the need. Increase your knowledge about ADHD—both a general understanding of the disorder and recommended strategies and interventions to help. This information will be necessary in guiding you on how to instruct the student, organize the environment, and use behavioral supports and interventions. Teachers or other school professionals should consider the following suggestions when they wish to initiate an evaluation for students suspected of having ADHD.

Initiating an Evaluation

• Keep records of interventions you are attempting, anecdotal records regarding the student's behaviors and classroom performance, work samples, and notes on any phone contacts or conferences with parents.

• Communicate with the student's previous year's teachers to see if your areas of concern were also an issue last year. If so, find out what strategies and interventions were used successfully or unsuccessfully by that teacher.

• Consult informally with appropriate support staff, such as the school counselor, school nurse, psychologist, or special education teacher. Always share your concerns, and ask for advice and assistance as needed. Often, alerting one of the support team members or administrators will suggest a need to schedule a multidisciplinary team meeting, the student support team (SST), to discuss the student. (This team goes by different names and acronyms in school districts around the country.)

• Most schools recommend the SST process for the next step if a teacher believes a student has a disability or disorder of any kind affecting his or her educational performance. The process generally consists of the following:

> • The teacher submits a meeting request form or referral to the SST coordinator. Most districts' SST process requires that the teacher first document strategies and interventions already tried and communicate and share concerns with the parents prior to bringing the child up for discussion at an SST meeting.
>
> • The SST meeting is scheduled to discuss the student. Together with the teachers and generally the parents, the team shares information and strategies and develops a plan of action to support the student.
>
> • Teachers and other team members will be asked to bring to the meeting any documentation or data collected on the student that may be helpful in sharing how the child is functioning academically, behaviorally, and socially.

• At the SST meeting, the classroom teachers, parents, and other team members (counselor, school psychologist, resource teacher, administrator, other support staff and instructional specialists) generally:

> • Review the student's school history and other relevant information.
>
> • Share information about the child's strengths, interests, and areas of difficulty.
>
> • Discuss interventions implemented in the past and currently.
>
> • Determine strategies and develop a plan of action, which may include implementing some additional interventions in school (various classroom strategies and accommodations, school counseling, non–special education academic supports, behavioral contracts and plans, organizational assistance) and recommendations to parents.

- This is often the time and place that parents will be told that their child exhibits behaviors symptomatic of what *may* be ADHD or perhaps another condition or disorder.
- Information and resources can be provided to parents if they are interested in learning more about ADHD.
- Parents may be informed at this time of what the diagnostic process involves and given the options of how to proceed with an evaluation for ADHD if they interested in doing so. *See checklists 1.11 and 2.17.*

- It is very important that teachers are cautious in the way in which they express to parents their concern that a child might have ADHD. The best forum for this discussion is generally through a team. It is strongly recommended that an individual teacher not conference alone with a parent when making recommendations for an ADHD evaluation, but to do so with at least one other school professional, if not the full team.
- The following are some professionally worded statements to consider using in communicating with parents:

  - "These are the behaviors we have been observing at school that have been . . ." Indicate how the behaviors are affecting their child in a negative way, such as: "making it difficult for your child to learn and keep up with class work"; "interfering with your child's academic and behavioral success"; "impairing your child's learning and social functioning"; "causing your child to have significant difficulty getting along with other students and producing work."
  - "A lot of these behaviors that we are seeing are symptoms of what could possibly be attention deficit/hyperactivity disorder"; or, "Sometimes there are medical or physiological reasons a child [is distractible; has trouble paying attention; is active and restless; has difficulty with self-control; exhibits impulsive behavior]."
  - "But of course, we couldn't know that without your child being evaluated."
  - "You may want to consider having your child evaluated," or "We recommend that you share these concerns with your child's doctor."

Points to Keep in Mind

• It is important to state your concerns by sharing objective information and descriptions of the student's behaviors and symptoms with the school team and parents. Teachers need to communicate their concerns, but to do so professionally, being careful not to sound as though they are diagnosing the child as having ADHD (which teachers are, of course, not qualified to do).

• Let parents know you are sincerely interested and committed to putting forth extra effort into helping their child succeed.

• An ADHD diagnosis requires collection of significant data that must be interpreted by the appropriate professionals to determine if the child meets the diagnostic criteria for ADHD. Be prepared to provide information and data that will enable the evaluator to determine how the symptoms are affecting the student, to what degree they are impairing school functioning, and what kinds of supports, strategies, and accommodations you have been implementing to address the behaviors and symptoms.

• For a medical or clinical diagnosis of ADHD to be made, the parents will need to have the school supply data to the physician or mental health professional conducting the assessment. Before the school is permitted to share any confidential information, parents must sign a release of information form that is kept on file at the school.

• Any possible medical conditions that may cause symptoms of ADHD or look like ADHD would have to be determined or ruled out by a medical professional, not school professionals.

• A school-based evaluation for ADHD can be conducted for educational purposes. If inattention or other behaviors are significant and impairing the student's school functioning, indicating the possible need for special education or related services or accommodations, an evaluation should be conducted by the school to determine eligibility for an individualized education program (IEP) or 504 accommodation plan.

• If parents wish to pursue any evaluation (school based or clinically based) once they sign the necessary permission forms, the school will start gathering the appropriate data and information: records indicating school history and indicators of current performance such as rating scales, questionnaires, observation forms, and screening and assessments.

• If the IEP process is initiated, the school must adhere to IEP time lines and procedures according to special education law and state and district guidelines.

• For more related information, *see checklists 1.11, 2.17, 5.1, and 5.7.*

Academic Strategies for Home and School

4.1 COMMON READING DIFFICULTIES

Many individuals with ADHD are strong readers. Those who do not have a coexisting learning disability often read fluently and skillfully. If the reading material is interesting and holds their attention, they can get lost in the book and read for hours with comprehension and recall of the material. But if they perceive the text to be boring, difficult, and not of their choice or interest, they can easily lose focus and persistence to stick to the task of reading. In spite of their reading aptitude, because of the inherent difficulties associated with inattention, distractibility, and poor executive functioning, children and teens with ADHD commonly have spotty comprehension and are not strategic readers.

Inattention-Related Reading Difficulties

• Students can be drawn off task while reading and therefore miss words and important details.

• Maintaining their attention and focusing on what they are reading, particularly when reading silently, can be a challenge.

• When students' attention drifts, so do their eyes from the page, and they lose their place when reading.

• They have trouble paying attention to stories and text that is read out loud in class. When one person is reading orally, students with

ADHD commonly have a hard time following along with the rest of the class. They are frequently on the wrong page of the book and especially struggle to follow the reader if he or she lacks fluency and expression.

Executive Functioning–Related Reading Difficulties

• Students with ADHD fail to use metacognitive strategies. This refers to the practice of self-monitoring their comprehension of the text, that is, paying attention to and thinking about whether what they are reading makes sense. When they recognize that they are not comprehending or processing the information well, they have difficulty going back and applying strategies to fix this.

• When reading, they may not be using their internal language and self-talk to actively engage the text, such as asking themselves:

- • "What is the main idea?"
- • "What is the author trying to say in this paragraph?"
- • "What does that remind me of?"
- • "What do I predict is going to happen next?"

• Another aspect of executive functioning weaknesses is poor working memory, which can affect their comprehension of the text, such as their ability to summarize, retell, and respond to questions related to the reading.

• Getting started and keeping up the level of effort and motivation to complete reading assignments, particularly material that is dry, lengthy, and tedious to read, can be a challenge.

Other Important Information

• Roughly 25 to 50 percent of children with ADHD also have specific learning disabilities, and reading disorders are the most common. Some children have specific processing deficiencies (for example, auditory or visual perception, short-term memory, phonological awareness, receptive and expressive language) that affect their acquisition of reading skills. Dyslexia, the most common reading disorder, is language-based and usually characterized by a deficit in phonological processing (being able to detect and manipulate the sounds in words), causing difficulties in reading and spelling.

• Children with ADHD who also are dyslexic generally have weak decoding skills in sounding out words, learning and remembering letter and sound association, and word recognition. Their reading is slow and labored and lacks fluency.

• Poor readers who struggle to decode unfamiliar words are generally weak in knowing how to use one or more of the cueing systems:

> • Semantic clues ("Does that make sense?")
>
> • Syntactic clues ("Does that sound right grammatically?")
>
> • Graphophonic clues ("What does that word look like?" "How do I sound out that word?")

• Children with language-based learning disabilities may have significant difficulties with vocabulary and reading comprehension as well.

4.2 READING STRATEGIES AND INTERVENTIONS

• Good readers are adept at:

> • Decoding and recognizing words at a rate that enables them to read with fluency and automaticity
>
> • Using all cueing systems (semantic, syntactic, and graphophonic) to figure out unfamiliar words or language
>
> • Understanding and figuring out challenging vocabulary and word meanings
>
> • Knowing how to read for a specific purpose
>
> • Using whatever background or prior knowledge they have about the subject to make inferences and get meaning out of what they are reading
>
> • Making connections as they read the text to other books previously read, their own life and experiences, and other information and concepts they know
>
> • Reflecting as they read

- Using effective metacognitive strategies to think about what they are reading and self-monitoring their comprehension and understanding

- Understanding organization and structure for different types of text (literary and expository)

- Applying a host of strategies in the process of actively reading for meaning.

- *Checklist 4.1* discusses reading difficulties that children and teens with ADHD may experience due to inattention and executive functioning weaknesses. Those ADHD-related issues most typically affect getting through the reading assignment with full comprehension and recall of the material read.

Strategies to Use Before, During, and After Reading

- Key strategies for readers with ADHD are those that keep them actively engaged throughout the reading process. They need to be taught to use metacognitive techniques and strategies that require their thinking about, questioning, and responding to the reading material. A number of strategies are helpful and effective prior to reading, during reading, and after completing the reading assignment to aid with recall and comprehension.

STRATEGIES FOR BEFORE READING

- Prereading strategies are important for activating the reader's prior knowledge about the topic, building connections and comprehension of the text, and generating interest and the motivation to read the material.

- Prior to reading, relate the story or reading material to the students' experiences and background knowledge through discussions, brainstorming, and charting prior knowledge ("What do we already know about . . . ?").

- Set the stage and establish the purpose for what they are about to read—for example: "As you read, think about what you would do if . . ."

- Ask them to make predictions prior to reading.

- Generate interest and increase their background knowledge and frame of reference before reading by using concrete objects and audiovisuals related to the topic of study, such as maps, music, photos, and videos.

• Provide time to preview the key information in the text (illustrations, captions, headings, chapter questions) before reading through the material. Another way to preview is to have the students listen to passages read aloud first before independently studying and rereading.

• To activate prior knowledge, they may be asked to write down everything they know about the topic in their learning log or to brainstorm and record on the first section of a KWL chart (what I **know** . . . what I **want** to know . . . what I **learned**).

• Discuss selected vocabulary that may be challenging in the text.

• Link prior knowledge to new concepts and information that will be studied using advance organizers, anticipation guides, and other prereading strategies and tools. My other books (*see checklist 5.8*) provide detailed information on these strategies.

STRATEGIES FOR DURING READING

• These strategies should be taught and modeled in order to encourage the child to think about and interact with the reading material. This is crucial for comprehension and maintaining focus on the text.

• Teach the student how to paraphrase a paragraph or section, putting into his or her own words the main idea and significant details. Paraphrasing and stating it into a recorder is a helpful technique.

• Give a few stopping points at strategic locations throughout the text for readers to interact with the material in some manner: to stop and question, react to, discuss, summarize, predict, clarify, or record.

• Teach the student how to find and pay attention to the introductory and summary paragraphs, how to find the subject and main ideas, and how to sift out the key facts and important details from the irrelevant and redundant words and text.

• Provide a pad of sticky notes. Encourage students to jot down notes, unfamiliar words to clarify, and questions by items they do not understand as they read. They can place the sticky note next to key points and main ideas for fast reference.

• Teach story mapping: identifying the setting (time and place), characters, conflicts and problems, action and events, climax, and resolution of conflicts.

• Help children learn to self-monitor their own comprehension by asking themselves questions while reading: "What is the problem or conflict?" "What might the character do to resolve the problem?" "Why did she say that?" "What was the main point of this section?" "Did I understand this?" "What were the steps for this procedure?" "What part does not make sense?" Questioning and self-questioning keep readers actively thinking about and processing the material.

• Teach and model strategies for resolving difficulties when comprehension breaks down: slowing the pace, going back and rereading, reading ahead to see if their questions are clarified later, talking with someone about their confusion, or jotting down questions to check later.

• Students who have trouble maintaining their attention when reading silently can go to a quiet corner and read to themselves aloud. Whisper-reading also helps. Consider providing a whisper-phone for this purpose: a curved, hollow plastic tube that the child holds like a telephone. When whisper-reading into it, the child clearly hears his or her voice without disturbing others. One such device is the Toobaloo (available at www.superduperinc.com and www .linguisystems.com). Whisper phones can also be constructed with two elbow-shaped PVC pipes.

• Encourage the student to set mini-goals in pacing his or her reading, such as reading a specified number of pages or reading to a certain point in the text before taking a break.

• For children who have trouble staying visually focused on the text and lose their place while reading, try using some form of marker such as a strip of cardboard or a boxed frame with a piece of colored transparent paper inside to place on the book. Such frames are available at www.HeadsUpNow.com.

• Teach clustering, webbing, and mapping to pull out the main idea and supporting details from the text.

• Photocopy chapter pages, and have the child color-highlight important information directly on those pages; they can use one color for key vocabulary and definitions, another for topic sentences and main ideas, and so forth.

• Provide study guides to aid in looking for key information in the text.

• Make or obtain an audio recording of books for individual or group listening at a listening post. While listening to the recording, the child should be following along in the text.

• Use any of the instructional strategies involving collaborative reading and analysis of the material, such as reciprocal teaching, book clubs, and buddy or partner reading. Learning and recall are greatly enhanced by the act of talking about the text. These and other such techniques are described in detail in my other books. *See checklist 5.8.*

STRATEGIES FOR AFTER READING

• These strategies involve the reader in deeper thinking and exploration of the reading material.

• After reading the text, students use their new insights and understanding to complete filling out charts and graphic organizers such as KWL charts and learning logs that were partially filled out during the prereading and during-reading stages.

• Have deep discussions about the concepts or events in the text or in character analysis.

• Make connections through related writing activities.

• Do further extension activities related to the theme and content of the reading to apply the learning.

• Many of the strategies used during reading are also continued or completed after the reading.

Graphic Organizers

The following graphic organizers are useful for increasing comprehension and recall of text:

- *Framed outlines.* Students are given copies of a teacher-prepared outline that contains missing information for them to fill in during and after the reading.

- *Storyboards.* Divide a board or piece of paper into sections, and have students draw or write story events in sequence in each box or frame.

- *Story frames.* These are sentence starters to fill in that provide a skeleton of the story or chapter. For example: "The setting of this chapter takes place _____. The character faced a problem when _____. First he _____. Next, _____. Then _____. I predict in the next chapter _____."

- *Time lines.* These are used to help the student visualize chronological text and the sequence of events.

- *Plot charts.* Students fill in the following information that cycles through the plot of a story: Somebody (list the character) . . . Wanted (goal) . . . But (what happened or interfered with the character achieving his or her goal) . . . And so (what happened next) . . .

- *Venn diagram.* Two overlapping circles are used to display differences and similarities between characters, books, settings, topics, or events.

- *Comparison chart.* Much like a Venn diagram, this chart compares and contrasts two or more items, events, concepts, characters, and themes.

- *Flowchart.* A flowchart organizes a series of items or thoughts in logical order.

- *Webs, cluster maps, and semantic maps.* A central concept or main idea is placed in the center of related subtopics, and further details extend from each of the subtopic areas. These are used to categorize or identify related information.

More Key Comprehension Strategies

- *Summarizing.* This is one of the most important reading comprehension skills. Sometimes the main idea is explicit and easy to find, and other times it is implied or embedded in the passage. Use techniques that require students to summarize what they have read at various stopping points throughout the text. For example, summarizing at the end of a passage with a one-sentence statement and at the end of chapters to write down the main event or two key points from the text on a sticky note.

- *Narrative text structure.* Explicitly teach story grammar or story mapping so students understand the structure of the narrative (literary) text. This includes setting, characters, problem or conflict, sequence of major events (actions), and the resolution or problem solution. Younger students generally focus on identifying the main characters, setting, and beginning, middle, and end of stories.

- *Expository or informational text structure.* Explicitly teach and provide practice in how to identify the main ideas and supportive details; textbook structure (the significance of boldface and italic type, headings, and subheadings); how to use the glossary, table of contents, index, and tables and graphs; and techniques for scanning and skimming to find the answers in textbooks and other expository materials.

Decoding, Fluency, and Vocabulary

• Because a number of children with ADHD also have language-based learning disabilities (dyslexia), they need strategies and interventions to build decoding skills, vocabulary, and reading fluency.

• Poor word recognition and fluency interfere with comprehension. In order to become fluent readers, children must first become skilled at decoding the printed word. They need direct, explicit instruction and early intervention to learn the skills of how to break the code in reading, which involves:

- Phonemic awareness—the auditory recognition of individual sounds and the ability to manipulate those sounds

- Alphabet knowledge

- Letter-sound association for all consonants, vowels, blends (e.g., *br, sl*), consonant digraphs (e.g., *ch, sh*), vowel digraphs and diphthongs (e.g., *oa, ea, ai, oi, ou*), and vowel patterns (e.g., final *e, r* controlled)

- Rapid blending of isolated sounds into words

- Recognition of patterns (rhyming, spelling, word families)

- Structural analysis of words—awareness of word parts such as root words, compounds, and prefixes and suffixes

- Knowledge of syllable types and strategies for decoding multisyllabic words

• Children need to be taught strategies and cueing systems to use as they read to decode the text correctly:

- *Semantic cues:* Determining if the word makes sense in the context of what is being read and being able to self-correct (substitute a different word if it does not make sense)

- *Syntactic cues:* Determining if the word sounds right grammatically and being able to self-correct (substitute a different word that grammatically fits in the context of what is being read)

- *Graphophonic cues:* Using recognition of the printed letters (graphemes) and their corresponding sounds (phonemes) to figure out unfamiliar words

• Students with reading disabilities are often weak in graphophonics and need intensive, systematic instruction in these and other language skills. Most research-validated programs for teaching decoding skills incorporate direct, multisensory instruction and use of mnemonics (memory devices).
  • Word recognition also involves teaching:

  - *Word patterns:* Grouping by rhyming sound families or visual patterns (rock/stock/flock, right/might/flight/bright). These are called word families or onset and rimes.

  - *Structural clues:* Recognition of prefixes, suffixes, base words, and their meanings.

  - *Automatic word recognition:* Some words must be learned and recalled at an automatic level such as high-frequency words and irregular or sight words such as *said, there,* and *they.*

Reading Fluency

• Fluency is the ability to recognize words and read with ease, speed, accuracy, and expression. Strategies to build fluency and practice oral reading include:

  - *Mirror or echo reading.* The adult reads first, providing a model of fluent reading. The students reread the same passage with adult coaching as needed. Read a certain amount of material, stop, and have students orally reread that passage.

  - *Choral reading:* The adult, fluent reader, and students read together in unison.

  - *Cloze technique:* Read (or reread) a passage orally to the class, leaving out key words. The students fill in the missing words aloud.

  - *Repeated readings:* Students read and reread the passage until they achieve a certain level of fluency.

  - *Fluency practice drills:* These drills give repeated practice reading single words, phrases, and passages.

- *Recorded-reading practice:* The child reads along while listening to a recorded book. This is practiced until the child can read the text independently.

- *Buddy or partner reading:* Students read orally with partners, either in unison or alternating between paragraphs or pages.

- *Reread in a variety of situations:* The process of rereading passages that have already been heard before increases fluency and comprehension and is particularly helpful for students with reading difficulties. In response to teacher prompts and questioning, students locate specific information and orally reread those passages. Try rereading in different formats: partners, small groups, adult, and into a recording device.

- *Practicing to perform:* Reader's theater, puppet shows, and plays provide motivating fluency practice.

- There are excellent resources for fluency practice, including those found in some of my other books (*see checklist 5.8*).

Vocabulary

• Some children with ADHD have language disorders as well and may be weak in vocabulary skills and use. Vocabulary can be taught through the following techniques and methods:

- Using a direct definition
- Explaining through words that are the same (synonyms) or opposite (antonyms)
- Using a description or metaphor
- Teaching the word through examples and nonexamples
- Using context clues
- Vocabulary word walls and word banks
- Instructing students to use a dictionary, glossary, or thesaurus to find the meaning
- Reading to students and providing other language experiences that will expose them to rich vocabulary

• A number of students have difficulty with the language and vocabulary of books at their grade level. However, all children should have the opportunity to hear and discuss literature and expository text that is interesting, motivating, and at a challenging level.

• Although the vocabulary may be difficult, a nonproficient reader can equally participate in reading of grade-level material through shared reading, read-alouds, teacher-guided reading, and the host of reading comprehension strategies in which students collaboratively read the text.

Additional Reading Tips for Parents

• Try to read to and with your child every day. You can do shared reading in a number of ways—for example, you read the pages on the left and your child reads the pages on the right, or "You read this paragraph, and I'll read the next."

• Consider purchasing or borrowing another set of school books to keep at home, so your child always has a copy at home and at school.

• Increase the motivation to read by providing books and other reading material that tap into your child's interests. Struggling readers are easily intimidated by lengthy books with few illustrations. There are wonderful options: picture books that are interesting and appropriate even for older children, joke and riddle books, magazines, comic books, informational books with color pictures and short reading passages, sheet music with lyrics of favorite songs, and so forth.

• Have your child participate in school book clubs, purchasing inexpensive books of their choice on a regular basis. Purchase your child a subscription to a magazine of interest, for example, *Sports Illustrated for Kids, Ranger Rick,* or *Cricket.*

• Children with a documented reading disability are entitled to a wonderful service of being provided recorded books through Recording for the Blind and Dyslexic (RFB&D), a nonprofit national educational library for those with documented print disabilities. RFB&D lends audiobooks (including all student textbooks) in a broad range of subjects at all levels, kindergarten through postgraduate, to those eligible for this service. In order to play RFB&D digitally recorded textbooks, the student needs specialized CD players or software. For more information, contact your school district's special education department or go to www.rfbd.org.

• E-books are highly engaging and multisensory and may interest and motivate your child even if he or she is a reluctant reader.

• A child who is a struggling reader and displays any of the types of reading difficulties described in *checklist 4.1* may have a learning disability in addition to ADHD. To determine if this is the case, the child will need a psychoeducational evaluation by the school district. *See checklists 1.20, 2.17, and 3.18* for information about requesting evaluations and educational rights under the law.

• See my other books and videos and DVDs in *checklist 5.8* for a host of strategies that parents and teachers can use to help children with ADHD and learning disabilities improve their reading skills. Also, browse the Web resources in *checklist 5.7*.

4.3 MATH DIFFICULTIES RELATED TO ADHD AND LEARNING DISABILITIES

Although many children with ADHD or learning disabilities (LD), or both, have strong mathematical aptitude and skills, some struggle with math computation and problem solving. Math difficulties may be due to ADHD-related weaknesses such as inattention, poor organization, working memory, and self-monitoring. Others may result from a learning disability, for example, sequential learning and memory, perceptual-motor, and language. Keep in mind that many children with ADHD have a coexisting LD.

Attention Weaknesses

• Attention weaknesses may affect:

  • Noticing processing and operational signs in math problems (for example, being aware that the plus sign changes to minus sign)

  • Paying attention to other details (for example, decimal points and other symbols)

  • Self-correcting and finding errors in computation

• Problems with attention result in numerous careless errors and inconsistent performance, even when the student is skilled at solving the math problems.

Memory Weaknesses

• Memory weaknesses may affect:

  • The learning and acquisition of basic math facts
  • Being able to recall math facts and retrieve those facts quickly and accurately
  • Computing multistep problems (forgetful of sequence and recalling where they are in the process)
  • Recalling rules, procedures, algorithms, teacher instruction, and directions

• Sequencing weaknesses may affect:

  • The ability to do algebra and other step-by-step equations
  • The execution of any multistep procedure
  • The ability to do skip counting (for example, 3, 6, 9, 12, 15 . . . and multiples of other numbers)
  • Recognition and use of patterns

Perceptual, Visual-Motor, Fine-Motor, and Spatial-Organization Weaknesses

• Perceptual, visual-motor, fine-motor, and spatial-organization weaknesses may affect:

  • Copying problems from the board or book onto paper
  • Aligning numbers, decimal points, and so forth accurately on paper
  • Writing and computing within the minimal amount of given space on the page, spacing between problems, and leaving enough room
  • Remembering and using correct directionality for solving math problems (for example, beginning with the column to the right and moving right to left, regrouping accurately)
  • Recognizing and not confusing symbols
  • Speed of writing down problems and answers—either too fast and illegible or too slow and cannot keep up or complete assignments and tests

• Difficulties in these weaknesses result in numerous errors and the need for frequent erasing and correction, causing the student much frustration.

Language Weaknesses

• These weaknesses may affect:

- • Understanding and relating to the numerous abstract terms in math
- • Solving word problems (interpreting and understanding what is being asked, separating relevant from irrelevant information provided)
- • Following directions

Executive Function Weaknesses

• Executive function weaknesses involving metacognitive skills, self-monitoring, and self-management may affect:

- • Planning and organizing strategies for solving a problem
- • Awareness if something is not working or making sense (for example, the answer is not close to the estimate) and readjusting or trying another strategy
- • Time awareness in pacing and working the problems given
- • Sustaining the level of attention, mental effort, and perseverance necessary to complete problems with accuracy
- • Being able to check for errors and self-correct

Written Expression Weaknesses

• Because writing is infused in all curricular areas in today's classrooms, students are generally expected to write about their thinking processes and how they solved problems. Consequently, a student who may be strong with numbers and mathematical problem solving but struggles in written expression may do poorly in math class as a result of language and writing difficulties.

4.4 MATH STRATEGIES AND INTERVENTIONS

The following strategies strengthen and build mathematical skills, and the accommodations and modifications support students with ADHD and learning disabilities who struggle with math.

Strategies for Increasing Focus and Attention

• Color-highlight or underline key words and vocabulary in word problems: *shared, doubled, product, average, larger, slower, difference, altogether, equal parts,* and so on.

• Color-dot the ones (units) column to remind students the direction of where to begin computation.

• Color-highlight processing signs so that students who are inattentive will notice the change in operational signs on a page. For example, color addition signs yellow, subtraction signs pink, and so forth.

• Color-highlight place value. For example, given the number 16,432,781, write the hundreds (781) in green, the thousands (432) in orange, and the millions (16) in blue.

• Reduce the number of problems on a page.

• Block part of the page while the student is working on problems, or fold the paper under to reveal just one or two rows at a time.

• Cut up a page of problems into strips or rows, and give one strip one at a time to students.

• Allow the child to stand up and stretch or take a break of some kind after completing a certain number of problems and checking them for accuracy.

Strategies for Memory and Recall of Math Facts and Procedures

• Have multiplication fact sheets, charts, and tables readily available for reference.

• Use mnemonic devices (memory clues, images, and associations) to help students remember facts, sequential steps, procedures, and abstract concepts and vocabulary.

• Make use of rhymes, chants, raps, or songs to help students memorize the multiplication tables. Children can make up their own or use those commercially available.

• Use mnemonics, such as *D*ead *M*onsters *S*mell *B*adly, for learning the steps of long division (*d*ivide, *m*ultiply, *s*ubtract, *b*ring down).

• Some mnemonic programs are available that use picture associations and clever stories to help master multiplication facts as well. One such program is *Time Tables the Fun Way: A Picture Method of Learning the Multiplication Facts* (by Judy and Dave Rodriguez, available at www.citycreek.com). Another is *Memory Joggers* (by Donnalyn Yates, available at www.memoryjoggers.com).

• Teach children to look for patterns to help them learn their math facts. One recommended program is *Teach Your Child the Multiplication Tables with Dazzling Patterns, Grids and Tricks!* (by Eugenia Francis, available at www.TeaChildMath.com).

• Once students know multiples of up to the 5 times tables, teach the 9 times table. Recognizing and recalling the commutative property of multiplication (for example, 3 × 7 = 7 × 3) significantly reduces the stress and feeling that there are so many facts to learn. Actually, there will only be twelve more facts left to memorize: 4 × 4, 4 × 6, 4 × 7, 4 × 8, 6 × 4, 6 × 6, 6 × 7, 6 × 8, 7 × 4, 7 × 7, 7 × 8, and 8 × 8.

• Practice one sequence of multiples at a time (the 2 or 3 times tables, for example) in a variety of multisensory formats until the child achieves mastery.

• Encourage students to keep a card file of specific math skills, concepts, rules, and algorithms taught, along with specific examples of each on the card for reference.

• Practice and review facts in frequent, brief sessions (five minutes per session a few times each day). This can be done at home in a fun, relaxed manner.

• Daily timings of basic facts can be great practice and motivation if students compete against themselves, not their classmates. Have students chart their own progress and mastery. Do not display this information for the whole class to see.

Strategies to Compensate for Spatial Organization and Perceptual-Motor Difficulties

• Encourage students to write and solve their computation problems on graph paper rather than notebook paper. Experiment with graph paper of varying square and grid sizes.

• Turning notebook paper sideways (with the lines running vertically rather than horizontally) makes it much easier for students to keep numbers aligned in columns and reduces careless errors.

• Reduce the requirement of copying problems from the board or book by photocopying the page or writing out the problems on paper for students who need this help.

• Provide a large work space on tests. If necessary, rewrite test items on other paper with lots of room for computation.

• Provide lots of space on the page between problems and the bottom of the page.

Self-Monitoring and Metacognitive Strategies

• Model how to first read problems (particularly word problems) and plan a strategy for solving them before beginning the work.

• Teach how to estimate and determine whether an answer given is reasonable.

• Have students keep a journal of their thinking, reasoning, questions, and understanding of math concepts. Also, have them write their understanding about mathematical concepts before and after the unit is taught.

• Model talking out loud while reasoning and thinking about a mathematical problem. Encourage students to do the same, externalizing their thinking and verbalizing while solving problems. Listen to students as they think out loud, and correct gaps in their comprehension when possible.

• Teach students to think about what they are being asked to figure out in the problem and state in their own words.

Instructional and Assessment Strategies and Modifications

• Reduce the number of problems assigned (half-page, evens only, odds only).

• Make the abstract more concrete. Provide many kinds of manipulatives to help students visualize and work out math problems. Cubes, chips, tiles, counters, beans, base-ten blocks, and number lines are some of the many possibilities.

• Model and encourage the use of drawing, diagramming, and labeling in the problem-solving process.

• Allow and encourage students to use calculators, particularly for checking their work.

• Allow extra time on math tests so students are not rushed and make careless errors.

• Avoid the anxiety of timed tests and drills, especially those posted for all students in the class to see, and extend the amount of time permitted for certain students as "passing."

• Grade by number of correct problems over the number assigned (which could be different for students receiving modified homework or class work).

• Provide frequent checks for accuracy and immediate feedback whenever possible. This reduces the frustration of having to erase and fix a number of problems done incorrectly. Set a certain number of problems to complete (for example, one row only or three to four problems) and then check students before they are permitted to continue. Student partners can also compare answers after working every few problems on their own. If they don't agree on any of the answers after reworking the problem together, those students can then ask other classmates or the teacher.

• List steps and procedures to multistep problems and algorithms. Post clear numbered steps, or give students a desk copy model of steps for solving problems.

• Keep sample math problems on the board, and have students keep them in a notebook for reference.

• Work problems on the board, overhead projector, or document camera using color to make the steps and processes visually clear.

• Teach key words that indicate the process. For example, the words *product, times, doubled,* and *tripled* all indicate multiplication. The words *average, quotient, equal parts, sharing,* and *divisible by* all indicate division.

• Teach and model a variety of problem-solving strategies: finding clue words, looking for a pattern, constructing a table, making an organized list, using objects, drawing a picture, working backward, making a model, eliminating possibilities, and guessing and checking, among others.

• Always build in time during the lesson for students to share how they solved the problem, and emphasize the variety of ways, not just one method, to solve them.

• Increase the amount of practice and review. Make sets of practice and review problems (a few per page) with answers on the back for independent practice.

• Use computer games for drill and practice of math skills. These programs have the benefit of being adjusted for speed and level of difficulty. They also provide immediate feedback and are fun, non-threatening, and motivating for children.

• Motivate the practice of skills through the use of games. Many board games and card games such as Battleship and Uno are excellent for building such math skills as counting, logic, probability, and strategic thinking.

• Provide many opportunities for using math in the context of real-life situations: using money, balancing a checkbook, determining mileage on a fantasy road trip, comparison shopping, and paying for a meal, with tax and tip, for example.

• Practice functional math skills (measurement, time concepts, counting money and change) as much as possible at home. These are critical skills that teachers often do not have enough time to teach until mastery. Parents can include their child in activities such as cooking, baking, constructing, sewing, gardening, and home improvements, which are great ways to teach and reinforce functional math skills and fun to do together.

4.5 WHY WRITING IS A STRUGGLE

Written language tends to be the most common area of academic weakness in children and teens with ADHD or learning disabilities because the process is complex. It involves the integration and often simultaneous use of several skills and brain functions (for example, organization, spelling, fine motor, planning, self-monitoring, memory, language). These children are often verbal and knowledgeable but struggle to effectively show what they know on paper.

Preplanning and Organization

• This requires being able to generate, plan, and organize ideas. When given a written assignment, students with ADHD often get stuck here. They do not know what to write about, how to organize and begin, or how to narrow down and focus on a topic.

Memory

• Working memory is necessary in order to juggle the many different thoughts that one might want to transcribe onto paper. It involves:

- Keeping ideas in mind long enough to remember what one wants to say.
- Maintaining focus on the train of thought so the flow of the writing will not veer off course
- Keeping in mind the big picture of what you want to communicate, while manipulating the ideas, details, and wording

- The process of writing also requires other memory functions:

  - Retrieval of assorted information from long-term memory, such as facts and experiences) to share about the writing topic
  - Recall of vocabulary words, spelling, mechanics, and grammatical use

Language

- Writing requires the ability to:

  - Express thoughts in a logical, fluid, and coherent manner
  - Use vocabulary and word knowledge to express oneself and communicate to the reader effectively
  - Use descriptive sentences while maintaining proper sentence and paragraph structure

Spelling

- People with attention difficulties are often:

  - Inattentive to visual detail and do not notice or recall the letters, sequence, or visual patterns within words
  - Prone to making many careless mistakes

- Those who also have coexisting learning disabilities are typically weak in spelling due to:

  - Auditory-sequential memory deficits, causing great difficulty learning letter-sound associations, as well as hearing and remembering and then writing those sounds in the correct order.

- Visual-sequential memory, causing them difficulty in recalling the way a word looks and getting it down in the correct order or sequence. This results in misspelling common high-frequency words, such as *said, they,* and *because,* which cannot be sounded out phonetically and must be recalled by sight.

Graphomotor Skills

- Many children with ADHD or LD have impairments in graphomotor skills, which affect the physical task of writing and organization of print on the page. They often have trouble:

  - Writing neatly on or within the given lines.
  - Spacing and organizing their writing on the page.
  - Copying from the board or book onto paper.
  - With fine-motor skills, causing the act of handwriting to be very inefficient, fatiguing, and frustrating. It can affect, for example, pencil grip, pressure exerted, and legibility.
  - Executing print or cursive with precision or speed.

Editing

- Individuals with ADHD often have significant difficulty during the revision and proofreading stage of the writing process. Many students with ADHD want to go directly from the initial draft to the final draft without making revisions, because it is tedious to do so (without the use of assistive technology and other assistance). They are typically inattentive to the task of finding and correcting errors. It is common to find lack of capitalization, punctuation, and complete sentences, along with numerous spelling errors, in their written products.

Self-Monitoring

- Fluent writing requires the following self-monitoring skills:

  - Thinking and planning ahead
  - Keeping the intended audience in mind and writing to that audience with a clear purpose

- Following and referring back to the specific structure of a writing genre, such as the steps of a complete paragraph, narrative account, persuasive essay, or friendly letter
- Knowing how to read one's own work critically in order to make revisions and develop ideas

Speed of Written Output and Production

• Some students with ADHD rush through writing assignments, producing illegible work with many careless errors. Others with ADHD write excruciatingly slowly. Although they know the answers and can verbally express their thoughts and ideas articulately, they are unable to put more than a few words or sentences down on paper. Needless to say, this is extremely frustrating. Part of the problem with speed of output may be due to:

- Impulsivity
- Difficulty sustaining attention to task and maintaining the mental energy required in written expression
- Graphomotor dysfunction

4.6 STRATEGIES TO HELP WITH PREWRITING: PLANNING AND ORGANIZING

Prewriting is a critical stage of the writing process, involving the generation, planning, and organization of ideas and deciding what and how to express ideas before beginning to write. This is a challenge for many students with ADHD. The prewriting techniques in this checklist are designed to stimulate ideas, topic selection, and effective planning and also provide much needed structure, organization, and motivation to write.

Tips for Parents for Helping Their Children Think of Writing Topics

• Look through family albums together and reminisce about people and events. Talk about happenings in your child's life (humorous incidents, scary moments, milestones) that your son or daughter may not remember. Share family stories, and discuss current events.

• Ask leading questions that encourage your child to open up and share his or her feelings, fears, dreams, aspirations, or likes and dislikes.

• Provide books, reference materials, access to the library, the Internet, and other resources.

• Encourage your child to keep a journal or file on the computer for jotting down thoughts or questions he or she is pondering; observations; things that have happened to him or her that caused embarrassment, fear, joy, or other strong feelings; reactions to events in the news; and connections he or she has made between movies seen, books read, music heard, and his or her own life. These are all possible topics for future essays, personal narratives, and other writing assignments.

Prewriting Techniques in the Classroom

• *Brainstorming.* Sessions are no more than three to five minutes and focused. Given a general theme or topic, students call out whatever comes to mind related to that topic, while someone records all responses from the class.

• *Quick writes.* Students have three to four minutes to write down everything that they can think of related to a given topic, which can be single words or phrases or simple pictures or symbols to represent ideas. Model the same uninterrupted writing or drawing on a topic of your choice to demonstrate the process to students.

• *Writing topic folders.* Students maintain a folder, card file, or notebook of possible ideas for writing topics. These might include hobbies, places visited, jobs they have done, personal interests, colorful and interesting people they know, pets, special field trips or activities, observations, wonderings, and so forth. The writing folder can also be in the form of a personal collage. Students can use words and pictures cut out of magazines, newspapers, and travel brochures and laminate the folder when done.

• *Writing topic computer file.* Students enter in a computer file the same potential writing ideas that might go into a writing topic folder. This may also include digital pictures of people, things, or occasions students want to remember or topics they found while exploring sites on the Internet that they find interesting.

• *Telling personal stories.* In cooperative groups, students orally respond to prompts by telling personal stories—for example, "Tell about a time you or someone you knew got lost." After the oral telling and sharing of stories in small, cooperative groups, students fill out a graphic organizer and then write a rough draft or outline of the story they told.

• *Writing prompts.* A stimulus is provided such as a poem, story, picture, song, or news item to prompt writing. It often helps to offer students a variety of sample topic sentences, story starters, and writing prompts when they are struggling for an idea.

• *Reference books.* Students browse through the books for writing topic ideas.

• *Verbalize ideas into a recording device.* Some students benefit from first verbalizing what they want to say into a digital or other recorder before transcribing ideas onto paper.

• *Draw first, then write.* For creative writing, have students first draw what they might want to write about. Then have them think of a few possible story plots and share their picture and ideas with a partner. After this process and receiving feedback at the oral language stage, they can then choose their best idea for a story line.

Using Visual Organization Strategies Prior to Writing

Graphic organizers. These are among the most effective ways to help writers generate their ideas, as well as formulate and organize their thoughts. The following are some examples of graphic organizers; others are found in *checklist 4.2:*

- *Clustering.* Write the main idea in a box or rectangle in the center of the page and surround the main idea box with bubbles containing the supporting ideas.

- *Mind mapping.* Draw a circle at the center of a page. Write the topic inside the center circle, and write related ideas on lines stemming from the circle. This technique is also called *webbing,* and the graphic is called a *web.*

- *Software organizers.* There is excellent software for creating mind maps, diagrams, and other visual organizers to aid in the prewriting process that are easy and motivating for children to use. Two examples are Inspiration and Kidspiration from www.inspiration.com. Inspiration also has an outlining feature built in. Categories listed in the graphic web format are automatically placed in outline form with the press of a button.

- *Story maps.* These are used in preplanning the critical elements to be included when writing a story: setting, characters, problem, action, and resolution.

• A helpful technique is to have the student write main ideas and supporting details on separate index cards, sticky notes, or sentence strips. That makes it easier to spread out and group, organize, and sequence those thoughts and ideas.

• There are also Web sites on the Internet with downloadable graphic organizers, such as Houghton Mifflin's Education Place www.eduplace.com.

Thinking and Questioning

• Planning and organization are some of the executive functions that are areas of weakness in many individuals with ADHD. Therefore, it is important to provide instruction and support to guide students in the kind of thinking and questioning that is needed to plan and organize before writing.

• It is valuable to provide a prewriting checklist that lists specific questions students need to ask themselves at this stage of the writing process. These help the writer think through, plan, and organize prior to drafting. Such questioning can be done independently, but it is also recommended that they engage in this questioning process with someone else (a peer or partner or with parent or teacher) and during guided writing.

• When creating a prewriting checklist, teachers may want to select a few questions such as these:

- Who is my target audience?
- What is my purpose for this writing: to persuade, inform, entertain, or something else?
- What do I already know about this topic?
- Can I write enough about my selected topic?
- Which writing genre am I going to use?

- In what style or voice will I write?
- What are some words, ideas, or phrases related to my topic?

• Prewriting checklists may be divided into specific questions for the beginning, middle, and end of the piece of writing. For example:

Beginning (Opening)
- How will I introduce the subject or topic?
- What kind of hook can I use in the introduction to capture the audience's attention and interest?
- What will be the main idea about my subject?

Middle (Body)
- What interesting details and examples might I use?
- What will be my flow and sequence of ideas?
- Where should I research and gather interesting information about my topic?

Ending (Conclusion)
- What is the message I want to share with readers?
- What would be an interesting or exciting ending?

4.7 STRATEGIES FOR COMPOSITION AND WRITTEN EXPRESSION

Written expression is the most common academic area of difficulty among students with ADHD. As discussed in *checklist 4.5,* several brain processes are involved and used simultaneously (language, attention, memory, sequencing, organization, planning, self-monitoring, and critical thinking) when composing a written piece of work. Students are expected to meet grade-level expectations and standards in a variety of writing formats and genres. Teachers are expected to differentiate instruction to teach writers of all levels and abilities. The following strategies and tips are designed to help students become more successful writers.

Vocabulary and Sentence Structure

• Teach sentence structure and build on sentence writing skills. Children need to understand that all complete sentences have a *subject* (a noun—a person, place, or thing) that tells who or what is doing something and a *predicate* (which includes a verb and prepositional phrases) telling "what about" the subject.

• Teach and guide children in writing interesting, expanded sentences. Start with a simple bare sentence: *The puppy cried.* Have them dress it up by adding colorful, descriptive adjectives and adverbs, more powerful verbs, and prepositional phrases (When? Where? How? Why?) Example: *The frightened puppy whimpered and whined as it hid shaking under the sofa during the thunderstorm.*

• Teach descriptive language and the use of figurative language to enhance writing style. Generate class and individual lists of examples of descriptive, figurative language found in literature or poetry: metaphors, similes, personification, analogies, personification, onomatopoeia, and others.

• Provide lists of powerful verbs, alternatives to *said, went,* and other overused words, and transition or linking words and phrases. Post these words and phrases, and provide a desk or notebook copy for reference. Here are some examples:

> • Words that signal sequence: *first of all, furthermore, meanwhile, next, then, subsequently, finally*
>
> • Words that signal compare and contrast of two or more things: *nevertheless, on the other hand*
>
> • Words that signal cause and effect: *consequently, as a result*
>
> • Words that indicate an author's point of view: *I suggest, I believe*

Writing Genres

• Students are expected to write in a number of genres (depending on their grade):

> • Paragraphs: summary, directional, compare and contrast, procedural, descriptive, and narrative. These have a clear beginning, middle, and end.

- Letters: both friendly and business.

- Informational or expository reports: topic, main ideas, supporting details, and a conclusion. These often involve research, observations, and analysis.

- Personal narrative: relating ideas, observations, or recollections of an event or experience. These include presenting information with descriptive details, as well as a beginning, middle, and end.

- Stories with literary story grammar: setting, characters, problem, sequence of events, climax, and resolution.

- Summaries (narrative and expository): introduction, body, and conclusion.

- Persuasive essays: in which the writer tries to change the reader's point of view by presenting facts and opinions and arguing a point.

- Responses to literature: demonstrating an understanding of the literary work and supporting judgments with examples from text and prior knowledge.

   • Clearly model, explain, and provide examples showing the structure or format for each genre taught.
   • A number of programs and curricula explicitly teach how to write in the various genres and build written expression and composition skills. Some recommended resources are *Empowering Writers,* by B. Mariconda and D. P. Auray (www.empoweringwriters.com), *Writing Connections,* by N. Fetzer (www.nancyfetzer.com), and *Step Up to Writing* (www.sopriswest.com).
   • Rubrics and scoring guides should be provided with all writing assignments. They significantly help students with writing difficulties in planning, structuring, and self-monitoring their written work. They also help parents by explaining from the beginning exactly what the teacher expects in the writing assignment and what is considered proficient performance for the grade level.
   • There are numerous rubrics and variations of scoring guides, typically on a 1 to 4 or 1 to 5 scale: for example, 1 = Novice, 2 = Apprentice, 3 = Practitioner, 4 = Expert; or 1 = Below standard (below basic), 2 = Approaching standard (basic), 3 = Meets standard (proficient), 4 = Exceeds standard (advanced proficient).

• Because many children with ADHD are capable of writing and expressing themselves once they get started, it helps to give them support to get them going. Once they begin writing, they are often on a roll and can work independently and successfully. One way to help is to provide a list of possible sentence starters, or topic sentences that they might select from and use to jump-start their paragraphs.

• Providing writing frames is another helpful scaffold or support. This example is for a summary: The author, _____ (insert name), wrote a/an _____ (insert genre) titled _____ (insert title), which took place _____ (insert where and when). In the story, the main character, _____ (insert the character's name and problem and the main event in the plot—what the character did or what happened to the character).

Self-Monitoring and Metacognition

• Written expression requires a great deal of self-monitoring. Writers need to put themselves in the place of their potential readers and keep asking themselves: "Does this make sense?" "Is this clear?" "Do my ideas flow logically?" "Am I using the best choice of words?" It is helpful to provide students a checklist of such self-monitoring questions as a guide when writing different types of assignments and genres. For example, with an expository (nonfiction) piece, some questions might be:

Opening

   • How am I introducing the subject or topic?

   • What will be the main ideas about my subject?

   • What kind of hook can I use to capture the reader's attention?

Body

   • How am I going to develop my main ideas?

   • What details and examples am I going to use?

   • What will be my flow and sequence of ideas?

Conclusion

   • What will be the final thought or wrap-up?

   • On what note am I leaving the reader?

More Tips for Parents and Teachers

• Even students with significant writing difficulties are often able to meet writing standards when they receive a high degree of explicit modeling of writing skills, guided assistance, and feedback as they proceed through the writing process.

• Teachers should try to provide a head start on writing assignments. It often takes children with ADHD much longer to produce written work than it does other students in the class. Getting them started early, notifying parents of the requirements, and jointly monitoring throughout the assignment is very helpful.

• Set mini-goals and incremental due dates so the assignment is broken down into steps and completed in a timely manner.

• Experiment with the various strategies, assistive technology, and other supports found in *checklist 4.11.*

• My books that are coauthored with Julie A. Heimburge contain many activities, tools, and strategies for teaching and supporting students in composition and expressive writing. *See checklist 5.8.*

4.8 STRATEGIES FOR REVISING AND EDITING

For children and teens with ADHD, this stage of the writing process (revising, proofreading, and making corrections) is extremely difficult. Understandably, they are often resistant to making changes after struggling to write the first draft.

• Revising is the step of the writing process that involves adding or deleting information, resequencing the order of sentences and paragraphs, and choosing words that better communicate what one wants to say. Revision requires self-monitoring and critically evaluating one's own work. Students with ADHD need a lot of direct instruction, modeling, and feedback to learn how to and be motivated to do so.

Revision Strategies for Teachers and Parents

• Encourage students to write rough drafts on every other line of the paper. This spacing makes it much easier to revise and edit.

• Composing on a computer is ideal for easily revising subsequent drafts. Another benefit of composing on the computer is being able to save various draft versions electronically rather than storing paper.

This significantly helps maintain better organization and management of written work.

• Provide checklists to help students self-monitor during the revision process. Select some (not all) of the following questions in creating a list appropriate to the age and developmental level of the child:

- Have I given enough information?
- Have I identified and written for my audience?
- Does my introduction capture the attention of my readers?
- Is my beginning interesting and exciting?
- Did I develop my ideas logically?
- Have I left out any important details?
- Does everything make sense?
- Did I stick to my topic?
- Have I presented my ideas clearly and in the right order?
- Have I given details and examples for each main idea?
- Have I included enough facts and details to support my subject?
- Have I used descriptive words to make my writing interesting?
- Do my paragraphs have a beginning, middle, and end?
- Have I chosen the right words?
- Does it read smoothly?
- Do I need to insert, move around, or delete any ideas?
- Did I write an interesting, powerful conclusion?
- Did my conclusion restate the main ideas or refer back to the introduction?
- Have I satisfied my purpose for writing?
- Have I said everything I need to say?

• Have students read their drafts to peers or partners for feedback. The partner listens, questions, and indicates when more information is needed, what points need clarification, and other suggestions. Parents provide this type of feedback as well to help in the revision process.

• When reading or listening to a child read his or her initial drafts, always provide positive feedback—something you like about the piece of writing, any growth in skills that is apparent, and recognition of the effort made. Ask probing questions when something is confusing or unclear and more information is needed.

• The questions listed above can also be adapted to serve as a guide when providing feedback to the writer.

Editing Strategies for Teachers and Parents

• Editing is proofreading for errors in grammar, mechanics, and spelling and polishing the final product. Children and teens with ADHD are typically weak in editing skills, because they do not pay attention to or notice details such as spelling and mechanical errors. It is best to provide them direct assistance with editing.

• Provide direct instruction and guided practice in the proper use of mechanics (punctuation and capitalization).

• Use peer editing as well as adult assistance. Point out run-on or incomplete sentences, missing or incorrect capitalization and punctuation, and misspelled words.

• Teach how to use the editing tools and options (thesaurus, spell-check, cut and paste) on a computer program.

• Although self-editing is hard and the child may not be successful in this effort, encourage him or her to self-edit by circling (or coding in some manner) words the child thinks are possibly misspelled. Later, with assistance, the child can go back and check the spelling of those words.

• Provide and encourage the use of an electronic spell-checking device for use at home and school. Handheld devices are available, as well as spell-check tools on computers.

• Teach the proofreading symbols, and provide a reference chart.

• Provide a self-editing checklist for proofreading work for capitalization, sentence structure, and mechanical errors. The following list of questions can be used to develop a proofreading self-edit list:

- Did I use complete sentences?
- Did I begin all sentences with a capital letter?
- Did I end my sentences with a final punctuation mark?
- Have I capitalized all proper nouns (names of specific people, places, things, and any titles)?
- Have I checked my spelling for correctness (seeing if all words look like they are spelled right and checking a resource if not)?

- Have I indented paragraphs?
- Are my verbs in the same tense?
- Did I check for run-on sentences?
- Is my paper neat and organized?
- Have I used adequate spacing?
- Have I erased carefully?
- Is my writing legible?

Other Teaching Tips

- Conduct teacher-student writing conferences, during which time students respond to their own writing: "My best sentence is . . . " or "A simile or metaphor I used was . . . " The student reflects on his or her own work, and both student and teacher share what they like about the piece of writing.
- Have the student self-evaluate improvement and the skills to target for continued improvement: "My writing has improved in: [sentence structure, paragraphing, fluency, creativity, organization, capitalization, punctuation, spelling]. I plan to work on . . . "
- Provide a rubric with all writing assignments, and show models of what "at standard" and "exceeding standard" work looks like for that grade level.
- *See checklist 5.8* for more on this topic.

4.9 MULTISENSORY SPELLING STRATEGIES

Motivate children to practice spelling words in a variety of formats through strategies that are multisensory and engaging.

Using Fun Materials and Tactile Strategies

- Dip a clean paintbrush in water, and write words on the tabletop or chalkboard.
- Write words in the air using a stiff arm and large muscle movements while sounding the words out (sky writing).
- Write words in a flat tray or box of colored sand or salt using one or two fingers.

• Write words in glue or liquid starch on pieces of cardboard. Then sprinkle any powdery material, glitter, yarn, beans, macaroni, sequins, or other material to create textured, three-dimensional spelling words. Substances such as sand, salt, and glitter are good to use for students who benefit from tracing the words with their fingers. *Note:* The act of tracing with fingers on a texture helps make a sensory imprint on the brain that increases memory and retention.

• Write words in a sandbox with a stick.

• Pair with another student and write words on each other's back with a finger, with the receiver identifying the word by feel.

• While sitting on the carpet, practice writing the words directly on the carpet with two fingers using large muscle movements.

• Practice writing words on individual chalkboards (or dry-erase boards) with colored chalk (or colored dry-erase pens).

• Fingerpaint words using shaving cream on tabletops. Or use pudding, whipped cream, or frosting on waxed paper or paper plates.

• Type each of the words in a variety of fonts, colors, and sizes.

• Write the words using alphabet manipulatives and tactile letters. Examples are magnetic letters, sponge letters, alphabet stamps, alphabet cereal, letter tiles, and linking letter cubes.

• Practice writing words with a glitter pen, a neon gel pen on black paper, or other special pen.

• Use a flashlight in a darkened room or laser pen to "write" the words on a wall.

• Write words forming the letters with clay or Wikki Stix (www .wikkistix.com).

Using Song and Movement

• Pair movement while spelling words aloud: clapping to each letter, bouncing a ball, using a yo-yo, jumping rope, or jumping on a trampoline are some of the many possibilities.

• Tap out the sounds or syllables in words using a pencil on a desk, fingertips to the desk or other arm, or spell words while tapping with one hand down the other arm, from shoulder to hand.

• Chant the spelling of words that are irregular and hard to sound out phonetically.

• Use kinesthetic cues for letters and sounds, and act out those motions or refer to those cues when segmenting words to spell. Various programs for teaching letter and sound association include body movements as a kinesthetic cue for each sound or call attention to the mouth and tongue positions and how sounds are formed and feel. *See checklist 5.8.*

• Sing spelling words to common tunes or melodies.

• Spell words standing up for consonant letters and sitting down for vowels.

Using Color

• Use the rainbow technique of tracing over each word at least three different times in different colors (pencils, crayons, chalk, or markers). Then, without looking, write the word from memory.

• Color-code tricky letters (silent letters) in hard-to-spell words.

• Write the words by syllables in different colors.

• Write silent letters (ghost letters) in white pen.

• After taking a pretest, color the known part of a word (correctly spelled letters) in one color. By the time the word is spelled correctly with further trials, the whole word should be written in color.

• Write all the vowels of the word in red.

• Color-code key elements and features of the word (for example, prefixes and suffixes, final *e*).

Other Ways to Practice, Study, and Learn Spelling

• Make a set of flash cards, and study each of the words with a partner or parent. Put the cards of the words that were missed aside, and restudy them.

• Make up word skeletons. Example: _ _ s _ r _ _ e _ t for the word *instrument*. The child needs to fill in the missing letters.

• Write out each of the words. Circle the silent letters, and underline the vowels.

• Dictate the words, and have the child write them on a dry-erase board.

• Practice using the copy, write, cover, check method (CWCC).

• Trace words with a pencil while spelling the word. Then trace with an eraser. Get up and do a brief physical activity, such as five jumping jacks. Now write the word, and check it for accuracy.

• Underline misspelled letters or trouble spots in words.

• Use the "look, say, write" method of practice: (1) look at the word, and trace it with your finger or pencil; (2) say the word, spelling it out loud while copying it; and (3) write the word without looking and check for accuracy. Fix any errors immediately because it helps with remembering the correct spelling of the word.

Instructional Suggestions for Teachers

• Introduce words on the board or projector. As a class, ask students to look at the configuration or shape of the word. Have them also look for little words within the word and any mnemonic clues that would be helpful in remembering how to spell the word. Write the word in syllables in different colored pens. Discuss its meaning, and use it in context.

• Have several resources readily available for student access, such as dictionaries, electronic spell-checkers, and lists of commonly used words.

• Teach students to look for patterns in words by using phonograms, word families, and onsets and rimes. Color-highlight patterns within the words.

• Provide systematic phonetic training to students who are deficient in this skill and are poor spellers. The majority of words in the English language are phonetically regular and can be decoded and spelled correctly with phonetic knowledge and strategy application.

• The high-frequency irregular words that students are expected to spell correctly in their written work should be posted in a highly visible location. In addition, student desk or notebook copies can be provided for reference.

• Maintain a word wall in the classroom that includes content-area words, high-frequency words, and other words deemed important listed under each letter of the alphabet.

• Use mnemonics whenever possible to help students remember and learn memory strategies to apply in the future. Examples: *friend*: I am a friEND to the END; *church:* You are (U/R) in church.

• Use choral, unison techniques for practicing the spelling of nonphonetic words. Practice irregular nonphonetic words by creative techniques to help in recall. For example, make up a chant; clap out the letters in the words; spell the words using American Sign Language; or use voice inflections to help call attention to certain letters (for example, emphasizing the tricky letters in a louder voice).

• Provide many peer tutoring and partner spelling opportunities such as quizzing and practicing together in fun ways.

• Post an example of a picture association for different phonograms for student reference—for example, a picture of an eagle for *ea,* a picture of a house for *ou,* and a train or snail for *ai.*

4.10 IMPROVING HANDWRITING AND THE LEGIBILITY OF WRITTEN WORK

Struggles with handwriting and written organization interfere with production and being able to show what you know. Paper-and-pencil tasks are a source of great frustration for many children with ADHD. When the physical act of writing is so tedious and the results of these efforts are messy and illegible, it is no wonder that children with ADHD often hate to write and resist doing so.

• If you observe a child struggling with the physical task of writing (correct letter formation, pencil grip, speed, and legibility), share these concerns, and request a consultation with a specialist. An evaluation and perhaps services from an occupational therapist or other specialist may be needed.

HANDWRITING TIPS AND STRATEGIES

• Group letters by similarity of formation (for example, l/t/i; a/c/d; v/w) when teaching and practicing how to write them.

• After first tracing over letters, have the child write a few independently, and then circle his or her best effort.

• A highly recommended program for teaching print and cursive to children, especially those with writing difficulties, is *Handwriting Without Tears,* developed by an occupational therapist, Jan Olsen (www.hwtears.com). The program uses multisensory techniques and mnemonic cues for helping children learn proper letter formation; it also structures the sequence of letters introduced by clusters. For example, cursive *o, w, b,* and *v* are taught together as the "tow-truck letters" because of their special high endings.

• Provide visual cues such as a starting dot and numbered arrows as a guide for the correct letter formation (direction and sequence of strokes).

• If the child struggles to hold and manipulate a pencil, there are pencil grips of different shapes, materials, and designs that can make it easier. Experiment with different kinds. See www.theraproducts .com and other companies that carry such products in *checklist 5.7.*

• Try self-drying clay around the pencil to mold to the size and shape of the child's fingers and grip.

• Try mechanical pencils for students who frequently break their pencil tips from applying too much pressure. Although mechanical pencil tips can also break easily, at least the student doesn't need to sharpen his or her pencil frequently throughout the day—pulling the student off-task.

• Use real-life situations to stress the need for legible writing (job applications, filling out checks), and share how studies have proven that teachers tend to give students the benefit of the doubt and grade higher if their papers are neat rather than sloppy or hard to read.

• Provide sufficient time to write in order to avoid time pressures.

• Set realistic, mutually agreed-on expectations for neatness.

• Some children find it easier to write using narrow-ruled paper with a shorter line height; others do better using paper with wider-ruled lines.

• Teach placing an index finger between words (finger spacing) to help children who run their words together without spacing.

• Remind the child to anchor his or her paper with the nonwriting hand or arm to keep it from moving while writing.

• If the student's paper is frequently sliding around, try attaching the paper to a clipboard.

• Provide a strip or chart of alphabet letters (manuscript or cursive) on the student's desk for reference for letter formation. Draw directional arrows on the letters the child finds confusing and difficult to write.

Tactile-Kinesthetic Techniques to Motivate Letter Formation

• Make a "gel bag" by placing some hair gel in a plastic bag with a zipper lock. With a permanent marker, write each letter for practice on the outside of the bag. While tracing the letter, the child feels the interesting texture of the gel inside the bag, especially when the gel or ooze bag is refrigerated.

• Color-code the strokes of a letter on the outside of the gel bag. The first phase of the stroke can be one color, and the second phase can be another color. Arrows can be drawn indicating the directions of the letter formation as well.

• Practice correct letter formation by tracing with their finger letters written with directionality arrows on a variety of textures (puff paint, which is a fabric paint with a 3-D effect when it dries, or sandpaper, for example). Have the child also practice writing the letters with two fingers in a colored salt or sand tray or on the carpet. The sensory input through the fingers helps in recalling the letter formation.

• Provide guided practice by modeling letter formation in large movements, talking through the steps while writing the letter in color.

• Write letters in the air with large muscle movements while giving a verbal prompt. Holding the child's wrist, write in large strokes in the air while talking through the strokes. For example, with the letter B, give the following instruction: "Start at the top. Straight line down. Back to the top. Sideways smile. Another sideways smile." Then repeat without guiding the child's hand, but observe that the formation is correct.

• See my early childhood books in *checklist 5.8.*

Additional Tips

• Provide a lot of practice at home and school when children are learning how to print or write in cursive. Observe carefully as the child practices, and intervene immediately when you notice errors in letter formation. Gently correct if you observe the child making the strokes incorrectly (for example, bottom-to-top rather than top-to-bottom or circles formed clockwise rather than counterclockwise).

• Teachers can provide parents with a model of how the letters are being taught in class and any verbal prompts so there is consistency between home and school in teaching handwriting.

• Provide prompts for correct letter formation and directionality by placing a green dot indicating the starting point for the stroke and arrows showing the direction to write the strokes of the letters.

• Provide frequent practice and corrective feedback using short trace and copy activities.

• Allow students for whom cursive is a struggle to print.

• Encourage appropriate sitting, posture, and anchoring of paper when writing.

• Add variety for motivational purposes, using different sizes, shapes, textures, and colors of paper and assorted writing instruments.

Also, have students write on individual chalkboards with colored chalk or dry-erase boards with colored pens.

• Provide a slant board for better wrist position. You can make one by covering an old three-ring notebook completely with contact paper. The child then places his or her paper on the slant board when writing.

• Teach and post your expectations—for example: writing on one side of the paper only, draft papers written on every other line, math papers with two or three line spaces between problems, heading on upper-right section of paper.

• Post and provide individual copies of handwriting checklists for students to self-monitor their own written work for legibility. This list contains possible questions that may be included on a student handwriting checklist (depending on age and developmental level and grade-level standards):

- Are my letters resting on the line?
- Do tall letters reach the top line, and do short letters reach the middle line?
- Do I have space between words?
- Are my letters the right size (not too small, not too large)?
- Am I writing within the lines?
- Are my words in lowercase unless there is supposed to be a capital?
- Am I consistent in my letters: all print or all cursive, not mixed?
- Have I stayed within the margins of the paper?

• For accommodations and modifications when handwriting and output difficulties interfere with school success, *see checklist 4.11.*

4.11 STRATEGIES FOR BYPASSING AND ACCOMMODATING WRITING DIFFICULTIES

• It commonly takes children with ADHD significantly longer than others their age or grade to produce written work. An assignment that takes most students twenty minutes or so to complete may take hours for a child with ADHD. So, keep that in mind when giving written assignments and homework to these students and when sending home incomplete work.

• Assign reasonable amounts of homework and writing assignments. Be willing to make adjustments, and accept modified homework and reduced written tasks.

• Substitute nonwritten, hands-on assignments and verbal reports and presentations for written assignments.

• Give students options and choices that do not require writing, but may involve investigating, building, drawing, constructing, creating, simulating, experimenting, researching, telling, demonstrating, singing, dancing, and so on.

• Reduce the need to copy from the board or book.

• Enlarge the space on math papers, tests, and worksheets for doing written work.

• Stress accuracy and quality of writing, not volume.

• Follow written exams with an oral exam, and average the two grades for students with ADHD.

• Allow oral responses for assignments and tests when appropriate.

• Permit the student to dictate his or her responses, and have someone else record or transcribe them onto paper.

• Allow the student to write in whichever is easier and more legible: print or cursive.

• Provide in-class time to get started on assignments.

• Provide note-taking assistance. Assign a buddy to take notes, share, and compare.

• Provide noncarbon replica (NCR) paper for the note taker to use. The bottom NCR copy is torn off and given to the student with ADHD, or a photocopy is made of his or her notes. Encourage the child to take his or her own notes, but supplement them with the more detailed and organized copies from the designated note taker.

• Teach keyboarding skills, and provide sufficient practice opportunities.

• Provide access to a computer and motivating writing programs.

• Provide assistance typing and printing final drafts of papers if needed.

• Help the student get started writing by talking or prompting through the first few sentences or so. Have the student dictate while an adult writes the first few sentences to get the student started.

• Provide extended time for testing, particularly written assessments, such as those with essay questions.

• Grade content and spelling and mechanics separately on writing assignments.

Use of Assistive Tools and Technology

• Provide tools such as highlighting tape, paper with wide and narrow lines, various types of pens and pencils, and different shapes of pencil grips.

• Allow the student to use a digital or tape recorder instead of writing for summarizing learning, responding to questions, planning and recording ideas, and instructions.

• Allow the use of electronic spell-checkers, dictionaries, thesauruses, calculators, personal digital assistants, and other electronic tools if helpful.

• Use quality software programs that are designed with features to support the writing process such as *Write: Outloud, Co-Writer 4000, Draft: Builder,* and *SOLO* at www.donjohnston.com; *Inspiration* and *Kidspiration* at www.inspiration.com; and *Read and Write Gold* from www.texthelp.com.

• Provide or allow the use of laptops or portable word processors as an alternative for students with writing disabilities. These are lightweight, inexpensive, assistive technology tools that are easy to use, flexible, and transport easily between home and school. See these companies for such products: www.alphasmart.com, www.writerlearning.com, and www.quickpad.com

• Some software programs are designed specifically for those with reading and writing disabilities. They have features such as speech recognition, word prediction, text-to-speech, and audible spell-check. A few companies that carry such software are TextHelp (www.texthelp .com), Kurzweil Educational Systems (www.kurzweiledu.com), Quillsoft (www.quillsoft.com), and Don Johnston (www.donjohnston.com).

• Other checklists in this book addressing reading, writing, math, and homework also contain strategies and accommodations to help students with writing difficulties. *See checklists 2.11, 3.12, 3.15, 3.16, 3.17, 4.2, 4.4, 4.6, 4.7, 4.8, 4.9, and 5.10.*

Other Important Checklists for Parents and Teachers

5.1 THE TEAM APPROACH

The success of children and teens with ADHD is dependent on team effort. It is critical that in the diagnostic process, as well as any treatment and intervention provided, to have close communication among all parties: home, school, physician, and other service providers.

The Diagnostic Process

• Parents provide information regarding their child's medical, school, and family history and behaviors, past and present, through interviews, rating forms, and questionnaires.

• Classroom teachers and other school personnel directly working with the student or observing the child's functioning in various school settings provide their observations and data regarding the student's symptoms and school functioning.

• A physician, psychologist, other licensed mental health professional, or clinician evaluates the child for ADHD using the information provided by parents or other caregivers and the school.

• Eligibility for special education, related services, and accommodations may be conducted by the school's multidisciplinary assessment team, which may involve a number of school district

professionals: special educator, psychologist, speech/language therapist, school nurse, occupational therapist, or others.
  • For more on the diagnostic process, *see checklist 1.1.*

The Treatment Plan

  • The most effective approach in treating ADHD is multimodal,
involving a number of interventions from a variety of different professionals and service providers. For more on multimodal treatment,
see checklist 1.12.
  • Treatments outside school may include counseling or therapy by
a psychologist or other mental health professional for the child or
teen with ADHD, his or her parents, or the rest of the family.
  • School interventions are generally provided through a variety of
school professionals and other resources that may include general and
special education teachers, school counselor, social worker, psychologist,
nurse, speech/language therapist, adapted physical education, occupational therapist, administrators, aides (instructional, guidance, management), tutors, and volunteers (peer, cross-age, parent, community).
  • Medical intervention can be provided by pediatricians, family practitioners, child psychiatrists, neurologists, or other medical doctors.
  • It is important for the child or teen to participate in activities that
build on his or her interests and strengths and provide an emotional
and physical outlet. This may involve the support of athletic coaches,
youth group leaders, scout leaders, mentors, or instructors working
with the child or teen in extracurricular activities.
  • The child or teen may be involved in other treatments and interventions to address specific needs, among them, social skills training,
private academic tutoring, and ADHD coaching.
  • Parent training groups may be provided by various community
professionals or other trained facilitators in behavior management and
positive discipline strategies.
  • The school's multidisciplinary team should monitor and revise as
needed any individualized education program, 504 accommodation
plan, or other school-based intervention plan developed for the student.
If the student is receiving special education, the school's special education
service providers will be involved in the implementation of all aspects of
the child's individualized education program. *See checklist 1.20.*
  • Support groups for parents of children and teens with ADHD
such as CHADD (Children and Adults with Attention Deficit/

Hyperactivity Disorder; www.chadd.org) are composed of a number of people in the community, both parents and professionals, who can serve as a resource and support, a very helpful intervention for parents.

More About the Team Approach

• Most students with ADHD require close monitoring between the home and school to be successful. Teachers need to keep parents well informed about work assignments, upcoming tests and projects, how the student is performing and keeping up with daily work, as well as behavior and other issues. Parents need to communicate with teachers regarding how the student is functioning at home, the child's stress level, and other issues. In addition, parents need to stay on top of monitoring that homework is being done and followed through with any home-school plans (for example, to aid and reinforce behavior, work production, and organization skills).

• A child or teen who is taking medication requires close and ongoing monitoring and communication between the teachers, parents, and physician. If there is a school nurse, he or she is often the liaison in this communication process regarding medication management. *See checklist 1.15.*

• Most students with ADHD are educated in general education classrooms. Some receive special education services, and others do not. Collaboration and consultation between special education and classroom teachers regarding effective strategies and accommodations is helpful in addressing the child's needs.

• The child or teen must be included in the team effort. Once students are old enough, they need to learn about ADHD and understand the reason for the treatments and interventions. If they are taking medication, they need to understand what it does and does not do. Older children and adolescents need to take an active role in his or her treatment plan.

5.2 MEMORY STRATEGIES AND ACCOMMODATIONS

Poor working memory and forgetfulness are characteristic of children and teens with ADHD. In addition, if their attention was not engaged throughout the instruction, they may not remember a lot of what the teacher presented. Many people with ADHD also have coexisting learning disabilities in auditory or visual sequential memory. This makes it very difficult to memorize, especially nonmeaningful symbols such as the sequence of letters in a word, numerals, and basic math facts. It is important to teach and build memory strategies, as well as provide accommodations for memory weaknesses.

Building Memory and Accommodating Weaknesses

• Use a dry-erase board and colored markers at home to write down all projects and progress on the stages of the project.

• Use a monthly calendar at home and school to enter all activities and projects due.

• Use to-do lists and checklists daily at home and school.

• Teach, model, and expect that all assignments are recorded. This often requires monitoring by way of the teacher's initialing the assignment calendar or planner or student partners checking and initialing each other's assignment calendar or planner.

• Provide simple written instructions and reminders of what the child or teen needs to do.

• Have the child paraphrase instructions or information to be remembered.

• Use color and pictures to aid memory.

• After directions are given, have the child repeat the directions to you or someone else, such as a peer partner.

• Increase the amount of practice and review in a variety of formats.

• Allow the use of tools and aids such as multiplication charts and tables, spell-check devices, digital recorders, and electronic organizers.

• Avoid timed tests. Give extra time for recalling and responding.

• Use visual or graphic depictions to help the child or teen remember routines, procedures, or sequences of steps.

• Use melody and rhythm to help remember information.

• Supply and use sticky notes for reminders, and encourage the child or teen to place them in strategic locations.

• Provide checklists, task cards, reminders of expectations, and directions for independent work activities.

• Use frequent review, repetition, rehearsal, and practice.

• After instruction, have students list all they remember, in whatever order, as fast as they can. This act of writing what they just learned increases recall and retention.

• Research shows that we remember best that which we practice by doing and when the information and material is used immediately, such as by teaching it to someone else.

• To help lock information into long-term memory, do something interactive or reflective with the material, such as discussing, paraphrasing, writing, jotting down notes, making a quick illustration, filling a learning log or journal entry, or making a story map.

• Motivation aids memory. Discuss the benefits of memorizing the information (for example, knowing math facts makes learning all mathematical concepts much easier).

• To remember and study reading material, use **RCRC**. Memorize chunks of information by **reading, covering** the words while **reciting** (verbalizing) the information read, and **checking** oneself for accuracy.

• Flag, tab, or color-highlight important information in the text to be remembered.

Using Mnemonics

• Mnemonics are memory devices such as acronyms, acrostics, peg words (short words that sound like numbers), and keywords. Use of mnemonics is an excellent means of helping memorize and recall information.

• Teach and encourage children to create first-letter mnemonics (acronyms and acrostics), which are very helpful in remembering steps in a process or procedure, a sequence of any kind, or other information.

Examples of Acronyms

- HOMES (the five Great Lakes): **H**uron, **O**ntario, **M**ichigan, **E**rie, and **S**uperior
- Roy G. Biv (the seven colors of the rainbow): **r**ed, **o**range, **y**ellow, **g**reen, **b**lue, **i**ndigo, violet

Examples of Acrostics

- Dead Monsters Smell Badly (steps for long division: **d**ivide, **m**ultiply, **s**ubtract, **b**ring down)
- Every Good Boy Does Fine (sequence of lines in the treble clef: **EGBDF**)

- Please Excuse My Dear Aunt Sally (the order for solving algebraic equations: parentheses, exponents, multiplication, division, addition, subtraction)

• Pair unfamiliar new vocabulary with similar-sounding familiar words. This is called the keyword mnemonic technique. For example, to remember that Amsterdam is the capital of Netherlands, one can think of hamsters running around in "Never Never Land"; or the word *felons* (which sounds like *melons*) can be recalled easily by picturing some melons in prison clothing marching off to jail. See www.vocabularycartoons.com (New Monic Books) for great examples of using this method to learn vocabulary.

• Use peg words for learning basic math facts: Three/Tree, Four/Door, Six/Sticks, Seven/Heaven, Eight/Gate, Nine/Line. Various programs use the peg word technique and imagery in memorizing and recalling math facts. See www.memoryjoggers.com and *Times Tables the Fun Way* by www.citycreek.com.

Other Memory Tips

• Memory is strengthened by creating meaningful links and associations. Look for ways items go together (perhaps they sound alike or look alike) to help remember.

• Link a series of events, terms, or facts together through a silly story. Try using a sequence of outlandish mental images.

• Create all associations (silly stories, linking, pairing, and other mnemonic techniques) using vivid imagery, color, and action. Make the imagery as absurd and exaggerated as possible to make it more memorable.

• Use melody and rhythm to help memorize information. There are raps, rhymes, and songs that help in learning multiplication tables and other information (days of the week, months of the year, U.S. presidents, steps in a cycle or process). A number of resources teach through this method, such as those at www.songsforteaching.com and www.musicallyaligned.com.

• Create your own verses of information to learn and memorize using a familiar melody, such as "Row, Row, Row Your Boat" or "Frère Jacques."

• Use rhymes to remember rules (for example, i before e except after c).

• Chunk information into small bites. Long series of numbers, such as Social Security numbers and phone numbers, are chunked for that reason.

• Emotional memory is very strong. When you can evoke an emotion when teaching something, it sticks. Teaching through use of storytelling is a powerful tool because stories often evoke emotions in the listener.

5.3 RELAXATION STRATEGIES, VISUALIZATION, EXERCISE, AND MORE

Learning relaxation and stress reduction strategies, as well as finding positive outlets to channel one's energy and emotions, is helpful to those who are hyperactive, emotionally overreactive, or anxious. The following have health and psychological benefits that are good for all of us and may be of particular importance for youngsters with ADHD.

Fun and Laughter

• Laughter is one of the best ways to release stress and feel good. The chemicals released in the body through laughter reduce pain and tension. There is probably no substitute for finding ways to have fun and to laugh.

Breathing Techniques

• Controlled, conscious breathing has the benefit of relaxing muscles and reducing stress. Many believe it is useful in the management of some physical ailments and disease.

• Teach children how to take conscious deep breaths to relax while listening to the sound of the air coming in and out. Show them how to inhale deeply (preferably through the nose) and slowly exhale through the mouth. The abdomen rises and expands during inhaling.

• Students can do relaxation breathing in their chairs, seated on the floor cross-legged with eyes closed, lying down, or even standing. Breathing exercises in yoga can be taught to children too.

• Teach progressive muscle relaxation by isolating different body parts and then tightening and relaxing them. For example, while they are lying on the floor, instruct them to tighten or squeeze their toes on the left foot while taking a deep breath in and then relax the toes with a slow breath out. Continue to do the same tightening and relaxing muscles up the left leg (calf muscles, knee, thigh). Proceed in this fashion to the right side of the lower body, to the abdomen and upper body, each arm, hands and fingers, chest, neck, jaw, and face.

• Teach children that when their bodies are relaxed, they are better able to think and plan. Help them understand that when they are nervous, stressed, and angry, there is a tensing of certain body parts that they should be able to feel. Once they learn to recognize when their fists clench, jaws tighten, and stomachs harden, there are strategies that can help reduce the tension and give them better self-control, such as by breathing deeply and "sending" their breaths consciously to relax body parts.

• Help guide children to visualize that with each breath they take in, their body becomes filled slowly with a soothing color, aroma, sound, light, warmth, or other pleasant, comfortable feeling. For example, ask students to think of a color that makes them feel comfortable, peaceful, and relaxed. Then practice with closed eyes, breathing in that color and "sending" it (blowing it) throughout the body—the color going down their throat, into the neck and chest, down to the stomach, and so on.

Yoga, Brain Gym, and Slow Movement Exercises

• Yoga has many health and psychological benefits, among them stress reduction and heightening one's focus and awareness.

• In addition to finding yoga classes for children in the community, there are DVDs and books available that teach yoga postures and slow movement games and exercises for children, such as *Children's Book of Yoga* (Luby, 1998), *Yoga Games for Children* (Bersma, Visscher, & Kooistra, 2003), *Fly Like a Butterfly* (Khalsa, 1999), *Yoga Kids* (Wenig, 2003), and *Yoga for You and Your Child* (Singleton, 2004).

• Sensory integration exercises such as those taught through Brain Gym may be useful to teach children as well. For more information, go to www.braingym.com.

Guided Imagery and Visualization

• The ability to visualize colorful, vivid images with rich imagination and detailed action is a natural skill of childhood. These same skills have been found useful in empowering people to help overcome obstacles in their lives. Visualization techniques are used to improve memory and learning, facilitate healing, and strengthen other important skills, such as studying, social skills, coping, and creative expression.

• Teach children to visualize themselves in situations where they are achieving and being successful. For example, prior to taking a test, they can visualize themselves in detail: focused, well prepared, and working diligently taking the test. Encourage them to see themselves persistently and carefully reading each item, pacing themselves, and confidently answering questions. They can imagine feeling relaxed, not nervous or anxious. Have students picture themselves finishing the test and going back to check for careless errors.

• Playing a motivational song, such as the theme song from the movie *Rocky*, can set a positive mood and help build confidence.

• Many resources use these techniques for self-help and management. For example *Imagery for Kids: Discovering Your Special Place*, by Charlotte Reznick (www.imageryforkids.com) combines gentle music and a guided journey. *Ready, Set, R.E.L.A.X.*, by Jeffrey Allen and Roger Klein and available through www.sensorycomfort.com and other companies, is a program designed to help reduce children's stress and anxiety by progressive muscle relaxation, guided visualization, and positive self-talk.

Music

• Music can be helpful for relaxation, as a previsualization activity, to soothe away worries and distractions, and to bring a sense of inner peace. Music also stimulates the brain. Many people find that they are better able to focus and are more motivated and productive when listening to music.

• Many teachers find that playing classical music, soothing environmental sounds, and instrumental arrangements contribute to better learning, attention, and behavior. Different forms of music have been found to be effective in increasing the ability to focus, soothe, and relax and to boost learning, creativity, and critical-thinking skills.

• Environmental sounds (of a rain forest, oceans, or waterfalls, for example) and classical music (such as Debussy's *Claire de Lune* and Vivaldi's *Four Seasons*) have a calming effect. Examples of contemporary artists whose music is calming are Kitaro, George Winston, Steven Halpern, Hillary Stagg, Zamfir, and Jim Chappell.

• Certain kinds of instrumental musical arrangements and rhythmic patterns are believed to have calming and focusing effects, such as arrangements at sixty beats per minute, the same tempo as a resting heart rate. Gary Lamb's music (www.garylamb.com) and REI Institute (www.reinstitute.com) are two sources for such music.

• Listening to energizing music can help children and teens with ADHD when they are cognitively fatigued or have low energy for tasks.

• Encourage and provide the opportunity for children to learn how to play musical instruments. The discipline of learning and practicing an instrument can be difficult, but if the child learns how to play an instrument and enjoys doing so, it will be a gift for life.

Art

• Drawing, painting, sculpting, photography, and other forms of visual art expression can have beneficial effects for children and teens, particularly if it is a means of expression that they find enjoyable.

• Any opportunity to give children creative outlets that they find pleasurable is well worth pursuing. Many children with ADHD and learning disabilities have strength and talent in these areas.

• The visual arts are a means of self-expression and enable one to express graphically what may be difficult to do verbally, such as talking about feelings and emotions.

• Art therapy is based on the belief that the creative process of art is both healing and life enhancing.

• Working with artistic materials such as clay and paint can be calming.

Exercise and Sports

• Exercise stimulates the central nervous system by increasing blood flow and oxygen to the brain. Some of the benefits of exercise are a boost in mood, increase in focus and alertness, learning, and memory. Exercise directly increases important brain chemical levels, enhancing our medical and mental health.

• For children who have an abundance of energy, exercise is a healthy, positive way to expend that energy. It is particularly important for children and teens with ADHD to exercise regularly.

• Exercise in the morning, such as a before-school jogging program or aerobic workout, may increase a child's academic and behavioral performance.

• Encourage exercise breaks to shoot baskets, dance, jump on a trampoline, or whatever else the child enjoys as rewards for accomplishing mini-goals. For example, a child who completes math homework can go outside and shoot baskets for twenty minutes before beginning the next assignment.

• Some children with ADHD have difficulty in team sports, especially those that require having to wait patiently for their turn to participate, such as baseball. Unfortunately, poor performance in a team sport can lead to ridicule and social rejection of a child with already fragile self-esteem. Children with ADHD may do better in sports such as swimming, track and field, gymnastics, and martial arts, particularly Tae Kwon Do.

Leisure Activities, Recreation, and Hobbies

• Try to minimize the amount of time your child is in front of a screen (TV, video games, and computer). Help him or her to find other forms of entertainment.

• Nurture a child's interests, and provide opportunities for him or her to develop hobbies and outlets in arts, crafts, music, mechanics, and many others. Some activities, such as knitting, also have obvious benefits for those with ADHD by calming and keeping busy hands productively engaged.

• Find recreation and leisure activities to enjoy as a family, such as bicycling, hiking, or skating.

• Build your child's repertoire of games that he or she plays that involve interaction and strengthen mental skills and concentration; examples are chess, other board games, and word games.

References

Bersma, D., Visscher, M., & Kooistra, A. (2003). *Yoga games for children: Fun and fitness with postures, movements and breath.* Alameda, CA: Hunter House.

Khalsa, S. K. (1999). *Fly like a butterfly.* New York: Sterling.

Luby, T. (1998). *Children's book of yoga.* Santa Fe: Clear Light Books.

Singleton, M. (2004). *Yoga for you and your child*. London, UK: Duncan
    Baird Publishers.
Wenig, M. (2003). *Yoga kids: Educating the whole child through yoga*.
    New York: Stewart, Tabori, and Chang.

5.4 ADHD AND SOCIAL SKILLS INTERVENTIONS

Many children and teens with ADHD tend to be deficient in social skill awareness and application, which affects their interpersonal relationships—getting along with others at home, school, and other settings. Although some children with ADHD are quite popular, others have a hard time establishing and maintaining friendships and experience social rejection. Social difficulties can lead to a host of negative outcomes and low self-esteem, as well as be a source of pain and frustration for not just the child but the entire family.

• Because of their developmental delay (approximately 30 percent) in self-management and self-control, children with ADHD often behave immaturely.

• Some children and teens with ADHD have social skill deficits. Others may know the appropriate social skills but because of their impulsivity, inattention, and difficulty inhibiting their behavior, fail to perform the skills when necessary.

• Common struggles in children and teens with ADHD that negatively affect their interactions and social acceptance are:

  • Poor self-control\, problem-solving skills, and overreactivity. They are easily provoked to fighting, arguing, name-calling, and inappropriate means of resolving conflicts.

  • Poor self-awareness. They are often unaware of their behaviors that others find annoying or intrusive.

  • Difficulty controlling or regulating their emotions, noise level, and activity level.

  • Poor communication skills. They may have trouble focusing and listening to others or refraining from interrupting.

• Research indicates that multimodal interventions are the most effective for addressing interpersonal and social skills difficulties of children and teens with ADHD. These involve a combination of school interventions, child interventions, and parent interventions.

School Interventions

• Every day teachers informally model and teach students prosocial behaviors. By setting behavioral standards and enforcing expectations for respectful, cooperative behavior and good manners, most students learn and practice social skills daily. Teachers infuse social skills training into daily instruction when they explicitly model, coach, prompt, monitor, and positively reinforce such skills as sharing and taking turns, listening without interrupting, participating in conversations without dominating them, encouraging and complimenting others, disagreeing and expressing opinions appropriately, and general manners of using respectful, polite, verbal and body language.

• Within the classroom, there is no better place and structure for teaching and practicing appropriate social skills than in the context of cooperative learning groups. Research has proven cooperative learning to be effective not only in increasing student learning but also in developing positive and supportive relationships, student acceptance, and the ability to see other points of view.

• Schoolwide programs that teach and reinforce positive, prosocial behavior in all school settings are highly effective. See the Web site of Positive Behavioral Interventions and Supports (www.pbis.org) for developing a comprehensive schoolwide system and a model that is being used in many schools throughout the United States.

• Some elementary schools provide social skill training through lessons and units taught by the classroom teacher to the whole class, or in sessions facilitated and presented by the counselor, either in the classroom or small-group sessions outside the classroom. There are some excellent programs and social skills curricula from which to choose.

• Social skill programs generally have the following format:

1. Explain the need or rationale for learning the skill.

2. Define the skill clearly.

3. Discuss and reinforce the skill by visual displays such as posters and photos.

4. Demonstrate appropriate and inappropriate skills through positive and negative examples.

5. Provide modeling of the skills through demonstrations, using puppets, and books, for instance.

6. As students role-play the appropriate skill, the adult provides feedback.

7. Ask students to look for and observe the skill being displayed in different settings.

8. Practice, practice, practice.

9. Reinforce students for performing the skill appropriately.

• Many schools are implementing character education programs or social-emotional learning programs that focus on teaching and positively reinforcing prosocial values and virtues to the whole school community. These include such character traits as trustworthiness, honesty, dependability, courtesy, sportsmanship, responsibility, and initiative.

• Increase student awareness of appropriate skills by modeling, giving positive attention to, and reinforcing displays of politeness, good manners, and the appropriate way to say and do things in classroom and out-of-classroom settings. Try to provide corrective feedback in a manner that is not judgmental or embarrassing, but focuses on teaching positive social skills.

• Help children weak in social skills by carefully pairing them with positive role models and assigning them to groups that will be tolerant and supportive.

• Teachers and other school staff may need to help facilitate the fostering of friendships for students who tend to be socially isolated or rejected. They can look for opportunities to engage the child in fun activities with compatible peers.

• Many schoolwide interventions can be employed to increase the social functioning and interpersonal relationships of students. Among them are conflict resolution, peer mediation, character education programs, cooperative learning opportunities, and antibullying programs.

• Specific social behaviors can be the target for improvement in designing daily report cards for individual students. *See checklist 1.14.*

Child Interventions

• Often children with ADHD are not socially accepted because they have poor skills in playing various games and sports, so other children don't want to play with them or have them on their team. It is a helpful intervention to build their skills and competencies in playing sports and games to raise their status with other children. Provide opportunities to learn and practice the strategies, rules, and skills of those sports and games and general sportsmanship so that their peers will want to include them in their play.

• Social skills training programs can be implemented in a variety of settings: after-school programs, summer treatment programs, clinical settings, and learning centers and recreation centers, for example.

• These programs commonly address some of the following areas: working and playing cooperatively, learning to join a game in progress, ignoring teasing, managing anger and using effective coping strategies, and solving problems peacefully and nonaggressively.

• Social skills programs are designed to teach specific skills within a small group (children and teens generally of the same age range). The trainer uses social skills curriculum. Most effective programs have sessions with these components:

> • A brief introduction to the skill, including examples and non-examples, role play, and rehearsal.
>
> • The bulk of the session involves playing an indoor or outdoor game or other activity.
>
> • Children are prompted and coached on the use of the skill.
>
> • There is a short debriefing with feedback and reinforcement for demonstrating the use of the targeted skill.

• Any social skill taught should be one that can be generalized across settings. This requires that the skills be practiced and reinforced at school, at home, and in other environments where the child spends time interacting with others.

• Many children and teens with ADHD do not have a social skill deficit, and social skills training is not necessary. They know the appropriate social skills but typically forget or fail to perform the appropriate skills in the situation or setting when needed. What they most benefit from is prompting, cueing, reminding them about the appropriate behavior, and reinforcing their use of good social skills in activities and environments where they have problems, such as on the playground, at the bus stop, in the cafeteria, and when playing competitive games with siblings or friends.

• Other child interventions involve teaching them some cognitive approaches and other methods to help improve interpersonal relationships, and self-regulation of behavior. This may include training in conflict resolution, anger management, self-monitoring, and problem-solving techniques (for example, identifying the problem, brainstorming possible solutions, selecting a solution to implement, and evaluating how that worked).

Parent Interventions

• Parents of children and teens with ADHD need to be part of the intervention plan to improve their child's social skills and interpersonal relationships. This includes training and skill building in:

- Behavior management techniques and positive discipline. *See checklists 2.2, 2.3, and 2.4.*
- Dealing with challenging behaviors effectively. *See checklists 2.5 and 1.1.*
- Communicating with effective messages, directions, and commands. *See checklist 2.7.*
- Working together with the school on joint goals and reinforcement of positive behaviors. *See checklists 1.12, 1.14, 2.6, and 5.1.*

• Parents of children with ADHD often need to help their child find compatible playmates and coach them to maintain friendships when their behaviors cause them to be rejected by peers. It might take effort to orchestrate opportunities for their son or daughter to socialize. One possibility is monitored play dates with another child.

• When having other children to the house to play (and just one other child at a time is generally preferable), parents can help reduce the chance of conflict by being prepared with enough activities to keep them busy, keeping the time together short, not having available certain toys that their child doesn't like to share with others, providing snacks, and monitoring from a distance in order to intervene if problems arise.

• Parents may try bringing to their child's attention the inappropriateness of some of his or her social behaviors and the negative impact they have on maintaining friendships. It is best to do so at more teachable moments, and never when emotions are running high. Parents may wish to discuss with their child why other children get angry with him or her and why he or she may be having trouble keeping friends. Perhaps practice or role-play appropriate ways to behave for some of the child's problem areas—for example, being a good sport when losing a game, taking turns, and being cooperative rather than bossy.

• Some communities have centers or clinics specializing in multimodal treatment approaches for children and teens with ADHD. They may offer a variety of services and supports for both children and their parents. For example, children may be participating in a social skills training group in one room, while parents are in a different room in a parent training session with a facilitator and group of other parents.

• Some summer camps and treatment programs have highly effective programs for children with ADHD. These are designed to used a strong behavioral and social skills component, along with parent training and other aspects of a multimodal approach. For information about such programs, see http://summertreatmentprogram.com and www.additudemag.com/directory.asp

Medication Intervention

• Medication is helpful for many children and teens with ADHD by enabling them to benefit more from such psychosocial interventions as behavior modification, ability to apply problem-solving and conflict-resolution strategies, managing anger and emotions, and so forth.

5.5 ADHD IN YOUNG CHILDREN

With very young children, it is hard to distinguish between what is normal rambunctious, inattentive, and uninhibited early childhood behavior and what may be abnormal, that is, maladaptive and outside the limits of what is developmentally appropriate behavior for that age. Although most children with ADHD are not diagnosed until first grade or higher, youngsters with more severe ADHD symptoms and behaviors can be identified and treated in kindergarten or preschool.

• Many children, not just those with ADHD, have difficulty adjusting to a classroom environment, the hours away from home, the structure and expectations of their preschool or kindergarten teacher, and relating to the other children. Sometimes it just takes time for them to make the adjustment and feel comfortable in the new environment. It is often the case that some of the behaviors that were problematic at the beginning of the year diminish and are no longer a significant issue once the children have learned the routine and structure, bonded with their teacher, and matured somewhat.

• If a child has ADHD, the preschool or kindergarten teacher will find the behaviors—impulsivity, hyperactivity, and inattention—to be very problematic and excessive in comparison to the other children. It is appropriate for the teacher to share observations and concerns with parents and support staff and to implement strategies and supports to address the needs of the child. Almost all of the teaching and parenting techniques recommended throughout this book are applicable and effective for children in this age bracket as well.

• Children with ADHD are developmentally delayed in their ability for self-control and stopping or inhibiting their behavior. They often behave like a younger child, even though they may be quite bright and have no learning weaknesses.

Early Intervention

• Often children with ADHD display other developmental delays such as in the areas of speech and language, gross or fine motor skills, or acquiring academic readiness skills, such as learning and remembering the ABCs, numbers, shapes, and letter-sound association. The child should be screened for possible vision or hearing deficits, and evaluation for these concerns is generally recommended, because there is great benefit from early intervention services, such as in speech and language, occupational therapy, adapted physical education, and skill training in areas of difficulty.

• If a child is diagnosed with ADHD in the preschool or kindergarten years, the symptoms are typically quite severe, with the child experiencing many behavioral, social, and other interpersonal difficulties. It is not uncommon for these children to be kicked out of one or more early childhood programs, often due to aggressive and oppositional behavior. These children are at high risk for many more problems down the road, and early intervention is critical.

• The first long-term comprehensive study of ADHD treatment in this population is the Preschool ADHD Treatment Study, conducted in 2006 by the National Institute of Mental Health. Behavioral therapy was found to be effective and is the intervention that almost all scientists and practitioners agree is essential. This includes parent training in effective behavioral management and discipline, proper and consistent use of positive and negative consequences, and other such strategies and interventions described in *checklists 1.12, 1.14, and 2.2–2.8.*

• The study also found low doses of methylphenidate medication, which must be closely monitored for side effects, to be effective. Most doctors are cautious about prescribing medication for young children. However, in more severe cases, particularly if the behavioral interventions are insufficient in helping the child, medication is an option.

• Early intervention is beneficial for children with disabilities and special needs. Federal law requires that school districts provide early identification and intervention services.

• The same principles of parenting, effective behavior management, and problem prevention described in *checklists 1.14 and 2.2–2.8* apply to parents of young children with ADHD as well.

• It is highly recommended that parents start early in seeking help from specialists to learn how to cope with and manage their young child's challenging behaviors and more difficult temperaments. There are many resources available to help parents learn how to do so: parenting classes, behavior management training, counseling, parent support groups such as CHADD (Children and Adults with Attention Deficit/Hyperactivity Disorder), books and DVDs, and other materials.

• Parents need to provide the necessary structure and manage the environmental factors to help their child be successful by anticipating potential problems and planning accordingly. For example, parents of highly active young children need to take great care to childproof the home for safety.

Strategies and Tips for Preschool and Kindergarten Teachers

• In preschool and kindergarten, every behavioral expectation and social skill must be taught. Teachers need to explain and model each desired behavior and practice until all students know precisely what is expected from them, including how to line up; stand in line; walk in line; move to groups, stations, and learning centers; sit on the rug or at the table; raise a hand to get the teacher's attention; and use indoor voices.

• Teachers need to model, role-play, and have children practice expectations—for example, "Show me what to do when you have something you want to say." "Who wants to show us how we get our lunch boxes and line up for lunch?"

• Literature that has manners and appropriate behavior as a theme, such as sharing and being a good friend, is helpful in teaching behavioral expectations and social skills. So are puppets, songs, games, visual display, role playing, and other such means.

• Behavior management techniques for children with ADHD in preschool and kindergarten are similar to those in higher grades: a high degree of feedback, visual prompting and cueing, proximity control, group positive reinforcement systems, corrective consequences that are applied consistently, and individualized behavioral plans and supports. *See checklists 1.14 and 3.1–3.10.*

• *Quiet space.* Sometimes children with ADHD are on sensory overload and can become agitated or disruptive. It is important to allow them time and space to settle, regroup, and get away from some of the overstimulation. It helps to have an area that is designed for this purpose, with calming music they can listen to with earphones, pillows, and stuffed animals, for example. Teachers may ask, "Do you need to move to . . . ?" "Is there a better place to do your work?" Or they can redirect the child to a quieter, calmer area by whispering to him or her, "Go to the pillow area and read [look at] a book."

• *Diversionary tactics.* The perceptive teacher will watch for signs of children who are beginning to get restless or agitated and try diverting their attention (for example, "Sara, come help me turn the pages of this book") to redirect their behavior. Most young children love to be the teacher's helper. They can be given a task such as wiping down tables, putting up chairs, or passing out papers.

• *Positive attention.* As with older children, the best way to manage is through watching for positive behaviors and recognizing children for what they are doing right. "I see how nicely Coby and Jason are taking turns. Thank you for working so cooperatively." Besides specific praise from teachers, positive recognition and appreciation from peers are important as well: "Let's give a big round of applause to . . ." (children clap finger-to-finger in a large circular movement). "Let's give ourselves a pat on the back" (children reach over and pat themselves on the back). "Let's give the silent cheer for . . ."

• *Check for specific behaviors.* Ask: "Are your eyes on me?" "Are your ears open and on full power?" "Where should you be sitting right now?" "Are we sitting criss-cross applesauce?"

• *Visual prompts.* Use these for all behavioral expectations. For example, make class charts with pictures depicting the behaviors you want students to demonstrate. Point to and refer to those visuals frequently. Keep your camera handy, and take photos of children who are sitting appropriately or raising their hand to speak, for example, and use those photos as reminders of appropriate behaviors.

• *Environmental structuring.* Children with ADHD often have difficulty knowing and understanding their physical boundaries. They tend to invade other people's space and react adversely to being crowded or bumped into. They are helped by having concrete visual structuring of their space, such as with colored duct tape to indicate their boundaries on the carpet area or at tables. Also, placing them in the front or back of the line (not in the middle) can avoid some problems when walking in lines.

• Some children need individualized behavior modification charts or daily report cards for working to improve one or two specific behaviors such as staying in their assigned place or keeping their hands and feet to themselves. Young children need to be reinforced frequently; short time frames of appropriate behavior can earn the child a star, a smiley face, a sticker on a chart, or some other reward. *See checklist 1.14.*

• Prepare and reassure children who are easily frustrated with tasks. For example, "Which do you think will be easier: the cutting or the gluing?" "I know you can do this, but if you need help . . . "

• In addition, early childhood classrooms need to be:

   • Rich in oral language, with children exposed to a lot of rhyme and verse, patterned literature, and fun, interesting stories

   • Colorful, warm, and comfortable

   • Well equipped with enriching materials, centers, literature, and hands-on activities

   • Full of activities and materials to develop language skills, fine motor skills, early literacy, and math

   • Clearly labeled for children to access materials and clean up independently

   • Embedded with music and movement in all aspects of the curriculum throughout the day

5.6 ADHD IN ADOLESCENTS

For most children with ADHD, the symptoms continue into adolescence to varying degrees. Some symptoms may diminish, but other problems may emerge or intensify during middle and high school. Many preteens and teenagers find these years to be the most difficult and stressful for themselves and their families.

• Hyperactivity in adolescence generally manifests more as restlessness rather than the more overt hyperactivity seen in younger children.

• Impulsivity can be more problematic during the teen years. Lack of self-control and inhibition in adolescence is associated with many risk factors, including significantly more than average traffic violations, accidents, and teen pregnancies, as well as conduct that results in conflict with school authorities, parents, and law enforcement.

• Some children with ADHD who were able to cope adequately in elementary school may find themselves overwhelmed and unable to do so with the high demands, requirements, and workload of middle and secondary school.

• Common difficulties in adolescents with ADHD that affect academic performance are directly related to their executive function deficits (*see checklist 1.5*). These issues become apparent and problematic during the middle and high school years:

- *Poor organization and time awareness and management,* resulting in missing and incomplete assignments, not meeting deadlines and due dates, and losing important materials

- *Poor working memory,* causing forgetfulness and affecting reading comprehension, mathematical problem solving, written composition, and other academic tasks

- *Poor planning and goal-directed behavior,* affecting success in long-term assignments and projects

• Inattention and distractibility cause difficulty in listening to and following directions and lessons, starting and completing assignments, staying on task, taking exams, making careless errors in their work, and so forth.

• Other issues and factors for teens and preteens with ADHD include:

- Poor study skills (work habits, note taking, test taking)
- Instruction that is not conducive to their learning styles, such as lecture and little opportunity for hands-on, active learning
- Managing multiple teachers' behavioral expectations, classroom procedures, and work requirements
- Social difficulties, such as being the victim of teasing or bullying, and social isolation, which can be devastating at this age
- Desire for peer approval, coupled with impulsivity and not stopping to think before they act, resulting in inappropriate conduct that gets them into trouble

• Besides these special challenges related to their ADHD, adolescents must also cope with the normal stresses and anxieties of this age, such as changes and transitions to a new school; dealing with several teachers, each with his or her own teaching style, expectations, and requirements; the enormous social and peer pressures such as the need to be accepted and fit in; and physical changes.

• Students in these grades often complain that school is boring and they do not see the connection between what is taught in school and their own lives. Instruction at this level must be meaningful, relevant, challenging, and motivating and designed for active participation and engagement. It also needs to tap into students' interests and strengths.

• It is very important for parents and teachers of students with ADHD to be aware of conditions that frequently co-occur with ADHD and may emerge in the middle and high school years. *See checklist 1.7.* Depression, anxiety, oppositional defiant disorder, and conduct disorder are common coexisting conditions requiring support from mental health professionals. There is also a high rate of learning disabilities (approximately 25 to 50 percent) among individuals with ADHD, with the teen generally in need of special education, related services, or academic accommodations. Other conditions, such as sleep disorders, are common as well.

• It is very important to reevaluate when other conditions are suspected or current treatment is not working well and implement whatever interventions may be necessary at this time: academic assistance, medical treatment or adjustment in medication, counseling, or something else.

• Adolescents with ADHD may appear mature physically and grown up, but looks are deceiving. They are typically far less mature behaviorally and emotionally than their same-age peers. They do not act their age because they have a developmental delay of approximately 30 percent in skills affecting their self-management, behavior, and executive functions. A fifteen year old with ADHD will likely behave like a ten or eleven year old in some respects and the twelve year old like an eight or nine year old due to this developmental lag. Do not let their intelligence and physical maturity mislead you.

• Although they may be of an age when the expectation is to demonstrate more independence, responsibility, and self-control, the reality is that adolescents with ADHD take longer to exhibit those behaviors. They need more adult monitoring and direct supports than their peers.

• Students of this age still benefit from incentive systems, daily report cards, contracts, and other forms of home and school monitoring plans. *See checklists 1.14, 2.4, 2.5, 2.11, 3.2, 3.4, and 3.12.*

• Adolescents with ADHD need the following from parents and teachers:

- Awareness and understanding of ADHD and strategies to help them deal with their challenges
- More frequent communication between home and school than is generally necessary for other students this age
- Reasonable and realistic expectations
- Use of a positive discipline approach rather than punishment as the primary mode of dealing with behavior
- Monitoring and supervision (although they may complain bitterly)
- Open channels of communication and efforts to strengthen the relationship
- Lots of encouragement and support

• Older children need to understand about ADHD, the nature of the disorder, and how they can best manage to deal with the symptoms. There are some excellent resources on ADHD geared to the older child or adolescent. Parents and doctors need to take the time to explain and educate the teen or preteen about ADHD. It is very important to acknowledge their feelings and elicit their participation in decision making, monitoring, and management.

• As students with ADHD enter the middle and high school grades, they need to advocate for themselves; they must understand their needs and learn how to approach teachers respectfully with requests for accommodations. Parents still need to take an active role in their child's education and maintain communication with teachers. However, it is also appropriate for students to speak directly with their teachers. Students with ADHD can politely explain to their teachers what makes it easier or harder for them to learn in the classroom and the kinds of supports and accommodations that help them, such as preferential seating.

• One of the advantages in middle and secondary school is the availability of more options in scheduling. Sometimes the best intervention is a change of classes or teachers. Other times, rescheduling a class with the same teacher but at a more optimal time of day makes a difference.

• Parents of adolescents with ADHD need to be vigilant in monitoring their child's performance in his or her classes. Teachers may be asked to send more frequent progress reports or be kept informed by e-mail or other communication system throughout the grading period.

• Teens with ADHD generally need an adult at school who serves officially or unofficially as a case manager to monitor progress, advise, and intervene in school situations. For students with individualized education programs, the special education teacher (resource teacher) is often the case manager. Sometimes a school counselor, homeroom teacher, or other staff member serves this function.

• Some middle and high schools have in place supportive interventions, or safety nets, available to students in need, such as mentors, homework and organization assistance, study skills and learning strategies classes, and tutoring. Teens with ADHD benefit from such school supports, as well as the opportunity to participate in clubs, sports, and electives to build on their interests and showcase their areas of strength.

• Teachers in middle and high schools typically have little training about ADHD, learning disabilities, or other special needs. It is important that they are able to receive professional development and training that is informative and relevant and helps them to understand and empathize with their students who struggle with these disorders.

• These are years when it is very difficult for parents and teachers to find that proper balance: how to teach children to assume responsibility for their own learning and behavioral choices and how to intervene as we guide and support them to success.

• The bulk of strategies and interventions for ADHD (instructional, environmental, organizational, and behavioral) recommended throughout this book are effective and appropriate for adolescents as well.

5.7 WEB RESOURCES TO UNDERSTAND AND SUPPORT CHILDREN WITH ADHD AND RELATED DISORDERS

ADHD National Organizations and Resource Centers

Attention Deficit Disorder Association, www.add.org

Children and Adults with Attention Deficit/Hyperactivity Disorder (CHADD), www.chadd.org

National Center for Girls and Women with AD/HD www.ncgiadd.org/

National Resource Center on AD/HD, a clearinghouse for science-based information—a CHADD program funded through a cooperative agreement with the Centers for Disease Control and Prevention, www.help4adhd.org/

Learning Disabilities Resources with Information About ADHD

International Dyslexia Association, www.interdys.org

Learning Disability Association of America, www.ldanatl.org

LD Online, www.ldonline.org

National Center for Learning Disabilities, www.ncld.org

Schwab Learning, a parent's guide to helping children with learning difficulties, www.schwablearning.org/

Smart Kids with Learning Disabilities, www.smartkidswithld.org/

Medical and Mental Health

American Academy of Child and Adolescent Psychiatry, www.aacap.org

American Academy of Pediatrics, www.aap.org

American Medical Association, www.ama-assn.org

American Psychiatric Association, www.psych.org/

American Psychological Association, www.apa.org/

Centers for Disease Control and Prevention, www.cdc.gov/ncbddd/adhd/

Federation of Families for Children's Mental Health, www.ffcmh.org

Health Central, www.healthcentral.com/adhd/

Mental Help Net, www.mentalhelp.net

National Alliance for the Mentally Ill, www.nami.org

National Association of School Psychologists, www.nasponline.org/

National Institute of Mental Health, www.nimh.nih.gov

National Mental Health Association, www.nmha.org

As there are a number of coexisting conditions with ADHD, also see the Web sites of the national organizations for those specific disorders.

Other Important Disability Resources

Alliance for Technology Access, www.ataccess.org

Council for Exceptional Children, www.cec.sped.org

Family Center on Technology and Disability, www.fctd.info

Internet Resources for Special Children, irsc.org

National Information Clearinghouse for Handicapped Children and Youth (also referred to as the National Dissemination Center for Children with Disabilities), www.nichcy.org/

Parent Advocacy Coalition for Educational Rights (PACER Center), www.pacer.org

Parent Training and Information Centers, www.taalliance.org

Recordings for the Blind and Dyslexic, www.rfbd.org

U.S. Department of Education, www.ed.gov/parents/needs/speced/resources.html

Gifted Children with Disabilities

Association for the Education of Gifted Underachieving Students, www.aegus1.org

Twice-Exceptional Newsletter, www.2eNewsletter.com

Educational Rights for Children with Disabilities

Council of Parent Attorneys and Advocates, www.copaa.org

Family and Advocates Partnership for Education, www.fape.org

Monahan and Cohen, www.monahan-cohen.com

Reed Martin, Esq, www.reedmartin.com

U.S. Department of Education on IDEA 2004, http://idea.ed.gov

U.S. Department of Education Office of Special Education Programs, www.ed.gov/policy/speced/guid/idea/letters/revpolicy/index.html

Wrightslaw, www.wrightslaw.com

Magazines, Newsletters, and Other ADHD Resources

ADD Warehouse, http://addwarehouse.com

ADDitude Magazine, www.additudemag.com

ADDvance On-line, www.addvance.com

ATTENTION!, www.chadd.org

Parent to Parent: Family Training on AD/HD, www.chadd.org

The ADHD Report, www.guilford.com

UB Center for Children and Families, State University of New York at Buffalo, http://ccf.buffalo.edu/resources_downloads.php

There are many other Web sites of experts in the field—researchers and other authorities who share their expertise in helping children and adults with ADHD. Just a few include www.drrobertbrooks.com, www.samgoldstein.com, www.russellbarkley.net, www.drthomasebrown.com, and www.helpforadd.com (David Rabiner's Web site).

There are some wonderful tools and resources available such as alternatives to hard chairs for seating, a variety of fidget toys, and products to help with fine motor difficulties. Some companies that carry such products include:

- Child Therapy Toys, www.childtherapytoys.com
- Heads Up Now!, www.headsupnow.com
- Pocket Full of Therapy, www.pfot.com
- Sensory Comfort, www.sensorycomfort.com
- Therapro, www.theraproducts.com
- Therapy Shoppe, www.therapyshoppe.com

There are numerous books, DVDs, and other resources on ADHD available—too many products and publishers to list here. My books and other commercial products are found in *checklist 5.8*, as well as at www.sandrarief.com.

5.8 BOOKS AND OTHER RESOURCES BY SANDRA RIEF

Books

Fetzer, N., & Rief, S. (2000). *Alphabet center learning activities kit.*
San Francisco: Jossey-Bass.

Rief, S. (2001). *Ready . . . start . . . school! Nurturing and guiding your child through preschool and kindergarten.* Paramus, NJ: Prentice Hall.

Rief, S. (2003). *The ADHD book of lists: A practical guide for helping children and teens with attention deficit disorders.* San Francisco: Jossey-Bass.

Rief, S. (2005). *How to reach and teach children with ADD/ADHD: Practical techniques, strategies and interventions* (2nd ed.).
San Francisco: Jossey-Bass.

Rief, S., & Heimburge, J. (2006). *How to reach and teach all children in the inclusive classroom: Practical strategies, lessons, and activities* (2nd ed.). San Francisco: Jossey-Bass.

Rief, S., & Heimburge, J. (2007). *How to reach and teach all children through balanced literacy: User-friendly strategies, tools, activities, and ready-to-use materials.* San Francisco: Jossey-Bass.

Rief, S., & Stern, J. (forthcoming). *The dyslexia checklist: A practical reference for parents and teachers.* San Francisco: Jossey-Bass.

Other Resources

The following resources are available through Educational Resource Specialists (www.sandrarief.com):

ADHD and LD powerful teaching strategies and accommodations (DVD)

ADHD and LD: Strategies at your finger tips (Reference card)

How to help your child succeed in school: Strategies and guidance for parents of children with ADHD and/or learning disabilities (DVD)

Successful classrooms: Effective teaching strategies for raising achievement in reading and writing (DVD)

Successful schools: How to raise achievement and support "at-risk" students (DVD)

For more information, go to www.sandrarief.com.

~ Index

How to Reach and Teach Children with ADD/ADHD

Practical Techniques, Strategies, and Interventions

Second Edition

Sandra F. Rief

ISBN 978-0-7879-7295-0
Paperback • 464 pages

This second edition of the best-selling book, *How to Reach and Teach Children with ADD/ADHD*, is completely revised and updated with the most current research-based information about ADHD for continued service as a leading resource for teachers, school professionals, parents, and clinicians. *How to Reach and Teach Children with ADD/ADHD, 2nd edition* is filled with practical strategies and techniques to improve the academic, behavioral, and social performance of students with ADHD.

In addition to real-life case studies, interviews, and student intervention plans for children with ADD/ADHD, this invaluable resource offers proven suggestions for:

* Engaging students' attention and active participation
* Keeping students on-task and productive
* Preventing and managing behavioral problems in the classroom
* Differentiating instruction and addressing students' diverse learning styles
* Building a partnership with parents

"One of the most comprehensive ADHD reference guides ever compiled...Whether you are a teacher, parent, or mental health professional, this book belongs in your ADHD resource library."
—**Kathleen Nadeau, Ph.D.**, co-publisher, *ADDvance* magazine; coauthor, *Learning to Slow Down and Pay Attention*

"An invaluable resource that is as clear and comprehensive as it is well-organized and readable. This exceptional book has so many lists brimming with helpful tips, valuable insights, and useful strategies that it deserves to be on everyone's short list of great ADHD books!"
—**Dr. Andrew Adesman**, associate professor of pediatrics, Albert Einstein College of Medicine

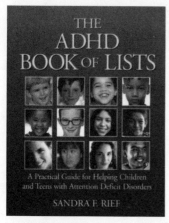

The ADHD Book of Lists

A Practical Guide for Helping Children and Teens with Attention Deficit Disorders

Sandra F. Rief

ISBN 978-0-7879-6591-4
Paperback • 496 pages

The ADHD Book of Lists is a comprehensive, reliable source of answers, practical strategies, and tools based on the most current information about Attention Deficit/Hyperactivity Disorder (ADHD). Created for teachers (K-12), parents, school psychologists, medical and mental health professionals, counselors, and other school personnel, this important resource contains a wealth of information to guide in the management of ADHD in school and at home. It is filled with the strategies, supports, and interventions that have been found to be the most effective in minimizing the problems and optimizing the success of children and teens with ADHD.

The ADHD Book of Lists, with its convenient list format and 8½" x 11" lay flat reproducible checklists, forms, tools, and resources, is easy to use and apply in both home and school environments.

"When Sandra Rief writes about ADHD and educational issues, people listen! Rief, widely recognized as the leading authority on these topics, has an extraordinary gift for identifying key challenges and providing practical, effective tips for helping children succeed in school. The ADHD Book of Lists is another indispensable tool for both parents and teachers! As the author of two popular books on ADHD, I always use Sandra's books as primary references."
—**Chris A. Zeigler Dendy**, author,
Teenagers with ADD and *Teaching Teens with ADD and ADHD*

"Educating ADHD kids can be a real challenge for everyone involved. The ADHD Book of Lists *combines Sandra Rief's classroom-proven techniques with current information about this condition and should be required reading for all teachers and parents of ADHD children."*
—**Harlan R. Gephart, M.D.**, Center for ADHD, Bellevue, Washington

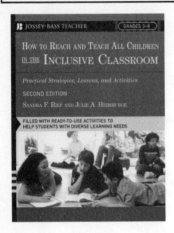

How to Reach and Teach All Children in the Inclusive Classroom

Practical Strategies, Lessons, and Activities

2nd Edition

Sandra F. Rief & Julie A. Heimburge

ISBN 978-0-7879-8154-9
Paperback • 480 pages

The second edition of *How to Reach and Teach All Children in the Inclusive Classroom* continues to provide classroom teachers, special educators, parents, and administrators with a wealth of adaptable and ready-to-use strategies, lessons, and activities to aid in reaching students with varied learning styles, ability levels, skills, and behaviors. The authors enable teachers to guide diverse groups of students in grades 3–8 toward academic, social, and emotional success by advocating a team approach that includes parents, colleagues, and learning specialists.

This resource is invaluable for educators who want to successfully reach and teach all of the children in a mainstream general education classroom.
Topics include how to:

- Effectively differentiate instruction
- Make accommodations and modifications for students based on their learning styles, abilities, and behaviors
- Engage reluctant readers and writers
- Motivate all students to be successful mathematicians
- Increase communication and collaboration between home and school
- Build students' organization, time management, and study skills
- Implement positive behavioral supports and interventions
- Create classroom and schoolwide programs designed to enhance students' resiliency and self-esteem

"Rief and Heimburge's new work provides the novice/beginning and experienced professional educator with a plethora of valuable ideas and techniques for promoting pro-social behaviors in school and raising the academic achievement of all learners."

—**Dr. Bob Bayuk**, school psychologist;
past president of Wyoming School Psychology Association